"My aim in this inquiry is to ascertain beyond preadventure whether protection or free trade best accords with the interests of those who live by their labor"

protection
or
free trade

Henry George

protection
or
free trade

*An examination
of the tariff question,
with especial regard to
the interests of labor*

Henry George

ROBERT SCHALKENBACH FOUNDATION
5 East 44th Street, New York
1980

George, Henry, 1839-1897.
  Protection or free trade.

  Includes index.
  1. Free trade and protection—Free trade.
  2. Tariff—United States. I. Title.
  [HF1755.G355 1980]   382.7'0973   80-14436
  ISBN 0-914016-70-9

Printed in the United States of America by Courier Printing Company
Binding by New Hampshire Bindery
Design by A.L. Morris

To the memory of those illustrious Frenchmen of a century ago... Quesnay, Turgot, Mirabeau, Condorcet, Dupont and their fellows who in the night of despotism foresaw the glories of the coming day.

CONTENTS

PREFACE

to the

CURRENT EDITION / 1980

T HE LONG CRUSADE for freedom of international trade began with the French Physiocrats, the economic philosophers of the 18th century who, with Adam Smith, laid the foundations of contemporary economic science. Henry George, the American economist and social philosopher who was one of the three Americans in the 19th century to make original systematic contributions to political economy, very properly dedicated his book, *Protection or Free Trade,* to these pioneers in the modern struggle for human rights, human freedom.

The Physiocrats numbered in their circle some very great thinkers, among them Francois Quesnay, Jean Claude Gournay, R. Cantillon (the first to set their principles on paper), A. R. J. Turgot and P. S. Dupont de Nemours. They raised the banner of Freedom of Exchange so that each person might make the most of his or her labor; and of unrestricted competition in the market, unfettered by monopolies and privilege, to insure to each person "such natural enjoyments" as he or she could acquire by his or her labor. They believed that society exists on the basis of an implicit contract between individuals which limits the "natural" freedom of each only so far as it is inconsistent with the rights of others.

It is within the context of human rights and human freedom that they initiated the campaign against a system that in our day is based not only on tariffs and duties but on quotas, most-favored-nation treatment, bilateral treaties, negotiated terms of trade, manipulated exchange rates, subsidies, central bank arrangements, instructions to customs appraisers and a host of other devices to restrict trade as a means of achieving competitive advantage in the world or the domestic market. Or as a means of waging economic warfare.

The campaign the Physiocrats started, taken up by the English and American economists of the classical school, produced several classics. The eloquent addresses of the English statesman, John Bright, were one; they won him recognition as the last great practitioner of the formal art of oratory. Another English statesman shared with Bright the leadership of the movement that achieved relative freedom of trade during the administration of Sir Robert Peel: Richard Cobden. Their achievement laid the basis for Britain's late 19th century prosperity, after tariffs, the exactions of land monopolists and other restrictions on economic activity had produced the "Hungry Forties," the mid-century period when the poor and the workers starved. Cobden's writings and speeches have immortalized him as one of the great heroes in the struggle for justice and liberty.

Another classic was produced by Frederic Bastiat, one of Cobden's French disciples. The work, *Sophismes Economiques,* was pronounced by the *Encyclopedia Brittanica* "the completest and most effective, the wisest and the wittiest exposure of protectionism"—and certainly it ranked among the few works qualified for that category.

The other great classic of the campaign is Henry George's masterly polemic, *Protection or Free Trade.* The merit of the book is not in the formidable case it makes against restriction of international competition; the others also do that. Nor even in its demonstration that free competition in the world market place as well as the domestic achieves the most efficient allocation of labor, capital and resources in each participating country. Its unique contribution is in the way it shows how the campaign for free trade is an essential element of the crusade for human freedom; how the trade monopoly is akin to the monopolies of land and all other natural resources, the monopolies of production and distribution, the privileges granted by despots, kings and even democratic governments, and all other abridgments of the right of each person to equality of opportunity in all areas of human activity. The campaign for justice and liberty cannot rest until these ideals prevail everywhere.

In our day only special interests defend protectionism. The case for free trade has persuaded every thinking man and woman. Still, the nations negotiate endlessly to achieve it. We must not delude ourselves that the fight has been won. Only the argument has.

In our day the fight for human rights has forced the nations of the world to subscribe to a universal charter "guaranteeing" them, and to a convention calling for its monitoring. Even the most barbaric despots have signed them—with tongue in cheek. So the struggle goes on. In the worst despotisms dissidents are fighting for liberty. Those who, like these heroes, enjoy a similar dedication will find *Protection or Free Trade* a weapon worth an armory full.

Will Lissner, Ed.D.
Editor-in-chief
American Journal of Economics and Sociology

PREFACE

to the

ORIGINAL EDITION / 1886

I N THIS BOOK I have endeavored to determine whether protection or free trade better accords with the interests of labor, and to bring to a common conclusion on this subject those who really desire to raise wages.

I have not only gone over the ground generally traversed, and examined the arguments commonly used, but, carrying the inquiry further than the controversialists on either side have yet ventured to go, I have sought to discover why protection retains such popular strength in spite of all exposures of its fallacies; to trace the connection between the tariff question and those still more important social questions, now rapidly becoming the "burning questions" of our times; and to show to what radical measures the principle of free trade logically leads. While pointing out the falsity of the belief that tariffs can protect labor, I have not failed to recognize the facts which give this brief vitality, and, by an examination of these facts, have shown, not only how little the working-classes can hope from that mere "revenue reform" which is miscalled "free trade," but how much they have to hope from real free trade. By thus harmonizing the truths which free traders perceive with the facts that to protectionists make their own theory plausible, I believe I have opened ground upon which those separated by seemingly irreconcilable differences of opinion may unite for that full application of the free trade principle which would secure both the largest production and the fairest distribution of wealth.

By thus carrying the inquiry beyond the point where Adam Smith and the writers who have followed him have stopped, I believe I have stripped the vexed tariff question of its greatest difficulties, and have cleared the way for the settlement of a dispute which otherwise might go on interminably. The conclusions thus reached raise the doctrine of free trade from the emasculated form in which it has been taught by the English economists to the fullness in which it was held by the predecessors of Adam Smith, those illustrious Frenchmen, with whom originated the motto *Laissez faire,* and who, whatever may have been the confusions of their terminology or the faults of their method, grasped a central truth which free traders since their time have ignored.

My effort, in short, has been to make such a candid and thorough examination of the tariff question, in all its phases, as would aid men to whom the subject is now a perplexing maze to reach clear and firm conclusions. In this I trust I have done something to inspire a movement now faint-hearted with the earnestness and strength of radical conviction, to prevent the division into hostile camps of those whom a common purpose ought to unite, to give to efforts for the emancipation of labor greater definiteness of purpose, and to eradicate that belief in the opposition of national interests which leads peoples, even of the same blood and tongue, to regard each other as natural antagonists.

To avoid any appearance of culling absurdities, I have, in referring to the protectionist position, quoted mainly from the latest writer who seems to be regarded by American protectionists as an authoritative exponent of their views —Professor Thompson of the University of Pennsylvania.

                                                            Henry George

protection
or
free trade

CHAPTER I.

INTRODUCTORY.

NEAR the window by which I write, a great bull is
tethered by a ring in his nose. Grazing round and
round he has wound his rope about the stake until now
he stands a close prisoner, tantalized by rich grass he
cannot reach, unable even to toss his head to rid him of
the flies that cluster on his shoulders. Now and again
he struggles vainly, and then, after pitiful bellowings,
relapses into silent misery.

This bull, a very type of massive strength, who, because
he has not wit enough to see how he might be free,
suffers want in sight of plenty, and is helplessly preyed
upon by weaker creatures, seems to me no unfit emblem
of the working masses.

In all lands, men whose toil creates abounding wealth
are pinched with poverty, and, while advancing civilization opens wider vistas and awakens new desires, are
held down to brutish levels by animal needs. Bitterly
conscious of injustice, feeling in their inmost souls that
they were made for more than so narrow a life, they, too,
spasmodically struggle and cry out. But until they trace

1

effect to cause, until they see how they are fettered and
how they may be freed, their struggles and outcries are
as vain as those of the bull. Nay, they are vainer. I
shall go out and drive the bull in the way that will
untwist his rope. But who shall drive men into freedom? Till they use the reason with which they have
been gifted, nothing can avail. For them there is no
special providence.

Under all forms of government the ultimate power lies
with the masses. It is not kings nor aristocracies, nor
landowners nor capitalists, that anywhere really enslave
the people. It is their own ignorance. Most clear is
this where governments rest on universal suffrage. The
working-men of the United States may mold to their will
legislatures, courts and constitutions. Politicians strive
for their favor and political parties bid against one
another for their vote. But what avails this? The little
finger of aggregated capital must be thicker than the
loins of the working masses so long as they do not know
how to use their power. And how far from any agreement as to practical reform are even those who most feel
the injustice of existing conditions may be seen in the
labor organizations. Though beginning to realize the
wastefulness of strikes and to feel the necessity of acting
on general conditions through legislation, these organizations when they come to formulate political demands
seem unable to unite upon any measures capable of large
results.

This political impotency must continue until the
masses, or at least that sprinkling of more thoughtful
men who are the file-leaders of popular opinion, shall
give such heed to larger questions as will enable them to
agree on the path reform should take.

It is with the hope of promoting such agreement that
I propose in these pages to examine a vexed question

which must be settled before there can be any efficient union in political action for social reform—the question whether protective tariffs are or are not helpful to those who get their living by their labor.

This is a question important in itself, yet far more important in what it involves. Not only is it true that its examination cannot fail to throw light upon other social-economic questions, but it leads directly to that great "Labor Question" which every day as it passes brings more and more to the foreground in every country of the civilized world. For it is a question of direction— a question which of two divergent roads shall be taken. Whether labor is to be benefited by governmental restrictions or by the abolition of such restrictions is, in short, the question of how the bull shall go to untwist his rope.

In one way or another, we must act upon the tariff question. Throughout the civilized world it everywhere lies within the range of practical politics. Even when protection is most thoroughly accepted there not only exists a more or less active minority who seek its over· throw, but the constant modifications that are being made or proposed in existing tariffs are as constantly bringing the subject into the sphere of political action, while even in that country in which free trade has seemed to be most strongly rooted, the policy of protection is again raising its head. Here it is evident that the tariff question is the great political question of the immediate future. For more than a generation the slavery agitation, the war to which it led and the problems growing out of that war have absorbed political attention in the United States. That era has passed, and a new one is beginning, in which economic questions must force themselves to the front. First among these questions, upon which party lines must soon be drawn and political discussion must rage, is the tariff question.

It behooves not merely those who aspire to political leadership, but those who would conscientiously use their influence and their votes, to come to intelligent conclusions upon this question, and especially is this incumbent upon the men whose aim is the emancipation of labor. Some of these men are now supporters of protection; others are opposed to it. This division, which must place in political opposition to each other those who are at one in ultimate purpose, ought not to exist. One thing or the other must be true—either protection does give better opportunities to labor and raises wages, or it does not. If it does, we who feel that labor has not its rightful opportunities and does not get its fair wages should know it, that we may unite, not merely in sustaining present protection, but in demanding far more. If it does not, then, even if not positively harmful to the working-classes, protection is a delusion and a snare, which distracts attention and divides strength, and the quicker it is seen that tariffs cannot raise wages the quicker are those who wish to raise wages likely to find out what can. The next thing to knowing how anything can be done, is to know how it cannot be done. If the bull I speak of had wit enough to see the uselessness of going one way, he would surely try the other.

My aim in this inquiry is to ascertain beyond peradventure whether protection or free trade best accords with the interests of those who live by their labor. I differ with those who say that with the rate of wages the state has no concern. I hold with those who deem the increase of wages a legitimate purpose of public policy. To raise and maintain wages is the great object that all who live by wages ought to seek, and workingmen are right in supporting any measure that will attain that object. Nor in this are they acting selfishly, for, while the question of wages is the most important of questions to laborers, it is also the most important of questions to society at large. Whatever improves the condition of the lowest and broadest social stratum must promote the true interests of all. Where the wages of common labor are high and remunerative employment is easy to obtain, prosperity will be general. Where wages are highest, there will be the largest production and the most equitable distribution of wealth. There will invention be most active and the brain best guide the hand. There will be the greatest comfort, the widest diffusion of knowledge, the purest morals and the truest patriotism. If we would have a healthy, a happy, an enlightened and a virtuous people, if we would have a pure government, firmly based on the popular will and quickly responsive to it, we must strive to raise wages and keep them high. I accept as good and praiseworthy the ends avowed by the advocates of protective tariffs. What I propose to inquire is whether protective tariffs are in reality conducive to these ends. To do this thoroughly I wish to go over all the ground upon which protective tariffs are advocated or defended, to consider what effect the opposite policy of free trade would have, and to stop not until conclusions are reached of which we may feel absolutely sure.

To some it may seem too much to think that this can be done. For a century no question of public policy has been so widely and persistently debated as that of Protection *vs.* Free Trade. Yet it seems to-day as far as ever from settlement—so far, indeed, that many have come to deem it a question as to which no certain conclusions can be reached, and many more to regard it as too complex and abstruse to be understood by those who have not equipped themselves by long study.

This is, indeed, a hopeless view. We may safely leave many branches of knowledge to such as can devote themselves to special pursuits. We may safely accept what chemists tell us of chemistry, or astronomers of astronomy, or philologists of the development of language, or anatomists of our internal structure, for not only are there in such investigations no pecuniary temptations to warp the judgment, but the ordinary duties of men and of citizens do not call for such special knowledge, and the great body of a people may entertain the crudest notions as to such things and yet lead happy and useful lives. Far different, however, is it with matters which relate to the production and distribution of wealth, and which thus directly affect the comfort and livelihood of men. The intelligence which can alone safely guide in these matters must be the intelligence of the masses, for as to such things it is the common opinion, and not the opinion of the learned few, that finds expression in legislation.

If the knowledge required for the proper ordering of public affairs be like the knowledge required for the prediction of an eclipse, the making of a chemical analysis, or the decipherment of a cuneiform inscription, or even like the knowledge required in any branch of art or handicraft, then the shortness of human life and the necessities of human existence must forever condemn the masses of men to ignorance of matters which directly affect their means of subsistence. If this be so, then popular government is hopeless, and, confronted on one side by the fact, to which all experience testifies, that a people can never safely trust to any portion of their number the making of regulations which affect their earnings, and on the other by the fact that the masses can never see for themselves the effect of such regulations, the only prospect before mankind is that the many must always be ruled and robbed by the few.

But this is not so. Political economy is only the economy of human aggregates, and its laws are laws which

we may individually recognize. What is required for
their elucidation is not long arrays of statistics nor the
collocation of laboriously ascertained facts, but that sort
of clear thinking which, keeping in mind the distinction
between the part and the whole, seeks the relations of
familiar things, and which is as possible for the unlearned
as for the learned.

Whether protection does or does not increase national
wealth, whether it does or does not benefit the laborer,
are questions that from their nature must admit of decisive answers. That the controversy between protection
and free trade, widely and energetically as it has been
carried on, has as yet led to no accepted conclusion cannot therefore be due to difficulties inherent in the subject.
It may in part be accounted for by the fact that powerful
pecuniary interests are concerned in the issue, for it is
true, as Macaulay said, that if large pecuniary interests
were concerned in denying the attraction of gravitation,
that most obvious of physical facts would have disputers.
But that so many fair-minded men who have no special
interests to serve are still at variance on this subject can,
it seems to me, be fully explained only on the assumption that the discussion has not been carried far enough
to bring out that full truth which harmonizes all partial
truths.

The present condition of the controversy, indeed,
shows this to be the fact. In the literature of the subject, I know of no work in which the inquiry has yet
been carried to its proper end. As to the effect of protection upon the production of wealth, all has probably
been said that can be said; but that part of the question
which relates to wages and which is primarily concerned
with the distribution of wealth has not been adequately
treated. Yet this is the very heart of the controversy,
the ground from which, until it is thoroughly explored,

fallacies and confusions must constantly arise, to envelop in obscurity even that which has of itself been sufficiently explained.

The reason of this failure is not far to seek. Political economy is the simplest of the sciences. It is but the intellectual recognition, as related to social life, of laws which in their moral aspect men instinctively recognize, and which are embodied in the simple teachings of Him whom the common people heard gladly. But, like Christianity, political economy has been warped by institutions which, denying the equality and brotherhood of man, have enlisted authority, silenced objection, and ingrained themselves in custom and habit of thought. Its professors and teachers have almost invariably belonged to or been dominated by that class which tolerates no questioning of social adjustments that give to those who do not labor the fruits of labor's toil. They have been like physicians employed to make a diagnosis on condition that they shall discover no unpleasant truth. Given social conditions such as those that throughout the civilized world to-day shock the moral sense, and political economy, fearlessly pursued, must lead to conclusions that will be as a lion in the way to those who have any tenderness for "vested interests." But in the colleges and universities of our time, as in the Sanhedrim of old, it is idle to expect any enunciation of truths unwelcome to the powers that be.

Adam Smith demonstrated clearly enough that protective tariffs hamper the production of wealth. But Adam Smith—the university professor, the tutor and pensioner of the Duke of Buccleuch, the prospective holder of a government place—either did not deem it prudent to go further, or, as is more probable, was prevented from seeing the necessity of doing so by the atmosphere of his time and place. He at any rate failed to carry his great inquiry into the causes which from "that original state

of things in which the production of labor constitutes
the natural recompense or wages of labor " had developed
a state of things in which natural wages seemed to be
only such part of the produce of labor as would enable
the laborer to exist. And, following Smith, came Mal-
thus, to formulate a doctrine which throws upon the
Creator the responsibility for the want and vice that flow
from man's injustice—a doctrine which has barred from
the inquiry which Smith did not pursue even such high
and generous minds as that of John Stuart Mill. Some
of the publications of the Anti-Corn-Law League contain
indications that if the struggle over the English corn-
laws had been longer continued, the discussion might
have been pushed further than the question of revenue
tariff or protective tariff; but, ending as it did, the capitalists of the Manchester school were satisfied, and in
such discussion as has since ensued English free traders,
with few exceptions, have made no further advance,
while American advocates of free trade have merely
followed the English free traders.

On the other hand, the advocates of protection have
evinced a like indisposition to venture on burning
ground. They extol the virtues of protection as furnish-
ing employment, without asking how it comes that any
one should need to be furnished with employment; they
assert that protection maintains the rate of wages, without explaining what determines the rate of wages. The
ablest of them, under the lead of Carey, have rejected the
Malthusian doctrine, but only to set up an equally untenable optimistic theory which serves the same purpose of
barring inquiry into the wrongs of labor, and which has
been borrowed by Continental free traders as a weapon
with which to fight the agitation for social reform.

That, so far as it has yet gone, the controversy
between protection and free trade has not been carried
to its logical conclusions is evident from the positions

which both sides occupy. Protectionists and free traders alike seem to lack the courage of their convictions. If protection have the virtues claimed for it, why should it be confined to the restriction of imports from foreign countries? If it really "provides employment" and raises wages, then a condition of things in which hundreds of thousands vainly seek employment, and wages touch the point of bare subsistence, demands a far more vigorous application of this beneficent principle than any protectionist has yet proposed. On the other hand, if the principle of free trade be true, the substitution of a revenue tariff for a protective tariff is a ridiculously inefficient application of it.

Like the two knights of allegory, who, halting one on each side of the shield, continued to dispute about it when the advance of either must have revealed a truth that would have ended their controversy, protectionists and free traders stand to-day. Let it be ours to carry the inquiry wherever it may lead. The fact is, that fully to understand the tariff question we must go beyond the tariff question as ordinarily debated. And here, it may be, we shall find ground on which honest divergences of opinion may be reconciled, and facts which seem conflicting may fall into harmonious relations.

CHAPTER II.

CLEARING GROUND.

THE protective theory has certainly the weight of most general acceptance. Forty years ago all civilized countries based their policy upon it; and though Great Britain has since discarded it, she remains the only considerable nation that has done so, while not only have her own colonies, as soon as they have obtained the power, shown a disposition to revert to it, but such a disposition has of late years been growing in Great Britain herself.

It should be remembered, however, that the presumption in favor of any belief generally entertained has existed in favor of many beliefs now known to be entirely erroneous, and is especially weak in the case of a theory which, like that of protection, enlists the support of powerful special interests. The history of mankind everywhere shows the power that special interests, capable of organization and action, may exert in securing the acceptance of the most monstrous doctrines. We have, indeed, only to look around us to see how easily a small special interest may exert greater influence in forming opinion and making laws than a large general interest. As what is everybody's business is nobody's business, so what is everybody's interest is nobody's interest. Two or three citizens of a seaside town see

that the building of a custom-house or the dredging of a
creek will put money in their pockets; a few silver-
miners conclude that it will be a good thing for them to
have the government stow away some millions of silver
every month; a navy contractor wants the profit of
repairing useless ironclads or building needless cruisers,
and again and again such petty interests have their way
against the larger interests of the whole people. What
can be clearer than that a note directly issued by the
government is at least as good as a note based on a
government bond? Yet special interests have sufficed
with us to institute and maintain a hybrid currency for
which no other valid reason can be assigned than private
profit.

Those who are specially interested in protective tariffs
find it easy to believe that protection is of general benefit.
The directness of their interest makes them active in
spreading their views, and having control of large means
—for the protected industries are those in which large
capitals are engaged—and being ready on occasion, as a
matter of business, to spend money in propagating their
doctrines, they exert great influence upon the organs of
public opinion. Free trade, on the contrary, offers no
special advantage to any particular interest, and in the
present state of social morality benefits or injuries which
men share in common with their fellows are not felt so
intensely as those which affect them specially.

I do not mean to say that the pecuniary interests
which protection enlists suffice to explain the wide-spread
acceptance of its theories and the tenacity with which
they are held. But it is plain that these interests do
constitute a power of the kind most potent in forming
opinion and influencing legislation, and that this fact
weakens the presumption the wide acceptance of protection might otherwise afford, and is a reason why those

who believe in protection merely because they have constantly heard it praised should examine the question for themselves.

Protection, moreover, has always found an effective ally in those national prejudices and hatreds which are in part the cause and in part the result of the wars that have made the annals of mankind a record of bloodshed and devastation—prejudices and hatreds which have everywhere been the means by which the masses have been induced to use their own power for their own enslavement.

For the first half-century of our national existence American protectionists pointed to the protective tariff of Great Britain as an example to be followed; but since that country, in 1846, discarded protection, its American advocates have endeavored to utilize national prejudice by constantly speaking of protection as an American system and of free trade as a British invention. Just now they are endeavoring to utilize in the same way the enmity against everything British which long oppressions and insults have engendered in the Irish heart, and, in the words of a recent political platform, Irish-Americans are called upon "to resist the introduction into America of the English theory of free trade, which has been so successfully used as a means to destroy the industries and oppress the people of Ireland."

Even if free trade had originated in Great Britain we should be as foolish in rejecting it on that account as we should be in refusing to speak our mother tongue because it is of British origin, or in going back to hand-and water-power because steam-engines were first introduced in Great Britain. But, in truth, free trade no more originated in Great Britain than did the habit of walking on the feet. Free trade is the natural trade—the trade that goes on in the absence of artificial restrictions. It is protection that had to be invented. But instead of being invented in the United States, it was in full force in Great Britain long before the United States were thought of. It would be nearer the truth to say that protection originated in Great Britain, for, if the system did not originate there, it was fully developed there, and it is from that country that it has been derived by us. Nor yet did the reaction against it originate in Great Britain, but in France, among a school of eminent men headed by Quesnay, who were Adam Smith's predecessors and in many things his teachers. These French economists were what neither Smith nor any subsequent British economist or statesman has been —true free traders. They wished to sweep away not merely protective duties, but all taxes, direct and indirect, save a single tax upon land values. This logical conclusion of free-trade principles the so-called British free traders have shirked, and it meets to-day as bitter opposition from the Cobden Club as from American protectionists. The only sense in which we can properly speak of "British free trade" is the same sense in which we speak of a certain imitation metal as "German silver." "British free trade" is spurious free trade. Great Britain does not really enjoy free trade. To say nothing of internal taxes, inconsistent with true free trade, she still maintains a cordon of custom-house officers, coast-guards and baggage-searchers, and still collects over a hundred million dollars of her revenue from import duties. To be sure, her tariff is "for revenue only," but a tariff for revenue only is not free trade. The ruling classes of Great Britain have adopted only so much free trade as suits their class interests, and the battle for free trade in that country has yet to be fought.

On the other hand, it is absurd to talk of protection as an American system. It had been fully developed in

Europe before the American colonies were planted, and
during our colonial period England maintained a more
thorough system of protection than now anywhere exists
—a system which aimed at building up English industries not merely by protective duties, but by the repres-
sion of like industries in Ireland and the colonies, and
wherever else throughout the world English power could
be exerted. What we got of protection was the wrong
side of it, in regulations intended to prevent American
industries from competing with those of the mother
country and to give to her a monopoly of the American
trade.

The irritation produced in the growing colonies by
these restrictions was the main cause of the Revolution
which made of them an independent nation. Protectionist ideas were doubtless at that time latent among
our people, for they permeated the mental atmosphere of
the civilized world, but so little disposition was there to
embody those ideas in a national policy, that the American representatives in negotiating the treaty of peace
endeavored to secure complete freedom of trade between
the United States and Great Britain. This was refused
by England, then and for a long time afterwards completely dominated by protective ideas. But during the
period following the Revolution in which the American
Union existed under the Articles of Confederation, no
tariff hampered importations into the American States.

The adoption of the Constitution made a Federal tariff
possible, and to give the Federal Government an independent revenue a tariff was soon imposed; but although
protection had then begun to find advocates in the
United States, this first American tariff was almost
nominal as compared with what the British tariff was
then or our tariff is now. And in the Federal Constitution State tariffs were prohibited—a step which has re-

sulted in giving to the principle of free trade the greatest extension it has had in modern times. Nothing could more clearly show how far the American people then were from accepting the theories of protection since popularized among them, for the national idea had not then acquired the force it has since gained, and if protection had then been looked upon as necessary the different States would not without a struggle have given up the power of imposing tariffs of their own.

Nor could protection have reached its present height in the United States but for the civil war. While attention was concentrated on the struggle and mothers were sending their sons to the battle-field, the interests that sought protection took advantage of the patriotism that was ready for any sacrifice to secure protective taxes such as had never before been dreamed of—taxes which they have ever since managed to keep in force, and even in many cases to increase.

The truth is that protection is no more American than is the distinction made in our regular army and navy between commissioned officers and enlisted men—a distinction not of degree but of kind, so that there is between the highest non-commissioned officer and the lowest commissioned officer a deep gulf fixed, a gulf which can only be likened to that which exists between white and black where the color-line is drawn sharpest. This distinction is historically a survival of that made in the armies of aristocratic Europe, when they were officered by nobles and recruited from peasants, and has been copied by us in the same spirit of imitation that has led us to copy other undemocratic customs and institutions. Though we preserve this aristocratic distinction after it has been abandoned in some European countries, it is in no sense American. It neither originated with us nor does it consort with our distinctive ideas and institutions. So it is with protection. Whatever be its economic merits there can be no doubt that it conflicts with those ideas of natural right and personal freedom which received national expression in the establishment of the American Republic, and which we have been accustomed to regard as distinctively American. What more incongruous than the administering of custom-house oaths and the searching of trunks and hand-bags under the shadow of "Liberty Enlightening the World"?

As for the assertion that "the English theory of free trade" has been used "to destroy the industries and oppress the people of Ireland," the truth is that it was "the English theory of protection" that was so used. The restrictions which British protection imposed upon the American colonies were trivial as compared with those imposed upon Ireland. The successful resistance of the colonies roused in Ireland the same spirit, and led to the great movement of "Irish Volunteers," who, with cannon bearing the inscription "Free Trade or —— !" forced the repeal of those restrictions and won for a time Irish legislative independence.

Whether Irish industries that were unquestionably hampered and throttled by British protection could now be benefited by Irish protection, like the question whether protection benefits the United States, is only to be settled by a determination of the effects of protection upon the country that imposes it. But without going into that, it is evident that the free trade between Great Britain and Ireland which has existed since the union in 1801, has *not* been the cause of the backwardness of Irish industry. There is one part of Ireland which has enjoyed comparative prosperity and in which important industries have grown up—some of them, such as the building of iron ships, for which natural advantages cannot be claimed. How can this be explained on the theory that Irish industries cannot be reëstablished with-out protection?

If the very men who are now trying to persuade Irish-American voters that Ireland has been impoverished by "British free trade" were privately asked the cause of the greater prosperity of Ulster over other parts of Ire-land, they would probably give the answer made familiar by religious bigotry—that Ulster is enterprising and prosperous because it is Protestant, while the rest of Ireland is sluggish and poor because it is Catholic. But the true reason is plain. It is, that the land tenure in Ulster has been such that a larger portion of the wealth produced has been left there than in other parts of Ire-land, and that the mass of the people have not been so remorselessly hunted and oppressed. In Presbyterian Skye the same general poverty, the same primitive condi-tions of industry exist as in Catholic Connemara, and its cause is to be seen in the same rapacious system of land-lordism which has carried off the fruits of industry and prevented the accumulation of capital. To attribute the backwardness of industry among a people who are steadily stripped of all they can produce above a bare living to the want of a protective tariff or to religious opinions is like attributing the sinking of a scuttled ship to the loss of her figurehead or the color of her paint.

What, however, in the United States at least, has tended more than any appeals to national feeling to dispose the masses in favor of protection, has been the difference of attitude toward the working-classes assumed by the contending policies. In its beginnings in this country protection was strongest in those sections where labor had the largest opportunities and was held in the highest esteem, while the strength of free trade has been the greatest in the section in which up to the civil war slavery prevailed. The political party which successfully challenged the aggressions of the slave power also declared for a protective tariff, while the men who tried to rend the Union in order to establish a nation based upon the right of capital to own labor, prohibited protection in the constitution they formed. The explanation of these facts is, that in one section of the country there were many industries that could be protected, while in the other section there were few. While American cotton culture was in its earlier stages, Southern cotton-planters were willing enough to avail themselves of a heavy duty on India cottons, and Louisiana sugar-growers have always been persistent sticklers for protection. But when cotton raised for export became the great staple of the South, protection, in the absence of manufactures, was not only clearly opposed to dominant Southern interests, but assumed the character of a sectional imposition by which the South was taxed for the benefit of the North. This sectional division on the tariff question had no reference whatever to the conditions of labor, but in many minds its effect has been to associate protection with respect for labor and free trade with its enslavement.

Irrespective of this there has been much in the presentation of the two theories to dispose the working-classes toward protection and against free trade. Working-men generally feel that they do not get a fair reward for their labor. They know that what prevents them from successfully demanding higher wages is the competition of others anxious for work, and they are naturally disposed to favor the doctrine or party that proposes to shield them from competition. This, its advocates urge, is the aim of protection. And whatever protection accomplishes, protectionists at least profess regard for the working-classes, and proclaim their desire to use the powers of government to raise and maintain wages.

Protection, they declare, means the protection of labor. So constantly is this reiterated that many suppose that this is the real derivation of the term, and that "protection" is short for "protection of labor."

On the other hand, the opponents of protection have, for the most part, not only professed no special interest in the well-being of the working-classes and no desire to raise wages, but have denied the justice of attempting to use the powers of government for this purpose. The doctrines of free trade have been intertwined with teachings that throw upon the laws of nature responsibility for the poverty of the laboring-class, and foster a callous indifference to their sufferings. On the same grounds on which they have condemned legislative interference with commerce, free-trade economists have condemned interference with hours of labor, with the rate of wages, and even with the employment of women and children, and have united protectionism and trades-unionism in the same denunciation, proclaiming supply and demand to be the only true and rightful regulator of the price of labor as of the price of pig-iron. While protesting against restrictions upon the production of wealth they have ignored the monstrous injustice of its distribution, and have treated as fair and normal that competition in which human beings, deprived of their natural opportunities of employing themselves, are compelled by biting want to bid against one another.

All this is true. But it is also true that the needs of labor require more than kind words, and are not to be satisfied by such soft phrases as we address to a horse when we want to catch him that we may put a bit in his mouth and a saddle on his back. Let me ask those who are disposed to regard protection as favorable to the aspirations of labor, to consider whether it can be true that what labor needs is to be protected?

To admit that labor needs protection is to acknowledge its inferiority; it is to acquiesce in an assumption that degrades the workman to the position of a dependent, and leads logically to the claim that the employee is bound to vote in the interest of the employer who *provides* him with work. There is something in the very word "protection" that ought to make working-men cautious of accepting anything presented to them under it. The protection of the masses has in all times been the pretense of tyranny—the plea of monarchy, of aristocracy, of special privilege of every kind. The slave-owners justified slavery as protecting the slaves. British misrule in Ireland is upheld on the ground that it is for the protection of the Irish. But, whether under a monarchy or under a republic, is there an instance in the history of the world in which the "protection" of the laboring masses has not meant their oppression? The protection that those who have got the law-making power into their hands have given to labor, has at best always been the protection that man gives to cattle—he protects them that he may use and eat them.

There runs through protectionist professions of concern for labor a tone of condescending patronage more insulting to men who feel the true dignity of labor than frankly expressed contempt could be—an assumption that pauperism is the natural condition of labor, to which it must everywhere fall unless benevolently protected. It is never intimated that the landowner or the capitalist needs protection. They, it is always assumed, can take care of themselves. It is only the poor working-man who must be protected.

What is labor that it should so need protection? Is not labor the creator of capital, the producer of all wealth? Is it not the men who labor that feed and clothe all others? Is it not true, as has been said, that the three great orders of society are "working-men, beggar-men and thieves"? How, then, does it come that working-men alone need protection? When the first man came upon the earth who was there to protect him or to provide him with employment? Yet whenever or however he came, he must have managed to get a living and raise a family!

When we consider that labor is the producer of all wealth, is it not evident that the impoverishment and dependence of labor are abnormal conditions resulting from restrictions and usurpations, and that instead of accepting protection, what labor should demand is freedom? That those who advocate any extension of freedom choose to go no further than suits their own special purpose is no reason why freedom itself should be distrusted. For years it was held that the assertion of our Declaration of Independence that all men are created equal and endowed by their Creator with unalienable rights, applied only to white men. But this in no wise vitiated the principle. Nor does it vitiate the principle that it is still held to apply only to political rights.

And so, that freedom of trade has been advocated by those who have no sympathy with labor should not prejudice us against it. Can the road to the industrial emancipation of the masses be any other than that of freedom?

CHAPTER III.

OF METHOD.

ON the deck of a ship men are pulling on a rope, and on her mast a yard is rising. A man aloft is clinging to the tackle that raises the yard. Is his weight assisting its rise or retarding it? That, of course, depends on what part of the tackle his weight is thrown upon, and can be told only by noticing whether its tendency is with or against the efforts of those who pull on deck.

If in things so simple we may easily err in assuming cause from effect, how much more liable to error are such assumptions in regard to the complicated phenomena of social life.

Much that is urged in current discussions of the tariff question is of no validity whatever, and however it may serve the purpose of controversy, cannot aid in the discovery of truth. That a thing exists with or follows another thing is no proof that it is because of that other thing. This assumption is the fallacy *post hoc, ergo propter hoc*, which leads, if admitted, to the most preposterous conclusions. Wages in the United States are higher than in England, and we differ from England in having a protective tariff. But the assumption that the one fact is because of the other, is no more valid than would be the assumption that these higher wages are due to our decimal coinage or to our republican form of

government. That England has grown in wealth since
the abolition of protection proves no more for free trade
than the growth of the United States under a protective
tariff does for protection. It does not follow that an
institution is good because a country has prospered
under it, nor bad because a country in which it exists is
not prosperous. It does not even follow that institutions to be found in all prosperous countries and not to
be found in backward countries are therefore beneficial.
For this, at various times, might have been confidently
asserted of slavery, of polygamy, of aristocracy, of established churches, and it may still be asserted of public
debts, of private property in land, of pauperism, or of
the existence of distinctively vicious or criminal classes.
Nor even when it can be shown that certain changes in
the prosperity of a country, of an industry, or of a class,
have followed certain other changes in laws or institutions can it be inferred that the two are related to each
other as effect and cause, unless it can also be shown
that the assigned cause tends to produce the assigned
effect, or unless, what is clearly impossible in most cases,
it can be shown that there is no other cause to which the
effect can be attributed. The almost endless multiplicity
of causes constantly operating in human societies, and
the almost endless interference of effect with effect, make
that popular mode of reasoning which logicians call the
method of simple enumeration worse than useless in
social investigations.

As for reliance upon statistics, that involves the additional difficulty of knowing whether we have the right
statistics. Though "figures cannot lie," there is in their
collection and grouping such liability to oversight and
such temptation to bias that they are to be distrusted in
matters of controversy until they have been subjected to

rigid examination. The value of most arguments turning upon statistics is well illustrated in the story of the government clerk who, being told to get up the statistics of a certain question, wished first to know which side it was desired that they should support. Under their imposing appearance of exactness may lurk the gravest errors and wildest assumptions.

To ascertain the effect of protective tariffs, we must inquire what they are and how they operate. When we thus discover their nature and tendencies, we shall be able to weigh what is said for or against them, and have a clue by which we may trace their results amid the complications of social phenomena. For the largest communities are but expansions of the smallest communities, and the rules of arithmetic by which we calculate gain or loss on transactions of dollars apply as well to transactions of hundreds of millions.

Thus the facts we must use and the principles we must apply are common facts that are known to all and principles that are recognized in every-day life. Starting from premises as to which there can be no dispute, we have only to be careful as to our steps in order to reach conclusions of which we may feel sure. We cannot experiment with communities as the chemist can with material substances, or as the physiologist can with animals. Nor can we find nations so alike in all other respects that we can safely attribute any difference in their conditions to the presence or absence of a single cause without first assuring ourselves of the tendency of that cause. But the imagination puts at our command a method of investigating economic problems which is within certain limits hardly less useful than actual experiment. We may test the working of known principles by mentally separating, combining or eliminating

conditions. Let me explain what I mean by an illustration I have once before used.*

When I was a boy I went down to the wharf with
another boy to see the first iron steamship that had ever
crossed the ocean to Philadelphia. Now, hearing of an
iron steamship seemed to us then a good deal like hearing
of a leaden kite or a wooden cooking-stove. But we had
not been long aboard of her, before my comrade said in
a tone of contemptuous disgust: "Pooh! I see how it is.
She's all lined with wood; that's the reason she floats."
I could not controvert him for the moment, but I was
not satisfied, and sitting down on the wharf when he left
me, I set to work trying mental experiments. If it was
the wood inside of her that made her float, then the more
wood the higher she would float; and, mentally, I loaded
her up with wood. But, as I was familiar with the process of making boats out of blocks of wood, I at once
saw that, instead of floating higher, she would sink
deeper. Then, I mentally took all the wood out of her,
as we dug out our wooden boats, and saw that thus
lightened she would float higher still. Then, in imagination, I jammed a hole in her, and saw that the water
would run in and she would sink, as did our wooden
boats when ballasted with leaden keels. And thus I
saw, as clearly as though I could have actually made
these experiments with the steamer, that it was not
the wooden lining that made her float, but her hollow-
ness, or, as I would now phrase it, her displacement of
water.

In such ways as this, with which we are all familiar,
we can isolate, analyze or combine economic principles,
and, by extending or diminishing the scale of proposi-

---

* Lecture before the students of the University of California, on
the "Study of Political Economy," April, 1877.

tions, either subject them to inspection through a mental magnifying-glass or bring a larger field into view. And this each one can do for himself. In the inquiry upon which we are about to enter, all I ask of the reader is that he shall in nothing trust to me.

CHAPTER IV.

TO understand a thing it is often well to begin by looking at it, as it were, from the outside and observing its relations, before examining it in detail. Let us do this with the protective theory.

Protection, as the term has come to signify a certain national policy, means the levying of duties upon imported commodities for the purpose of protecting from competition the home producers of such commodities. Protectionists contend that to secure the highest prosperity of each nation it should produce for itself everything it is capable of producing, and that to this end its home industries should be protected against the competition of foreign industries. They also contend (in the United States at least) that to enable workmen to obtain as high wages as possible they should be protected by tariff duties against the competition of goods produced in countries where wages are lower. Without disputing the correctness of this theory, let us consider its larger relations.

The protective theory, it is to be observed, asserts a general law, as true in one country as in another. However protectionists in the United States may talk of "American protection" and "British free trade," protection is, and of necessity must be, advocated as of universal application. American protectionists use the arguments of foreign protectionists, and even where they complain that the protective policy of other countries is injurious to us, commend it as an example which we should follow. They contend that (at least up to a certain point in national development) protection is everywhere beneficial to a nation, and free trade everywhere injurious; that the prosperous nations have built up their prosperity by protection, and that all nations that would be prosperous must adopt that policy. And their arguments must be universal to have any plausibility, for it would be absurd to assert that a theory of national growth and prosperity applies to some countries and not to others.

Let me ask the reader who has hitherto accepted the protective theory to consider what its necessarily universal character involves. It was the realization of this that first led me to question that theory. I was for a number of years after I had come of age a protectionist, or rather, I supposed I was, for, without real examination, I had accepted the belief, as in the first place we all accept our beliefs, on the authority of others. So far, however, as I thought at all on the subject, I was logical, and I well remember how when the *Florida* and *Alabama* were sinking American ships at sea, I thought their depredations, after all, a good thing for the State in which I lived—California—since the increased risk and cost of ocean carriage in American ships (then the only way of bringing goods from the Eastern States to California) would give to her infant industries something of that needed protection against the lower wages and better established industries of the Eastern States which the Federal Constitution prevented her from securing by a State tariff. The full bearing of such notions never occurred to me till I happened to hear the protective theory elaborately expounded by an able man. As he urged that American industries must be protected from the competition of foreign countries, that we ought to work up our own raw materials and allow nothing to be imported that we could produce for ourselves, I began to realize that these propositions, if true, must be universally true, and that not only should every nation shut itself out from every other nation; not only should the various sections of every large country institute tariffs of their own to shelter their industries from the competition of other sections, but that the reason given why no people should obtain from abroad anything they might make at home, must apply as well to the family. It was this that led me to weigh arguments I had before accepted without real examination.

It seems to me impossible to consider the necessarily universal character of the protective theory without feeling it to be repugnant to moral perceptions and inconsistent with the simplicity and harmony which we everywhere discover in natural law. What should we think of human laws framed for the government of a country which should compel each family to keep constantly on their guard against every other family, to expend a large part of their time and labor in preventing exchanges with their neighbors, and to seek their own prosperity by opposing the natural efforts of other families to become prosperous? Yet the protective theory implies that laws such as these have been imposed by the Creator upon the families of men who tenant this earth. It implies that by virtue of social laws, as immutable as the physical laws, each nation must stand jealously on guard against every other nation and erect artificial obstacles to national intercourse. It implies that a federation of mankind, such as that which prevents the establishment of tariffs between the States of the American Union, would be a disaster to the race, and that in an ideal world each nation would be protected from every other nation by a cordon of tax-collectors, with their attendant spies and informers.

Such a theory might consort with that form of poly-theism which assigned to each nation a separate and hostile God; but it is hard to reconcile it with the idea of the unity of the Creative Mind and the universality of law. Imagine a Christian missionary expounding to a newly discovered people the sublime truths of the gospel of peace and love—the fatherhood of God; the brother-hood of man; the duty of regarding the interests of our neighbors equally with our own, and of doing to others as we would have them do to us. Could he, in the same breath, go on to declare that, by virtue of the laws of this same God, each nation, to prosper, must defend itself against all other nations by a protective tariff?

Religion and experience alike teach us that the highest good of each is to be sought in the good of others; that the true interests of men are harmonious, not antago-nistic; that prosperity is the daughter of good will and peace; and that want and destruction follow enmity and strife. The protective theory, on the other hand, implies the opposition of national interests; that the gain of one people is the loss of others; that each must seek its own good by constant efforts to get advantage over others and to prevent others from getting advantage over it. It makes of nations rivals instead of coöperators; it inculcates a warfare of restrictions and prohibitions and searchings and seizures, which differs in weapons, but not in spirit, from that warfare which sinks ships and burns cities. Can we imagine the nations beating their swords into plowshares and their spears into pruning-hooks and yet maintaining hostile tariffs?

No matter whether he call himself Christian or Deist, or Agnostic or Atheist, who can look about him without seeing that want and suffering flow inevitably from self-ishness, and that in any community the golden rule which teaches us to regard the interests of others as carefully as our own would bring not only peace but plenty? Can it be that what is true of individuals ceases to be true of nations—that in one sphere the law of prosperity is the law of love; in the other that of strife? On the contrary, universal history testifies that poverty, degradation and enslavement are the inevitable results of that spirit which leads nations to regard each other as rivals and enemies.

Every political truth must be a moral truth. Yet who can accept the protective theory as a moral truth?

A few months ago I found myself one night, with four other passengers, in the smoking-car of a Pennsylvania limited express-train traveling west. The conversation, beginning with fast trains, turned to fast steamers, and then to custom-house experiences. One told how, coming from Europe with a trunk filled with presents for his wife, he had significantly said to the custom-house inspector detailed to examine his trunks that he was in a hurry. "How much of a hurry?" said the officer. "Ten dollars' worth of a hurry," was the reply. The officer took a quick look through the trunk and remarked, "That's not much of a hurry for all this." "I gave him ten more," said the story-teller, "and he chalked the trunk."

Then another told how under similar circumstances he had placed a magnificent meerschaum pipe so that it would be the first thing seen on lifting the trunk-lid, and, when the officer admired it, had replied that it was his. The third said he simply put a greenback conspicu-ously in the first article of luggage; and the fourth told how his plan was to crumple up a note, and put it with his keys in the officer's hands.

Here were four reputable business men, as I afterward found them to be—one an iron-worker, one a coal-producer, and the other two manufacturers—men of at least average morality and patriotism, who not only thought it no harm to evade the tariff, but who made no scruple of the false oath necessary, and regarded the bribery of customs officers as a good joke. I had the curiosity to edge the conversation from this to the subject of free trade, when I found that all four were stanch protectionists, and by edging it a little further I found that all four were thorough believers in the right of an employer to discharge any workman who voted for a free-trade candidate, holding, as they put it, that no one ought to eat the bread of an employer whose interests he opposed.

I recall this conversation because it is typical. Whoever has traveled on trans-Atlantic steamers has listened to such conversations, and is aware that the great majority of the American protectionists who visit Europe return with purchases which they smuggle through, even at the expense of a "custom-house oath" and a greenback to the examining officer. Many of our largest undervaluation smugglers have been men of the highest social and religious standing, who gave freely of their spoils to churches and benevolent societies. Not long ago a highly respected banker, an extremely religious man, who had probably neglected the precautions of my smoking-car friends, was detected in the endeavor to smuggle through in his luggage (which he had of course taken a "custom-house oath" did not contain anything dutiable) a lot of very valuable presents to a church!

Conscientious men will (until they get used to them) shrink from false oaths, from bribery, or from other

means necessary to evade a tariff, but even of believers
in protection are there any who really think such eva-
sions wrong in themselves?   What theoretical protectionist is there, who, if no one was watching him, would
scruple to carry a box of cigars or a dress-pattern, or
anything else that could be carried, across a steamer
wharf or across Niagara bridge?   And why should he
scruple to carry such things across a wharf, a river, or
an imaginary line, since once inside the custom-house
frontier no one would object to his carrying them thousands of miles?

That unscrupulous men, for their own private advantage, break laws intended for the general good proves
nothing; but that no one really feels smuggling to be
wrong proves a good deal. Whether we hold the basis
of moral ideas to be intuitive or utilitarian, is not the
fact that protection thus lacks the support of the moral
sentiment inconsistent with the idea that tariffs are
necessary to the well-being and progress of mankind?
If, as is held by some, moral perceptions are implanted
in our nature as a means whereby our conduct may be
instinctively guided in such way as to conduce to the
general well-being, how is it, if the Creator has ordained
that man should prosper by protective tariffs, that the
moral sense takes no cognizance of such a law? If, as
others hold, what we call moral perceptions be the result
of general experience of what conduces to the common
good, how is it that the beneficial effects of protection
have not developed moral recognition?

To make that a crime by statute which is no crime in
morals, is inevitably to destroy respect for law; to resort
to oaths to prevent men from doing what they feel
injures no one, is to weaken the sanctity of oaths. Corruption, evasion and false swearing are inseparable from
tariffs. Can that be good of which these are the fruits?

A system which requires such spying and searching, such invoking of the Almighty to witness the contents of every box, bundle and package—a system which always has provoked, and in the nature of man always must provoke, corruption and fraud—can it be necessary to the prosperity and progress of mankind?

Consider, moreover, how sharply this theory of protection conflicts with common experience and habits of thought. Who would think of recommending a site for a proposed city or a new colony because it was very difficult to get at? Yet, if the protective theory be true, this would really be an advantage. Who would regard piracy as promotive of civilization? Yet a discriminating pirate, who would confine his seizures to goods which might be produced in the country to which they were being carried, would be as beneficial to that country as a tariff.

Whether protectionists or free traders, we all hear with interest and pleasure of improvements in transportation by water or land; we are all disposed to regard the opening of canals, the building of railways, the deepening of harbors, the improvement of steamships, as beneficial. But if such things are beneficial, how can tariffs be beneficial? The effect of such things is to lessen the cost of transporting commodities; the effect of tariffs is to increase it. If the protective theory be true, every improvement that cheapens the carriage of goods between country and country is an injury to mankind unless tariffs be commensurately increased.

The directness, the swiftness and the ease with which birds cleave the air, naturally excite man's desire. His fancy has always given angels wings, and he has ever dreamed of a time when the power of traversing those unobstructed fields might also be his. That this triumph is within the power of human ingenuity who in this age

of marvels can doubt? And who would not hail with
delight the news that invention had at last brought to
realization the dream of ages, and made navigation of
the atmosphere as practicable as navigation of the ocean?
Yet if the protective theory be true this mastery of
another element would be a misfortune to man. For it
would make protection impossible. Every inland town
and village, every rood of ground on the whole earth's
surface, would at once become a port of an all-embracing
ocean, and the only way in which any people could continue to enjoy the blessings of protection would be to
roof their country in.

It is not only improvements in transportation that are
antagonistic to protection; but all labor-saving invention
and discovery. The utilization of natural gas bids fair
to lessen the demand for native coal far more than could
the free importation of foreign coal. Borings in Central
New York have recently revealed vast beds of pure salt,
the working of which will destroy the industry of salt-
making, to encourage which we impose a duty on foreign
salt. We maintain a tariff for the avowed purpose of
keeping out the products of cheap foreign labor; yet
machines are daily invented that produce goods cheaper
than the cheapest foreign labor. Clearly the only con-
sistent protectionism is that of China, which would not
only prohibit foreign commerce, but forbid the introduction of labor-saving machinery.

The aim of protection, in short, is to prevent the
bringing into a country of things in themselves useful
and valuable, in order to compel the making of such
things. But what all mankind, in the individual affairs
of every-day life, regard as to be desired is not the
making of things, but the possession of things.

CHAPTER V.

THE more one considers the theory that every nation ought to "protect" itself against every other nation, the more inconsistent does it seem.

Is there not, in the first place, an obvious absurdity in taking the nation or country as the protective unit and saying that each should have a protective tariff?* What is meant by nation or country in the protectionist theory is an independent political division. Thus Great Britain and Ireland are considered one nation, France another,

---

* That protectionist writers are themselves conscious of this absurdity is to be seen in their constant effort to suggest the idea, too preposterous to be broadly stated, that nations, instead of being purely arbitrary political divisions of mankind, are natural, or divinely appointed, divisions. Thus, not to multiply instances, Professor Robert Ellis Thompson ("Political Economy," p. 34) defines a nation as "a people speaking one language, living under one government, and occupying a continuous area. This area is a district whose natural boundaries designate it as intended for the site of an independent people." This definition is given in large type, while underneath is appended in small type: "No one point of this definition is essential save the second." Yet in spite of this admission that the "nation" is a purely arbitrary political division, Professor Thompson endeavors throughout his book to suggest a different impression to the mind of the reader, by talking of "the existence of nations as parts of the world's *providential* order," the "*providential* boundaries of nations," etc.

Germany another, Switzerland another, the United States, Canada, Mexico, and each of the Central and South American republics are others. But these divisions are arbitrary. They do not coincide with any differences in soil, climate, race or industry—they have no maximum or minimum of area or population. They are, moreover, continually changing. The maps of Europe and America used by school-children to-day are very different from the maps their fathers used. The difference a hundred years ago was greater yet; and as we go further back still greater differences appear. According to this theory, when the three British kingdoms had separate governments it was necessary for the well-being of all that they should be protected from each other, and should Ireland achieve independence that necessity would recur; but while the three countries are united under one government, it does not exist. The petty states of which a few years ago Germany and Italy consisted ought upon this theory to have had, as they once had, tariffs between them. Yet, now, upon the same theory, they no longer need these tariffs. Alsace and Lorraine when provinces of France needed to be protected against Germany. Now that they are German provinces they need protection against France. Texas, when part of Mexico, required a protective tariff against the United States. Now, being a part of the United States, it requires a protective tariff against Mexico. We of the United States require a protective tariff against Canada, and the Canadians a tariff against us, but if Canada were to come into the Union the necessity for both of these tariffs would disappear.

Do not these incongruities show that the protective theory is destitute of scientific basis; that instead of originating in any deduction from principles or induction from facts, it has been invented merely to serve the pur-

poses of its inventors? Political changes in no wise alter
soil, climate or industrial needs. If the three British
kingdoms do not now need tariffs against one another,
they could not have needed them before the union. If it
is not injurious to the various states of Italy or Germany
to trade freely with each other now, it could not have
been injurious before they were united. If Alsace and
Lorraine are benefited by free trade with Germany now,
they would have been benefited by it when French provinces. If the people of the opposite shores of the Great
Lakes and St. Lawrence River would not be injured by
the free exchange of their products should Canada enter
the American Union, they could not be injured by freedom to exchange their products now.

Consider how inconsistent with the protective theory
is the free trade that prevails between the States of the
American Union. Our Union includes an area almost as
large as Europe, yet the protectionists who hold that
each European country ought to protect itself against all
the rest make no objections to the free trade that exists
between the American States, though some of these
States are larger than European kingdoms, and the differences between them, as to natural resources and industrial development, are at least as great. If it is for the
benefit of Germany and France that they should be separated by protective tariffs, does not New Jersey need the
protection of a tariff from New York and Pennsylvania?
and do not New York and Pennsylvania also need to be
protected from New Jersey? And if New England needs
protection against the Province of Quebec, and Ohio,
Illinois and Michigan against the Province of Ontario, is
it not clear that these States also need protection from
the States which adjoin them on the south? What difference does it make that one set of States belong to
the American Union and the other to the Canadian Con-

federation? Industry and commerce, when left to themselves, pay no more attention to political lines than do
birds or fishes.

Clearly, if there is any truth in the protective theory it
must apply not only to the grand political divisions but
to all their parts. If a country ought not to import
from other countries anything which its own people can
produce, the same principle must apply to every sub-
division; and each State, each county and each township
must need its own protective tariff.

And further than this, the proper application of the
protective theory *requires* the separation of mankind into
the smallest possible political divisions, each defended
against the rest by its own tariff. For the larger the
area of the protective unit, the more difficult does it
become to apply the protective theory. With every
extension of such countries as the United States the
possibility of protection, if it can be applied only to the
major political divisions, becomes less, and were the
poet's dream realized, and mankind united in a " Federation of the World," the possibility of protection would
vanish. On the other hand, the smaller the protective
unit the better can the theory of protection be applied.
Protectionists do not go so far as to aver that all trade
is injurious. They hold that each country may safely
import what it cannot produce, but should restrict the
importation of what it can produce. Thus discrimination is required, which becomes more possible the smaller
the protective unit.

Upon protective principles the same tariff will no
better suit all the States of our Union than the same
sized shoes will fit all our sixty million people. Massachusetts, for instance, does not produce coal, iron or
sugar. These, then, on protective principles, ought to
come into Massachusetts free, while Pennsylvania enjoyed

protection on iron and coal, and Louisiana on sugar. Oranges may be grown in Florida, but not in Minnesota; therefore, while Florida needs a protective duty on oranges, Minnesota does not. And so on through the whole list of States. To "protect" them all with the same tariff is to ignore as to each that part of the protective theory which permits the free importation of commodities that cannot be produced at home; and, by compelling them to pay higher prices for what they cannot produce, to neutralize the benefits arising from the protection of such commodities as they do produce.

Furthermore, while Massachusetts, on the protective theory, does not need protection on coal, iron and sugar, which she cannot produce, she does need protection against the beef, hogs and breadstuffs with which she is "deluged" from the West to the injury of her agricultural industries, and of which protection would enable her to raise enough for her home consumption. On the other hand, the West needs protection against the boots and shoes and woolens of Massachusetts, so that Western leather and wool could be worked up at home, instead of being carried long distances in raw form, to be brought back in finished form. In the same way the iron-workers of Ohio need protection against Pennsylvania more than they do against England, while it is only mockery to protect Rocky Mountain coal-miners against the coal of Nova Scotia, British Columbia and Australia, which cannot come into competition with them, while not protecting them against the coal of Iowa; or to protect the infant cotton-mills of the South against Old England while giving them no protection against New England.

Upon the protective theory protection is most needed against like industries. All protectionists agree that the United States has greater need of protection against Great Britain than against Brazil; and Canada against the United States than against India—all agree that if we must have free trade it should be with the countries most widely differing as to their productions from our own. Now there is far less difference between the productions and productive capacities of New Hampshire and Vermont, of Indiana and Illinois, or of Kansas and Nebraska, than there is between the United States as a whole and any foreign country. Therefore, on the protective theory, tariffs between these States are more needed than between the United States and foreign countries. And since adjoining townships differ less in industrial capacities than adjoining States, they require protective tariffs all the more.

The thirteen American colonies came together as thirteen independent sovereignties, each retaining the full power of taxation, including that of levying duty on imports, which was not given up by them until 1787, eleven years after the Declaration of Independence, when the Federal Constitution was adopted. If the protective theory, then dominant in Great Britain, had at that time had the hold upon the American people which it afterwards obtained, it is certain that the power of protecting themselves would never have been given up by the States. And had the Union continued as at first formed, or had the framers of the Constitution lacked the foresight to prohibit State tariffs, there is no doubt that when we came to imitate the British system of protection we should have had as strong a demand in the various States for protection against other States as we have had for protection against foreign countries, and the arguments now used against free trade with foreign countries would to-day be urged against free trade between the States.

Nor can there be any doubt that if our political organization made our townships independent of one another,

we should have, in our townships and villages, the same
clamor for protection against the industries of other
townships and villages that we have now for the protection of the nation against other nations.

I am writing on Long Island, near the town of
Jamaica. I think I could make as good an argument to
the people of that little town as is made by the protectionists to the people of the United States. I could say
to the shopkeepers of Jamaica, "Your townsmen now go
to New York when they want to purchase a suit of
clothes or a bill of dry-goods, leaving to you only the
fag-ends of their custom, while the farmers' wagons that
pass in a long line over the turnpike every night, carrying produce to New York and Brooklyn, bring back supplies the next day. A protective tariff will compel these
purchases to be made here. Thus profits that now go to
New York and Brooklyn will be retained in Jamaica;
you will want larger stores and better houses, can pay
your clerks and journeymen higher wages, will need
more banking accommodations, will advertise more
freely in Jamaican newspapers, and thus will the town
grow and prosper."

"Moreover," I might say, "what a useless waste of
labor there is in carrying milk and butter, chickens, eggs
and vegetables to New York and Brooklyn and bringing
back other things. How much better for our farmers if
they had a home market. This we can secure for them
by a tariff that will protect Jamaican industries against
those of New York and Brooklyn. Clothing, cigars,
boots and shoes, agricultural implements and furniture
may be manufactured here as well as in those cities.
Why should we not have a cotton-factory, a woolen-mill,
a foundry, and, in short, all the establishments necessary
to supply the wants of our people? To get them we
need only a protective tariff. Capital, when assured of

protection, will be gladly forthcoming for such enterprises, and we shall soon be exporting what we now import, while our farmers will find a demand at their doors for all their produce. Even if at first they do have to pay somewhat higher prices for what they buy they will be much more than compensated by the higher prices they will get for what they sell, and will save an eight- or ten-mile haul to Brooklyn or New York. Thus, instead of Jamaica remaining a little village, the industries which a protective tariff will build up here will make it a large town, while the increased demand for labor will make wages higher and employment steadier."

I submit that all this is at least as valid as the protective arguments that are addressed to the people of the whole United States, and no one who has listened to the talk of village shopkeepers or noticed the comments of local newspapers can doubt that were our townships independent, village protectionists could get as ready a hearing as national protectionists do now.

But to follow the protective theory to its logical conclusions we cannot stop with protection between State and State, township and township, village and village. If protection be needful between nations, it must be needful not only between political sub-divisions, but between family and family. If nations should never buy of other nations what they might produce at home, the same principle must forbid each family to buy anything it might produce. Social laws, like physical laws, must apply to the molecule as well as to the aggregate. But a social condition in which the principle of protection was thus fully carried out would be a condition of utter barbarism.

CHAPTER VI.

TRADE.

PROTECTION implies prevention. To protect is to preserve or defend.

What is it that protection by tariff prevents? It is trade. To speak more exactly, it is that part of trade which consists in bringing in from other countries commodities that might be produced at home.

But trade, from which "protection" essays to preserve and defend us, is not, like flood, earthquake, or tornado, something that comes without human agency. Trade implies human action. There can be no need of preserving from or defending against trade, unless there are men who want to trade and try to trade. Who, then, are the men against whose efforts to trade "protection" preserves and defends us?

If I had been asked this question before I had come to think over the matter for myself, I should have said that the men against whom "protection" defends us are foreign producers who wish to sell their goods in our home markets. This is the assumption that runs through all protectionist arguments — the assumption that foreigners are constantly trying to force their products upon us, and that a protective tariff is a means for defending ourselves against what *they* want to do.

Yet a moment's thought will show that no effort of foreigners to sell us their products could of itself make a

45

tariff necessary. For the desire of one party, however strong it may be, cannot of itself bring about trade. To every trade there must be two parties who mutually desire to trade, and whose actions are reciprocal. No one can buy unless he can find some one willing to sell; and no one can sell unless there is some other one willing to buy. If Americans did not want to buy foreign goods, foreign goods could not be sold here even if there were no tariff. The efficient cause of the trade which our tariff aims to prevent is the desire of Americans to buy foreign goods, not the desire of foreign producers to sell them. Thus protection really prevents what the "protected" themselves want to do. It is not from foreigners that protection preserves and defends us; it is from ourselves.

Trade is not invasion. It does not involve aggression on one side and resistance on the other, but mutual consent and gratification. There cannot be a trade unless the parties to it agree, any more than there can be a quarrel unless the parties to it differ. England, we say, forced trade with the outside world upon China, and the United States upon Japan. But, in both cases, what was done was not to force the people to trade, but to force their governments to let them. If the people had not wanted to trade, the opening of the ports would have been useless.

Civilized nations, however, do not use their armies and fleets to open one another's ports to trade. What they use their armies and fleets for, is, when they quarrel, to close one another's ports. And their effort then is to prevent the carrying in of things even more than the bringing out of things—importing rather than exporting. For a people can be more quickly injured by preventing them from getting things than by preventing them from sending things away. Trade does not require force.

Free trade consists simply in letting people buy and sell as they want to buy and sell. It is protection that requires force, for it consists in preventing people from doing what they want to do. Protective tariffs are as much applications of force as are blockading squadrons, and their object is the same—to prevent trade. The difference between the two is that blockading squadrons are a means whereby nations seek to prevent their enemies from trading; protective tariffs are a means whereby nations attempt to prevent their own people from trading. What protection teaches us, is to do to ourselves in time of peace what enemies seek to do to us in time of war..

Can there be any greater misuse of language than to apply to commerce terms suggesting strife, and to talk of one nation invading, deluging, overwhelming or inundating another with goods? Goods! what are they but good things—things we are all glad to get? Is it not preposterous to talk of one nation forcing its good things upon another nation? Who individually would wish to be preserved from such invasion? Who would object to being inundated with all the dress-goods his wife and daughters could want; deluged with a horse and buggy; overwhelmed with clothing, with groceries, with good cigars, fine pictures, or anything else that has value? And who would take it kindly if any one should assume to protect him by driving off those who wanted to bring him such things?

In point of fact, however, not only is it impossible for one nation to sell to another, unless that other wants to buy, but international trade does not consist in sending out goods to be sold. The great mass of the imports of every civilized country consists of goods that have been ordered by the people of that country and are imported at their risk. This is true even in our own case, although one of the effects of our tariff is that many goods that otherwise would be imported by Americans are sent here by European manufacturers, because undervaluation is thus made easier.

But it is not the importer who is the cause of importation. Whether goods are brought here by American importers or sent here by foreign exporters, the cause of their coming here is that they are asked for by the American people. It is the demand of purchasers at retail that causes goods to be imported. Thus a protective tariff is a prevention by a people not of what others want to do to them, but of what they themselves want to do.

When in the common use of the word we speak of individuals or communities protecting themselves, there is always implied the existence of some external enemy or danger, such as cold, heat or accident, savage beasts or noxious vermin, fire or disease, robbers or invaders; something disposed to do what the protected object to. The only cases in which the common meaning of the word does not imply some external enemy or danger are those in which it implies some protector of superior intelligence, as when we speak of imbeciles, lunatics, drunkards or young children being protected against their own irrational acts.

But the systems of restriction which their advocates have named "protective" lack both the one and the other of these essential qualities of real protection. What they defend a people against is not external enemies or dangers, but what that people themselves want to do. Yet this "protection" is not the protection of a superior intelligence, for human wit has not yet been able to devise any scheme by which any intelligence can be secured in a Parliament or Congress superior to that of the people it represents.

That where protective tariffs are imposed it is in accordance with the national will I do not deny. What I wish to point out is that even the people who thus impose protective tariffs upon themselves still want to do what by protective tariffs they strive to prevent themselves from doing. This is seen in the tendency of importation to continue in spite of tariffs, in the disposition of citizens to evade their tariff whenever they can, and in the fact that the very same individuals who demand the imposition of tariffs to prevent the importation of foreign commodities are among the individuals whose demand for those commodities is the cause of their importation. Given a people of which every man, woman and child is a protectionist, and a tariff unanimously agreed upon, and still that tariff will be a restriction upon what these people want to do and will still try to do. Protectionists are only protectionists in theory and in politics. When it comes to buying what they want all protectionists are free traders. I say this to point out not the inconsistency of protectionists, but something more significant.

"I write." "I breathe." Both propositions assert action on the part of the same individual, but action of different kinds. I write by conscious volition; I breathe instinctively. I am conscious that I breathe only when I think of it. Yet my breathing goes on whether I think of it or not—when my consciousness is absorbed in thought, or is dormant in sleep. Though with all my will I try to stop breathing, I yet, in spite of myself, try to breathe, and will continue that endeavor while life lasts. Other vital functions are even further beyond consciousness and will. We live by the continuous carrying on of multifarious and delicate processes apparent only in their results and utterly irresponsive to mental direction.

Between the man and the community there is in these respects an analogy which becomes closer as civilization progresses and social relations grow more complex. That power of the whole which is lodged in governments is limited in its field of consciousness and action much as the conscious will of the individual is limited, and even that consensus of personal beliefs and wishes termed public opinion is but little wider in its range. There is, beyond national direction and below national consciousness, a life and relation of parts and a performance of functions which are to the social body what the vital processes are to the physical body.

What would happen to the individual if all the functions of the body were placed under the control of the consciousness, and a man could forget to breathe, or miscalculate the amount of gastric juice needed by his stomach, or blunder as to what his kidneys should take from the blood, is what would happen to a nation in which all individual activities were directed by government.

And though a people collectively may institute a tariff to prevent trade, their individual wants and desires will still force them to try to trade, just as when a man ties a ligature round his arm, his blood will still try to circulate. For the effort of each to satisfy his desires with the least exertion, which is the motive of trade, is as instinctive and persistent as are the instigations which the vital organs of the body obey. It is not the importer and the exporter who are the cause of trade, but the daily and hourly demands of those who never think of importing or exporting, and to whom trade carries that which they demand, just as the blood carries to each fiber of the body that for which it calls.

It is as natural for men to trade as it is for blood to circulate. Man is by nature a trading animal, impelled to trade by persistent desires, placed in a world where everything shows that he was intended to trade, and finding in trade the possibility of social advance. Without trade man would be a savage.

Where each family raises its own food, builds its own house, makes its own clothes and manufactures its own tools, no one can have more than the barest necessaries of life, and every local failure of crops must bring famine. A people living in this way will be independent, but their independence will resemble that of the beasts. They will be poor, ignorant, and all but powerless against the forces of nature and the vicissitudes of the seasons.

This social condition, to which the protective theory would logically lead, is the lowest in which man is ever found—the condition from which he has toiled upward. He has progressed only as he has learned to satisfy his wants by exchanging with his fellows and has freed and extended trade. The difference between naked savages possessed of only the rudiments of the arts, cowering in ignorance and weakness before the forces of nature, and the wealth, the knowledge and the power of our highest civilization, is due to the exchange of the independence which is the aim of the protective system, for that interdependence which comes with trade. Men cannot apply themselves to the production of but one of the many things human wants demand unless they can exchange their products for the products of others. And thus it is only as the growth of trade permits the division of labor that, beyond the merest rudiments, skill can be developed, knowledge acquired and invention made; and that productive power can so gain upon the requirements for maintaining life that leisure becomes possible and capital can be accumulated.

If to prevent trade were to stimulate industry and promote prosperity, then the localities where he was most isolated would show the first advances of man. The natural protection to home industry afforded by rugged mountain-chains, by burning deserts, or by seas too wide and tempestuous for the frail bark of the early mariner, would have given us the first glimmerings of civilization and shown its most rapid growth. But, in fact, it is where trade could best be carried on that we find wealth first accumulating and civilization beginning. It is on accessible harbors, by navigable rivers and much-traveled highways that we find cities arising and the arts and sciences developing. And as trade becomes free and extensive—as roads are made and navigation improved; as pirates and robbers are extirpated and treaties of peace put an end to chronic warfare—so does wealth augment and civilization grow. All our great labor-saving inventions, from that of money to that of the steam-engine, spring from trade and promote its extension. Trade has ever been the extinguisher of war, the eradicator of prejudice, the diffuser of knowledge. It is by trade that useful seeds and animals, useful arts and inventions, have been carried over the world, and that men in one place have been enabled not only to obtain the products, but to profit by the observations, discoveries and inventions of men in other places.

In a world created on protective principles, all habitable parts would have the same soil and climate, and be fitted for the same productions, so that the inhabitants of each locality would be able to produce at home all they required. Its seas and rivers would not lend themselves to navigation, and every little section intended for the habitation of a separate community would be guarded by a protective mountain-chain. If we found ourselves in such a world, we might infer it to be the intent of nature that each people should develop its own industries independently of all others. But the world in which we do find ourselves is not merely adapted to intercommunication, but what it yields to man is so distributed as to compel the people of different localities to trade with each other to satisfy fully their desires. The diversities of soil and climate, the distribution of water, wood and mineral deposits, the currents of sea and air, produce infinite differences in the adaptation of different parts to different productions. It is not merely that one zone yields sugar and coffee, the banana and the pineapple, and another wheat and barley, the apple and the potato; that one supplies furs and another cotton; that here are hillsides adapted to pasture and there valleys fitted for the plow; here granite and there clay; in one place iron and coal and in another copper and lead; but that there are differences so delicate that, though experience tells us they exist, we cannot say to what they are due. Wine of a certain quality is produced in one place which cuttings from the same vines will not yield in another place, though soil and climate seem alike. Some localities, without assignable reason, become renowned for productions of one kind and some for productions of another kind; and experience often shows that plants thrive differently in different parts of the same field. These endless diversities, in the adaptation of different parts of the earth's surface to the production of the different things required by man, show that nature has not intended man to depend for the supply of his wants upon his own production, but to exchange with his fellows, just as the placing of the meat before one guest at table, the vegetables before another, and the bread before another, shows the intent of the host that they should help one another.

Other natural facts have similar bearing. It has long been known that to obtain the best crops the farmer should not sow with seed grown in his own fields, but with seed brought from afar. The strain of domestic animals seems always improved by imported stock, even poultry-breeders finding it best to sell the male birds they raise and supply their places with cocks brought from a distance. Whether or not the same law holds true with regard to the physical part of man, it is certain that the admixture of peoples produces stimulating mental effects. Prejudices are worn down, wits are sharpened, language enriched, habits and customs brought to the test of comparison and new ideas enkindled. The most progressive peoples, if not always of mixed blood, have always been the peoples who came most in contact with and learned most from others. "Home-keeping youths have ever homely wits" is true of nations.

And, further than this, it is characteristic of all the inventions and discoveries that are so rapidly increasing our power over nature that they require the greater division of labor, and extend trade. Thus every step in advance destroys the independence and increases the interdependence of men. The appointed condition of human progress is evidently that men shall come into closer relations and become more and more dependent upon each other.

Thus the restrictions which protectionism urges us to impose upon ourselves are about as well calculated to promote national prosperity as ligatures, that would impede the circulation of the blood, would be to promote bodily health and comfort. Protection calls upon us to pay officials, to encourage spies and informers, and to provoke fraud and perjury, for what? Why, to preserve ourselves from and protect ourselves against something which offends no moral law; something to which we are instinctively impelled; something without which we could never have emerged from barbarism, and something which physical nature and social laws alike prove to be in conformity with the creative intent.

It is true that protectionists do not condemn all trade, and though some of them have wished for an ocean of fire to bar out foreign products, others, more reasonable if less logical, would permit a country to import things it cannot produce. The international trade which they concede to be harmless amounts not to a tenth and perhaps not to a twentieth of the international trade of the world, and, so far as our own country is concerned, the things we could not obtain at home amount to little more than a few productions of the torrid zone, and even these, if properly protected, might be grown at home by artificial heat, to the incidental encouragement of the glass and coal industries. But, so far as the correctness of the theory goes, it does not matter whether the trade which "protection" would permit, as compared with that it would prevent, be more or less. What "protection" calls on us to preserve ourselves from, and guard ourselves against, is trade. And whether trade be between citizens of the same nation or citizens of different nations, and whether we get by it things that we could produce for ourselves or things that we could not produce for ourselves, the object of trade is always the same. If I trade with a Canadian, a Mexican, or an Englishman it is for the same reason that I trade with an American—that I would rather have the thing he gives me than the thing I give him. Why should I refuse to trade with a foreigner any more than with a fellow-citizen when my object in trading is my advantage, not his? And is it not in the one case, quite as much as in the other, an injury to me that my trade should be prevented? What difference does it make whether it would be possible or impossible for me to make for myself the thing for which I trade? If I did not want the thing I am to get more than the thing I am to give, I would not wish to make the trade. Here is a farmer who proposes to exchange with his neighbor a horse he does not want for a couple of cows he does want. Would it benefit these farmers to prevent this trade on the ground that one might breed his own horses and the other raise his own cows? Yet if one farmer lived on the American and the other lived on the Canadian side of the line this is just what both the American and Canadian governments would do. And this is called "protection."

It is only one of the many benefits of trade that it enables people to obtain what the natural conditions of their own localities would not enable them to produce. This is, however, so obvious a benefit that protectionists cannot altogether ignore it, and a favorite doctrine with American protectionists is that trade ought to follow meridians of longitude instead of parallels of latitude, because the great differences of climate and consequently of natural productions are between north and south.* The most desirable reconstruction of the world on this theory would be its division into "countries" consisting of narrow strips running from the equator to the poles, with high tariffs on either side and at the equatorial end, for the polar ice would serve the purpose at the other. But in the meantime, despite this notion that trade ought to be between north and south rather than between east and west, the fact is that the great commerce of the world is and always has been between east and west. And the reason is clear. It is that peoples

---

* "This, then, is our position respecting commerce . . . that it should interchange the productions of diverse zones and climates, following in its transoceanic voyages lines of longitude oftener than lines of latitude."—HORACE GREELEY, *Political Economy*, p. 39.

"Legitimate and natural commerce moves rather along the meridians than along the parallels of latitude."—PROFESSOR ROBERT ELLIS THOMPSON, *Political Economy*, p. 217.

most alike in habits and needs will call most largely for each other's productions, and that the course of migration and of assimilating influences has been rather between east and west than between north and south.

Difference in latitude is but one element of difference in climate, and difference in climate is but one element of the endless diversity in natural productions and capacities. In no one place will nature yield to labor all that man finds useful. Adaptation to one class of products involves non-adaptation to others. Trade, by permitting us to obtain each of the things we need from the locality best fitted for its production, enables us to utilize the highest powers of nature in the production of them all, and thus to increase enormously the sum of various things which a given quantity of labor expended in any locality can secure.

But, what is even more important, trade also enables us to utilize the highest powers of the human factor in production. All men cannot do all things equally well. There are differences in physical and mental powers which give different degrees of aptitude for different parts of the work of supplying human needs. And far more important still are the differences that arise from the development of special skill. By devoting himself to one branch of production a man can acquire skill which enables him, with the same labor, to produce enormously more than one who has not made that branch his specialty. Twenty boys may have equal aptitude for any one of twenty trades, but if every boy tries to learn the twenty trades, none of them can become a good workman in any; whereas, if each devotes himself to one trade, all may become good workmen. There will not only be a saving of the time and effort required for learning, but each, moreover, can in a single vocation work to much better advantage, and may acquire and use tools which it would be impossible to obtain and employ did each attempt the whole twenty.

And as there are differences between individuals which fit them for different branches of production, so, but to a much greater degree, are there such differences between communities. Not to speak again of the differences due to situation and natural facilities, some things can be produced with greater relative advantage where population is sparse, others where it is dense, and differences in industrial development, in habits, customs and related occupations, produce differences in relative adaptation. Such gains, moreover, as attend the division of labor between individuals, attend also the division of labor between communities, and lead to that localization of industry which causes different places to become noted for different industries. Wherever the production of some special thing becomes the leading industry, skill is more easily acquired, and is carried to a higher pitch, supplies are most readily procured, auxiliary and correlative occupations grow up, and a larger scale of production leads to the employment of more efficient methods. Thus in the natural development of society trade brings about differentiations of industry between communities as between individuals, and with similar benefits.

Men of different nations trade with each other for the same reason that men of the same nation do—because they find it profitable; because they thus obtain what they want with less labor than they otherwise could. Goods will not be imported into any country unless they can be obtained more easily by producing something else and exchanging it for them, than by producing them directly. And hence, to restrict importations must be to lessen productive power and reduce the fund from which all revenues are drawn.

Any one can see what would be the result of forbidding each individual to obtain from another any commodity or service which he himself was naturally fitted to produce or perform. Such a regulation, were any government mad enough to adopt it and powerful enough to maintain it, would paralyze the forces that make civilization possible and soon convert the most populous and wealthy country into a howling wilderness. The restrictions which protection would impose upon foreign trade differ only in degree, not in kind, from such restrictions as these. They would not reduce a nation to barbarism, because they do not affect all trade, and rather hamper than prohibit the trade they do affect; but they must prevent the people that adopt them from obtaining the abundance they might otherwise enjoy. If the end of labor be, not the expenditure of effort, but the securing of results, then whether any particular thing ought to be obtained in a country by home production, or by importation, depends solely upon which mode of obtaining it will give the largest result to the least labor. This is a question involving such complex considerations that what any country ought to obtain in this way or in that cannot be settled by any Congress or Parliament. It can safely be left only to those sure instincts which are to society what the vital instincts are to the body, and which always impel men to take the easiest way open to them to reach their ends.

When not caused by artificial obstacles, any tendency in trade to take a certain course is proof that it ought to take that course, and restrictions are harmful because they restrict, and in proportion as they restrict. To assert that the way for men to become healthy and strong is for them to force into their stomachs what nature tries to reject, to regulate the play of their lungs by bandages, or to control the circulation of their blood by ligatures, would be not a whit more absurd than to assert that the way for nations to become rich is for them to restrict the natural tendency to trade.

CHAPTER VII.

PRODUCTION AND PRODUCERS.

REMOTE from neighbors, in a part of the country where population is only beginning to come, stands the rude house of a new settler. As the stars come out, a ruddy light gleams from the little window. The housewife is preparing a meal. The wood that burns so cheerily was cut by the settler, the flour now turning into bread is from wheat of his raising; the fish hissing in the pan were caught by one of the boys, and the water bubbling in the kettle, in readiness to be poured on the tea, was brought from the spring by the eldest girl before the sun had set.

The settler cut the wood. But it took more than that to *produce* the wood. Had it been merely cut, it would still be lying where it fell. The labor of hauling it was as much a part of its production as the labor of cutting it. So the journey to and from the mill was as necessary to the production of the flour as the planting and reaping of the wheat. To produce the fish the boy had to walk to the lake and trudge back again. And the production of the water in the kettle required not merely the exertion of the girl who brought it from the spring, but also the sinking of the barrel in which it collected, and the making of the bucket in which it was carried.

As for the tea, it was grown in China, was carried on a bamboo pole upon the shoulders of a man to some river village, and sold to a Chinese merchant, who shipped it by boat to a treaty port. There, having been packed for ocean transportation, it was sold to the agency of some American house, and sent by steamer to San Francisco. Thence it passed by railroad, with another transfer of ownership, into the hands of a Chicago jobber. The jobber, in turn, in pursuance of another sale, shipped it to the village storekeeper, who held it so that the settler might get it when and in such quantities as he pleased, just as the water from the spring is held in the sunken barrel so that it may be had when needed.

The native dealer who first purchased this tea of the grower, the merchant who shipped it across the Pacific, the Chicago jobber who held it as in a reservoir until the storekeeper ordered it, the storekeeper who, bringing it from Chicago to the village, held it as in a smaller reservoir until the settler came for it, as well as those concerned in its transportation, from the coolie who carried it to the bank of the Chinese river to the brakemen of the train that brought it from Chicago—were they not all parties to the production of that tea to this family as truly as were the peasants who cultivated the plant and gathered its leaves?

The settler got the tea by exchanging for it money obtained in exchange for things produced from nature by the labor of himself and his boys. Has not this tea, then, been produced to this family by their labor as truly as the wood, the flour or the water? Is it not true that the labor of this family devoted to producing things which were exchanged for tea has really produced tea, even in the sense of causing it to be grown, cured and transported? It is not the growing of the tea in China that causes it to be brought to the United States. It is the demand for tea in the United States—that is to say, the readiness to give other products of labor for it—that

causes tea to be grown in China for shipment to the
United States.

To produce is to bring forth, or to bring to. There is
no other word in our language which includes at once
all the operations, such as catching, gathering, extracting,
growing, breeding or making, by which human labor
brings forth from nature, or brings to conditions adapted
to human uses, the material things desired by men and
which constitute wealth. When, therefore, we wish to
speak collectively of the operations by which things are
secured, or fitted for human use, as distinguished from
operations which consist in moving them from place to
place or passing them from hand to hand after they have
been so secured or fitted, we are obliged to use the word
production in distinction from transportation or exchange.
But we should always remember that this is but a narrow and special use of the word.

While in conformity with the usages of our language
we may properly speak of production as distinguished
from transportation and exchange, just as we may properly speak of men as distinguished from women and
children, yet in its full meaning, production includes
transportation and exchange, just as men includes
women and children. In the narrow meaning of the
word we speak of coal as having been produced when it
has been moved from its place in the vein to the surface
of the ground; but evidently the moving of the coal
from the mouth of the mine to those who are to use it is
as necessary a part of coal production, in the full sense,
as is the bringing of it to the surface. And while we
may produce coal in the United States by digging it out
of the ground, we may also just as truly produce it by
exchanging other products of labor for it. Whether we
get coal by digging it or by bringing it from Nova
Scotia or Australia or England in exchange for other

products of our labor, it is, in the one case as truly as in the other, produced here by our labor.

Through all protectionist arguments runs the notion that transporters and traders are non-producers, whose support lessens the amount of wealth which other classes can enjoy.* This is a short-sighted view. In the full sense of the term transporters and traders are as truly producers as are miners, farmers or manufacturers, since the transporting of things and the exchanging of things are as necessary to the enjoyment of things as is extracting, growing or making. There are some operations conducted under the forms of trade that are in reality gambling or blackmailing, but this does not alter the fact that real trade, which consists in exchanging and transporting commodities, is a part of production—a part so necessary and so important that without it the other operations of production could only be carried on in the most primitive manner and with the most niggard results.

And not least important of the functions of the trader is that of holding things in stock, so that those who wish to use them may be able to get them at such times and places, and in such quantities, as are most convenient. This is a service analogous to that performed by the sunken barrel which holds the water of a spring so that it can be had by the bucketful when needed, or by the

---

* "In my conception, the chief end of a true political economy is the conversion of idlers and useless exchangers and traffickers into habitual, effective producers of wealth."—HORACE GREELEY, *Political Economy*, p. 29.

The trader "adds nothing to the real wealth of society. He neither directs and manages a vital change in the form of matter as does the farmer, nor a chemical and mechanical change in form as does the manufacturer. He merely transfers things from the place of their production to the place of demand."—PROFESSOR R. E. THOMPSON, *Political Economy*, p. 198.

reservoirs and pipes which enable the inhabitant of a city
to obtain water by the turning of a faucet. The profits
of traders and "middlemen" may sometimes be excessive (and anything which hampers trade and increases
the capital necessary to carry it on tends to make them
excessive), but they are in reality based upon the performance of services in holding and distributing things
as well as in transporting things.

When Charles Fourier was young [says Professor Thompson
(*Political Economy*, p. 199)], he was on a visit to Paris, and priced at
a street stall some apples of a sort that grew abundantly in his
native province. He was amazed to find that they sold for many
times the sum they would bring at home, having passed through the
hands of a host of middlemen on their way from the owner of the
orchard to the eater of the fruit. The impression received at that
instant never left him; it gave the first impulse to his thinking out
his socialistic scheme for the reconstruction of society, in which
among other sweeping changes the whole class of traders and their
profits are to be abolished.

This story, quoted approvingly to convey an idea that
the trader is a mere toll-gatherer, simply shows what a
superficial thinker Fourier was. If he had undertaken
to bring with him to Paris a supply of apples and to
carry them around with him so that he could have one
when he felt like it he would have formed a much truer
idea of what he was really paying for in the increased
price. That price included not merely the cost of the
apple at its place of growth, plus the cost of transporting
it to Paris, the *octroi* at the Paris gates,* the loss of dam-
aged apples, and remuneration for the service and capital
of the wholesaler, who held the apples in stock until the

---

* The *octroi*, or municipal tariff on produce brought into a town,
is still levied in France, though abolished for a time by the Revolution. It is a survival of the local tariffs once common in Europe,
which separated province from province and town from country.

vender chose to take them, but also payment to the vender, for standing all day in the streets of Paris, in order to supply a few apples to those who wanted an apple *then* and *there.*

So when I go to a druggist's and buy a small quantity of medicine or chemicals I pay many times the original cost of those articles, but what I thus pay is in much larger degree wages than profit. Out of such small sales the druggist must get not only the cost of what he sells me, with other costs incidental to the business, but also payment for his services. These services consist not only in the actual exertion of giving me what I want, but in waiting there in readiness to serve me when I choose to come. In the price of what he sells me he makes a charge for what printers call "waiting time." And he must manifestly not merely charge "waiting time" for himself, but also for the stock of many different things only occasionally called for, which he must keep on hand. He has been waiting there, with his stock, in anticipation of the fact that such persons as myself, in sudden need of some small quantities of drugs or chemicals, would find it cheaper to pay him many times their wholesale cost than to go farther and buy larger quantities. What I pay him, even when it is not payment for the skilled labor of compounding, is largely a payment of the same nature as, were he not there, I might have had to make to a messenger.

If each consumer had to go to the producer for the small quantities individually demanded, the producer would have to charge a higher price on account of the greater labor and expense of attending to such small

Colbert, the first Napoleon, and the German Zollverein did much in reducing and abolishing these restrictions to trade, producing in this way good results which are sometimes attributed by protectionists to external tariffs.

transactions. A hundred cases of shoes may be sold at wholesale in less time than would be consumed in suiting a customer with a single pair. On the other hand, the going to the producer direct would involve an enormous increase of cost and trouble to the consumer, even when such a method of obtaining things would not be utterly impossible.

What "middlemen" do is to save to both parties this trouble and expense, and the profits which competition permits them to charge in return are infinitesimal as compared with the enormous savings effected—are like the charge made to each consumer for the cost of the aqueducts, mains and pumping-engines of a great system of water-supply as compared with the cost of providing a separate system for each house.

And further than this, these middlemen between producer and consumer effect an enormous economy in the amount of commodities that it is necessary to keep in stock to provide for a given consumption, and consequently vastly lessen the loss from deterioration and decay. Let any one consider what amount of stores would be needed to keep in their accustomed supply even for a month a family used to easy access to those handy magazines of commodities which retail dealers maintain. He will see at once that there are a number of things such as fresh meat, fish, fruits, etc., which it is impossible to keep on hand, so as to be sure of having them when needed. And of the things that would keep longer, such as flour, sugar, oil, etc., he will see that but for the retail dealer it would be necessary that much greater quantities should be kept in each house, with a much greater liability to loss from decay or accident. But it is when he comes to things not constantly needed, but which, when needed, though it may not be once a year or once a lifetime, may be needed very badly—that he will realize fully how the much-abused "middleman" economizes the capital of society and increases the opportunities of its members.

A retail dealer is called by the English a "shopkeeper" and by the Americans a "storekeeper." The American usage best expresses his real function. He is in reality a keeper of stores which otherwise his customers would have to keep on hand for themselves, or go without. The English speak of the shops of coöperative supply associations as "stores," since it is in them that the various things required from time to time by the members of those associations are stored until called for. But this is precisely what, without any formal association, the retail dealer does for those who buy of him. And though coöperative purchasing associations have to a certain extent succeeded in England (they have generally failed in the United States) there can be no question that the functions of keeping things in store and distributing them to consumers as needed are on the whole performed more satisfactorily and more economically by self-appointed store- or stock-keepers than they could be as yet by formal associations of consumers. And the tendencies of the time to economies in the distribution as well as in the production of commodities, are bringing about through the play of competition just such a saving of expense to the consumer as is aimed at by coöperative supply associations.

That in civilized society to-day there seem to be too many storekeepers and other distributors is quite true. But so there seem to be too many professional men, too many mechanics, too many farmers, and too many laborers. What may be the cause of this most curious state of things it may hereafter lie in our way to inquire, but at present I am only concerned in pointing out that the trader is not a mere "useless exchanger," who "adds nothing to the real wealth of society," but that the transporting, storing and exchanging of things are as necessary a part of the work of supplying human needs as is growing, extracting or making.

Nor should it be forgotten that the investigator, the philosopher, the teacher, the artist, the poet, the priest, though not engaged in the production of wealth, are not only engaged in the production of utilities and satisfactions to which the production of wealth is only a means, but by acquiring and diffusing knowledge, stimulating mental powers and elevating the moral sense, may greatly increase the ability to produce wealth. For man does not live by bread alone. He is not an engine, in which so much fuel gives so much power. On a capstan bar or a topsail halyard a good song tells like muscle, and a "Marseillaise" or a "Battle Hymn of the Republic" counts for bayonets. A hearty laugh, a noble thought, a perception of harmony, may add to the power of dealing even with material things.

He who by any exertion of mind or body adds to the aggregate of enjoyable wealth, increases the sum of human knowledge or gives to human life higher elevation or greater fullness—he is, in the large meaning of the words, a "producer," a "working-man," a "laborer," and is honestly earning honest wages. But he who without doing aught to make mankind richer, wiser, better, happier, lives on the toil of others—he, no matter by what name of honor he may be called, or how lustily the priests of Mammon may swing their censers before him, is in the last analysis but a beggar-man or a thief.

CHAPTER VIII.

TARIFFS may embrace duties on exports as well as on imports; but duties on exports are prohibited by the Constitution of the United States and are now levied only by a few countries, such as Brazil, and by them only on a few articles. The tariff, as we have to consider it, is a schedule of taxes upon imports.

The word "tariff" is said to be derived from the Spanish town of Tarifa, near Gibraltar, where the Moors in the days of their power collected duties, probably much after the manner of those Chinese local custom-houses called "squeeze stations." But the thing is older than the name. Augustus Cæsar levied duties on imports into Italy, and there were tariffs long before the Cæsars.

The purpose in which tariffs originate is that of raising revenue. The idea of using them for protection is an afterthought. And before considering the protective function of tariffs it will be well to consider them as a means for collecting revenue.

It is usually assumed, even by the opponents of protection, that tariffs should be maintained for revenue. Most of those who are commonly called free traders might more properly be called revenue-tariff men. They object, not to the tariff, but only to its protective features, and propose, not to abolish it, but only to restrict it to revenue purposes. Nearly all the opposition to the protective system in the United States is of this kind, and in current discussion a tariff for revenue only is usually assumed to be the sole alternative to a tariff for protection. But since there are other ways of raising revenue than by tariffs this manifestly is not so. And if not useful for protection, the only justification for any tariff is that it is a good means of raising revenue. Let us inquire as to this.

Duties on imports are indirect taxes. Therefore the question whether a tariff is a good means of raising revenue involves the question whether indirect taxation is a good means of raising revenue.

As to ease and cheapness of collection indirect taxation is certainly *not* a good means of raising revenue. While there are direct taxes, such as taxes on real estate and taxes on legacies and successions, from which great revenues can easily and cheaply be collected, the only indirect taxes from which any considerable revenue can be obtained require large and expensive staffs of officials and the enforcement of vexatious and injurious regulations. To collect the indirect tax on tobacco and cigars, France and some other countries make the trade and manufacture a strict government monopoly, while Great Britain prohibits the culture of tobacco under penalty of fine and imprisonment—a prohibition particularly injurious to Ireland, where the soil and climate are in some parts admirably adapted to the growth of certain kinds of tobacco. In the United States we maintain a costly inquisitorial system which assumes to trace every pound of tobacco raised or imported, through all its stages of manufacture, and requires the most elaborate returns of private business to be made to government officials. To collect more easily an indirect tax upon salt the government of British India cruelly prevents the making of salt in many places where the natives suffer from the want of it. While indirect taxes upon spirituous liquors, wherever resorted to, require the most elaborate system of prohibition, inspection and espionage.

So with the collection of indirect taxes upon imports. Land frontiers must be guarded and sea-coasts watched; imports must be forbidden except at certain places and under regulations which are always vexatious and frequently entail wasteful delays and expenses; consuls must be maintained all over the world, and no end of oaths required; vessels must be watched from the time they enter harbor until the time they leave, and everything landed from them examined, down to the trunks and satchels and sometimes the persons of passengers, while spies, informers and "bloodhounds" must be encouraged.

But in spite of prohibitions, restrictions, searchings, watchings and swearings, indirect taxes on commodities are largely evaded, sometimes by the bribery of officials and sometimes by the adoption of methods for eluding their vigilance, which though costly in themselves, cost less than the taxes. All these costs, however, whether borne by the government or by the first payers (or evaders) of the taxes, together with the increased charges due to increased prices, finally fall on consumers, and thus this method of taxation is extremely wasteful, taking from the people much more than the government obtains.

A still more important objection to indirect taxation is that when imposed on articles of general use (and it is only from such articles that large revenues can be had) it bears with far greater weight on the poor than on the rich. Since such taxation falls on people not according to what they have, but according to what they consume, it is heaviest on those whose consumption is largest in

proportion to their means. As much sugar is needed to
sweeten a cup of tea for a working-girl as for the richest
lady in the land, but the proportion of their means which
a tax on sugar compels each to contribute to the government is in the case of the one much greater than in the
case of the other. So it is with all taxes that increase
the cost of articles of general consumption. They bear
far more heavily on married men than on bachelors; on
those who have children than on those who have none;
on those barely able to support their families than on
those whose incomes leave them a large surplus. If the
millionaire chooses to live closely he need pay no more of
these indirect taxes than the mechanic. I have known
at least two millionaires—possessed not of one, but of
from six to ten millions each—who paid little more of
such taxes than ordinary day-laborers.

Even if cheaper articles were taxed at no higher rates
than the more costly, such taxation would be grossly
unjust; but in indirect taxation there is always a tendency to impose heavier taxes on the cheaper articles
used by all than on the more costly articles used only by
the rich. This arises from the necessities of the case.
Not only do the larger amounts of articles of common
consumption afford a wider basis for large revenues than
the smaller amounts of more costly articles, but taxes
imposed on them cannot be so easily evaded. For
instance, while articles in use by the poor as well as the
rich are under our tariff taxed fifty and a hundred, and
even a hundred and fifty per cent., the tax on diamonds
is only ten per cent., and this comparatively light tax is
most difficult to enforce, owing to the high value of
diamonds as compared with their bulk. Even where discrimination of this kind is not made in the imposition of
indirect taxation, it arises in its collection. Specific
taxes fall more heavily upon the cheaper than the costlier

grades of goods, while even in the case of *ad valorem* taxes, undervaluation and evasion are easier in regard to the more valuable grades.

That indirect taxes thus bear far more heavily on the poor than on the rich is undoubtedly one of the reasons why they have so readily been adopted. The rich are ever the powerful, and under all forms of government have most influence in forming public opinion and framing laws, while the poor are ever the voiceless. And while indirect taxation causes no loss to those who first pay it, it is collected in such insidious ways from those who finally pay it that they do not realize it. It thus affords the best means of getting the largest revenues from the body of the people with the least remonstrance against the amount collected or the uses to which it is put. This is the main reason that has induced governments to resort so largely to indirect taxation. A direct tax, where its justice and necessity are not clear, provokes outcry and opposition which may at times rise to successful resistance; but not only do those indirectly taxed seldom realize it, but it is extremely difficult for them to refuse payment. They are not called on at set times to pay definite sums to government agents, but the tax becomes indistinguishably blended with the cost of the goods they buy. When it reaches those who must finally pay it, together with all costs and profits of collection, it is not a tax yet to be paid, but a tax which has already been paid, some time ago, and many removes back, and which cannot be separated from other elements which go to make up the cost of goods. There is no choice save to pay the tax or go without the goods.

If a tax-gatherer stood at the door of every store, and levied a tax of twenty-five per cent. on every article bought, there would quickly be outcry; but the very people who would fight rather than pay a tax like this will uncomplainingly pay higher taxes when they are collected by storekeepers in increased prices. And even if an indirect tax is consciously realized, it cannot easily be opposed. At the beginning of our Revolution the indirect tax on tea levied by the British government, without the consent of the American colonies, was successfully resisted by preventing the landing of the tea; but if the tea had once got into the hands of the dealers, with the taxes on it paid, the English government could have laughed at the opposition of the patriots. When in Ireland, during the height of the Land League agitation, I was much struck with the ease and certainty with which an unpopular government can collect indirect taxes. At the beginning of the century the Irish people, without any assistance from America, proved in the famous Tithe war that the whole power of the English government could not collect direct taxes they had resolved not to pay; and the strike against rent, which so long as persisted in proved so effective, could readily have been made a strike against direct taxation. Had the government which was enforcing the claim of the landlords depended on direct taxation, its resources could thus have been seriously diminished by the same blow which crippled the landlords; but during all the time of this strike the force used to put down the popular movement was being supported by indirect taxation on the people who were in passive rebellion. The people who struck against rent could not strike against taxes paid in buying the commodities they used. Even had rebellion been active and general, the British government could have collected the bulk of its revenues from indirect taxation, so long as it retained command of the principal towns.

It is no wonder that princes and ministers anxious to make their revenues as large as possible should prefer a method that enables them to "pluck the goose without making it cry," nor is it wonderful that this preference should be shared by those who get control of popular governments; but the reason which renders indirect taxes so agreeable to those who levy taxes is a sufficient reason why a people jealous of their liberties should insist that taxes levied for revenue only should be direct, not indirect.

It is not merely the ease with which indirect taxes can be collected that urges to their adoption. Indirect taxes always enlist active private interests in their favor. The first rude device for making the collection of taxes easier to the governing power is to let them out to farm. Under this system, which existed in France up to the Revolution, and still exists in such countries as Turkey, persons called farmers of the revenue buy the privilege of collecting certain taxes and make their profits, frequently very large, out of the greater amount which their vigilance and extortion enable them to collect. The system of indirect taxation is essentially of the same nature.

The tendency of the restrictions and regulations necessary for the collection of indirect taxes is to concentrate business and give large capital an advantage. For instance, with a board, a knife, a kettle of paste and a few dollars' worth of tobacco, a competent cigar-maker could set up in business for himself, were it not for the revenue regulations. As it is, in the United States, the stock of tobacco which he must procure is not only increased in value some two or three times by a tax upon it; but before the cigar-maker can go to work he must buy a manufacturer's license and find bonds in the sum of five hundred dollars. Before he can sell the cigars he has made, he must furthermore pay a tax on them, and even then if he would sell cigars in less quantities than by the box he must buy a second license. The effect of all this is to give capital a great advantage, and to concentrate in the hands of large manufacturers a business in which, if free, workmen could easily set up for themselves.

But even in the absence of such regulations indirect taxation tends to concentration. Indirect taxes add to the price of goods not only the tax itself but also the profit upon the tax. If on goods costing a dollar a manufacturer or merchant has paid fifty cents in taxation, he will now expect profit on a dollar and fifty cents instead of upon a dollar. As, in the course of trade, these taxed goods pass from hand to hand, the amount which each successive purchaser pays on account of the tax is constantly augmenting. It is not merely inevitable that consumers have to pay considerably more than a dollar for every dollar the government receives, but larger capital is required by dealers. The need of larger capital for dealing in goods that have been enhanced in cost by taxation, the restrictions imposed on trade to secure the collection of the tax, and the better opportunities which those who do business on a large scale have of managing the payment or evading the tax, tend to concentrate business, and, by checking competition, to permit large profits, which must ultimately be paid by consumers. Thus the first payers of indirect taxes are generally not merely indifferent to the tax, but regard it with favor.

That indirect taxation is of the nature of farming the revenue to private parties is shown by the fact that those who pay such taxes to the government seldom or never ask for their reduction or repeal, but on the contrary generally oppose such propositions. The manufacturers and dealers in tobacco and cigars have never striven to secure any reduction in the heavy taxes on those articles, and the importers who pay directly the immense sums collected by our custom-houses have never grumbled at the duties, however they may grumble at the manner of their collection. When, at the time of the war, the national taxation was enormously increased there was no opposition to the imposition of indirect taxation from those who would thus be called upon to pay large sums to the government. On the contrary, the imposition of these taxes, by enhancing the value of stock in hand, made many fortunes. And since the war the main difficulty in reducing taxation has been the opposition of the very men who pay these taxes to the government. The reduction of the war tax on whisky was strongly opposed by the whisky ring, composed of great distillers. The match-manufacturers fought bitterly the abolition of the tax on matches. Whenever it has been proposed to reduce or repeal any indirect tax Congress has been beset by a persistent lobby urging that, whatever other taxes might be dispensed with, that particular tax might be left in full force. In order to provide an excuse for keeping up indirect taxes all sorts of extravagant expenditures of the national money have been made, and hundreds of millions have been voted away to get them out of the Treasury.* Despite all this extravagance, we have a surplus; yet we go on collecting taxes we do not need because of the opposition of interested parties to their reduction. This opposition is of the same kind and springs from the same motives as that which the farmers of the revenue under the old French system would have made to the abolition of a tax which enabled them to extort two millions of francs from the

---

* Just now (1886) the interests concerned in keeping up indirect taxation are urging a worse than useless scheme for spending enormous sums on iron-clad coast defenses.

French people for one million which they paid to the government.

Now, over and above the great loss to the people which indirect taxation thus imposes, the manner in which it gives individuals and corporations a direct and selfish interest in public affairs tends powerfully to the corruption of government. These moneyed interests enter into our politics as a potent demoralizing force. What to the ordinary citizen is a question of public policy, affecting him only as one of some sixty millions of people, is to them a question of special pecuniary interest. To this is largely due the state of things in which politics has become the trade of professional politicians; in which it is seldom that one who has not money to spend can, with any prospect of success, present himself for the suffrages of his fellow-citizens; in which Congress is surrounded by lobbyists, clamorous for special interests, and questions of the utmost general importance are lost sight of in the struggle which goes on for the spoils of taxation. That under such a system of taxation our government is not far more corrupt than it is, is the strongest proof of the essential goodness of republican institutions.

That indirect taxes may sometimes serve purposes other than the raising of revenue I do not deny. The license taxes exacted from the sellers of liquor may be defended on the ground that they diminish the number of saloons and lessen a traffic injurious to public morals. And so taxes on tobacco and spirits may be defended on the ground that the smoking of tobacco and the drinking of spirits are injurious vices, which may be lessened by making tobacco and spirits more expensive, so that (except the rich) those who smoke may be compelled to smoke poorer tobacco, and those who drink to drink viler liquor. But merely as a means of raising revenue, it is clear that indirect taxes are to be condemned, since they cost far more than they yield, bear with the greatest weight upon those least able to pay, add to corruptive influences, and lessen the control of the people over their government.

All the objections which apply to indirect taxes in general apply to import duties. Those protectionists are right who declare that protection is the only justification for a tariff,* and the advocates of "a tariff for revenue only" have no case. If we do not need a tariff for protection we need no tariff at all, and for the purpose of raising revenue should resort to some system which will not tax the mechanic as heavily as the millionaire, and will not call on the man who rears a family to pay on that account more than the man who shirks his natural obligation, and leaves some woman whom in the scheme of nature it was intended that he should support, to take care of herself as best she can.

---

* "Tariffs for revenue should have no existence. Interferences with trade are to be tolerated only as measures of self-protection." —H. C. CAREY, *Past, Present and Future*, p. 472.

"Taxes for the sake of revenue should be imposed directly, because such is the only mode in which the contribution of each individual can be adjusted in proportion to his means."—PROFESSOR E. P. SMITH, *Political Economy*, pp. 265-268.

"Duties for revenue . . . are highly unjust. They inflict all the hardship of indirect and unequal taxation without even the purpose of benefiting the consumer."—PROFESSOR R. E. THOMPSON, *Political Economy*, p. 232.

CHAPTER IX.

TARIFFS FOR PROTECTION.

PROTECTIVE tariffs differ from revenue tariffs in their object, which is not so much that of obtaining revenue as that of protecting home producers from the competition of imported commodities.

The two objects, revenue and protection, are not merely distinct, but antagonistic. The same duty may raise some revenue and give some protection, but, past a certain point at least, in proportion as one object is secured the other is sacrificed, since revenue depends on the bringing in of commodities; protection on keeping them out. So the same tariff may embrace both protective and revenue duties, but while the protective duties lessen its power of collecting revenue, the revenue duties by adding to the cost of home production lessen its power of encouraging home producers. The duties of a purely revenue tariff should fall only on commodities not produced in the country; or, if levied on commodities partly produced at home, should be balanced by equivalent internal taxes to prevent incidental protection. In a purely protective tariff, on the other hand, commodities not produced in the country should be free and duties should be levied on commodities that are or may be produced in the country. And, just in proportion as it accomplishes its object, the less revenue will it yield. The tariff of Great Britain is an example of a purely

revenue tariff, incidental protection being prevented by
excise duties. There is no example of a purely protective
tariff, the purpose of obtaining revenue seeming always to
be the original stock upon which protective features are
grafted. The tariff of the United States, like all actual
protective tariffs, is partly revenue and partly protective,
its original purpose of yielding revenue having been sub-
ordinated to that of giving protection, until it may now
be best described as a protective tariff yielding incidental
revenue.

As we have already considered the revenue functions
of tariffs, let us now consider their protective functions.

Protection, as the word has come to be used to denote
a scheme of national policy, signifies the levying of
duties on the importation of commodities (as a means) in
order (as an end) to encourage domestic industry.

Now, when the means proposed in any such scheme is
the only means by which the proposed end can be
reached, it is only needful to inquire as to the desira-
bility of the end; but when the proposed means is only
one of various means we must satisfy ourselves that it is
the best. If it is not, the scheme is condemned irrespective of the goodness of its end. Thus the advisability of
protection does not, as is generally assumed, follow the
admission of the advisability of encouraging domestic
industry. That granted, the advisability of protection is
still an open question, since it is clear that there are
other ways of encouraging home industry than by
import duties.

Instead of levying import duties, we might, for
instance, destroy a certain proportion of imported commodities, or require the ships bringing them to sail so
many times round the world before landing at our ports.
In either of these ways precisely the same protective
effect could be secured as by import duties, and in cases

where duties secure full protection by preventing importation, such methods would involve no more waste. Or,
instead of indirectly encouraging domestic producers by
levying duties on foreign goods, we might directly
encourage them by paying them bounties.

As a means of encouraging domestic industry the
bounty has over the protective system all the advantages
that the system of paying public officers fixed salaries
has over the system prevailing in some countries, and in
some instances in our own, of letting them make what
they can. As by paying fixed salaries we can get officials at such places and to perform such functions as we
wish, while under the make-what-you-can system they
can only be got at places and in capacities that will
enable them to pay themselves, so do bounties permit
the encouragement of any industry, while protection
permits only the encouragement of the comparatively
few industries with which imported commodities compete. As salaries enable us to know what we are
paying, to proportion the rewards of different offices to
their respective dignity, responsibility and arduousness,
while make-what-you-can may give to one official much
more than is necessary, and to others not enough, so do
bounties enable us to see and to fix the encouragement
to each industry, while the protective system leaves the
public in the dark and makes the encouragement to each
industry almost a matter of chance. And as salaries
impose on the people much lighter and more fairly
apportioned burdens than does the make-what-you-can
system, so is the difference between bounties and protection.

To illustrate the working of the two systems, let it be
assumed desirable to encourage aërial navigation at
public expense. Under the bounty system we should
offer premiums for the building and successful operation

of air-ships. Under the protective system we should impose deterrent taxes on all existing methods of transportation. In the one case we should have nothing to pay till we got what we wanted, and would then pay a definite sum which would fall on individuals and localities in general taxes. But in the other case we should have to suffer all the inconveniences of obstructed transportation before we got air-ships, and whether we got them or not; and while these obstructions would, in some cases, more seriously affect individuals, businesses and localities than in others, we should never be able to tell how much they distorted industry and cost the people, or how much they stimulated the invention and building of air-ships. In the one case, moreover, after aërial navigation had proved successful, and the stipulated bounties had been paid, the air-ship men would hardly have the audacity to ask for more bounties, and would not be likely to get them if they did. In the other case, the public would have grown accustomed to the taxes on surface transportation, while the air-ship proprietors, if they had not convinced themselves that these taxes were necessary to the continued prosperity of aërial navigation, could readily pretend so, and would have, in opposing their repeal, the advantage of that inertia which tends to the continuance of anything that is.

The superiority of the bounty system over the protective system for the encouragement of any single industry is very great; but it becomes greater as the number of industries to be encouraged is increased. When we encourage an industry by a bounty we do not discourage any other industry, except as the necessary increase in general taxation may have a discouraging effect. But when to encourage one industry we raise the price of its products by a protective duty, we at the same time produce a directly injurious effect upon other industries that

use those products. So complicated has production
become, so intimate are the relations between industries,
and in so many forms do the products of one industry
enter into the materials or processes of others, that what
will be the effect of a single protective duty it is hard for
an expert to say. But when it comes to encouraging not
one nor a dozen, but a thousand different industries, it
is impossible for human intelligence to trace the multifarious effects of raising the prices of so many products.
The people cannot tell what such a system costs them,
nor in most cases can even those who are supposed to be
its beneficiaries really tell how their gains under it compare with their losses from it.

The "drawback" system is an attempt to prevent, so
far as exports are concerned, the discouragement to
which the protection of one industry subjects others.
Drawbacks are bounties paid on exports of domestic
goods to an amount which it is calculated will compen-
sate for the addition a duty on material has made to
their cost. But drawbacks not only leave home prices
undiminished, but while fruitful of fraud, can only in
small part prevent the discouragement of exports, since
it is only on goods into which dutiable commodities have
entered in large proportion and obvious ways that drawbacks are allowed, or that it is worth the while of the
exporter to attempt to collect them. In 1884, for
instance, the United States paid out a larger sum in
drawbacks on copper than was received in duties on
copper, yet it is certain that very many exports into
which copper entered, and which were therefore
enhanced in cost by the duty, got no drawback whatever. And so of drawbacks on refined sugar, for which
we are paying a sum greatly in excess of the duties collected on the raw sugar, though many of our exports,
such as those of condensed milk, syrups and preserved
fruits, are much curtailed by these duties.

The substitution of bounties for protection in encouraging industry would do away with the necessity for such inefficient, fraud-provoking and back-action devices. Under the bounty system prices would not be raised, except as affected by general taxation. Each encouraged producer would know in dollars and cents how much encouragement he got, and the people at large would know how much they paid. In short, all and even more than protection can do to encourage home industries can be done more cheaply and more certainly by bounties.

It is sometimes asserted, as one of the advantages of tariff duties, that they fall on the producers of imported goods, and are thus paid by foreigners. This assertion contains a scintilla of truth. An import duty on a commodity of which the production is a closely controlled foreign monopoly may in some cases fall in part or in whole upon the foreign producer. For instance, let us say that a foreign house or combination has a monopoly in the production of a certain article. Within the limits of cost on the one hand and the highest rate at which any can be sold on the other, the price of such article can be fixed by the producers, who will naturally fix it at the point they conclude will give the largest aggregate profits. If we impose an import duty on such an article they may prefer to reduce their profit on what they sell to this country rather than have the sale diminished by the addition of the duty to the price. In such case the duty will fall upon them.

Or, again, let us suppose a Canadian farmer so situated that the only market in which he can conveniently sell his wheat is on the American side. Wheat being a commodity of which our home production not merely supplies home demands, but leaves a surplus for export, the duty on wheat does not add to price, and the Canadian farmer so exceptionally situated that he must send wheat to this side, although there is no general demand for Canadian wheat, cannot get back in enhanced price the duty he must pay.

The two classes represented by these instances suggest all the cases in which import duties fall on foreign producers.* Such cases, too unimportant to be considered in any estimates of national revenue, are only the rare exceptions to the general rule that the ability to tax ends with the territorial limits of the taxing power. And it is well for mankind that this is so. If it were possible for the government of one country, by any system of taxa-

---

* In certain cases where an import duty, levied in one country on the produce of another, has the effect of reducing price in the exporting country at the expense of rent, it may, in some part, fall upon foreign landowners. John Stuart Mill (" Political Economy," Book V., Chapter III.,) further maintains that taxes on imports fall in part, not on the foreign producer of whom we buy, but on the foreign consumer to whom we sell—since they increase the cost of products we export. But this is only to say that the injury which we do ourselves by protection must in some part fall upon those with whom we trade. And even if import duties do, in such ways, somewhat increase the cost to foreigners of what they get from us, and thus, in some degree, compel them to share our loss, yet they also handicap us when we come into competition with them. Thus, assuming that our tariff upon imports may at times, to some slight extent, have increased the price which English consumers have had to pay for our cotton, wheat or oil, the increased cost of production in the United States has certainly operated far more strongly to give English producers an advantage over American producers in markets in which they compete, and to enable England to take the lion's share of the ocean-borne commerce of the world.

The minute tracing of the actions and reactions of taxation upon international trade is, however, more a matter of theoretical nicety than of practical interest, since the general conclusion will be that stated in the text, that while we cannot injure ourselves without injuring others, the taxing power of a government is substantially restricted to its territorial limit. The clearest exception to this is in the case of export duties on articles of which the country levying the export duty has a monopoly, as Brazil has of india-rubber and Cuba of the Havana tobacco.

tion, to compel the people of other countries to pay its expenses, the world would soon be taxed into barbarism.

But the possibility of exceptional cases in which import duties may in part or in whole fall on foreign producers, instead of domestic consumers, has in it, even for those who would gladly tax "foreigners," no shadow of a recommendation for protection. For it will be noticed that the cases in which an import duty falls on foreign producers, are cases in which it can afford no encouragement to home producers. An import duty can only fall on foreign producers when its payment does not add to price; while the only possible way in which an import duty can encourage home producers is by adding to price.

It is sometimes said that protection does not increase prices. It is sufficient answer to ask, how then can it encourage? To say that a protective duty encourages the home producer without raising prices, is to say that it encourages him without doing anything for him. Wherever beneath this assertion, as regardless of fact as it is of theory, there is any glimmering of reason, it is either in the notion that protective duties do not permanently add to prices, because they bring about such a competition between home producers as finally carries prices down to the previous level; or else in a confused idea that it would be an advantage to home producers to be secured the whole home market, even if at no higher prices.

But as to the first, the only way in which a protective duty can increase home competition in the production of any commodity is by so increasing prices as to attract producers to the industry by the superior profits to be obtained. This competition, when free to operate, ultimately reduces profits to the general level.* But this is

---

* The effect of protection upon profits in the protected industries will be more fully examined in Chapter XVII.

not to say that it reduces prices to what they would be
without the duty. The profits of Louisiana sugar-grow-
ing are now, doubtless, no larger than in other occupations involving equal risks, but the duty on sugar does
make the price of sugar very much higher in the United
States than it is in England, where there is no duty upon
it. And even where there is no reason in natural or
social conditions why a commodity should not be produced as cheaply as in any foreign country, the effect of
the network of duties, of which the particular duty is
but a part, is to increase the cost of production, and thus,
though profits may fall, to keep prices above the point of
free importation. Did the price of a protected article
fall to the point at which the foreign product could not
be imported were there no duty, the duty would cease to
protect, since the foreign product would not be imported
if it were abolished, and the producers for whose protection it was imposed would cease to care for its retention.
In what instance has this been the case? Are any of
our protected industries less clamorous for protection
now than they were forty years ago?

As to the second notion, it is to be observed that the
only way in which a protective duty can give the home
market to home producers is by increasing the price at
which foreign products can be sold in it. Not merely
does this increase in the price of foreign products compel
an increase in the price of domestic products into which
they enter, but the shutting out of foreign products *must*
increase the price of similar domestic products. For it
is only where prices are fixed by the will of the producer
that increase or decrease in supply does not result in
increase or decrease of price. Thus, while the newspaper
business is not a monopoly, the publication of each individual paper is, and its price is fixed by the publisher. A
publisher may, and in most cases will, prefer increased cir-

culation to increased prices. And if competition were to
be lessened, or even cut off, as, for instance, by imposing
a stamp duty on, or prohibiting the publication of all the
newspapers of New York save one, it would not necessarily follow that the price of that paper would be
increased. But the prices of the great mass of commodities, and especially the great mass of commodities
which are exported and imported, are regulated by competition. They are not fixed by the will of producers,
but by the relative intensity of supply and demand,
which are brought to an equation in price by what Adam
Smith called "the higgling of the market," and hence
any lessening of supply caused by the shutting out of
importations will at once increase prices.

In short, the protective system is simply a system of
encouraging certain industries by enabling those carrying them on to obtain higher prices for the goods they
produce. It is a clumsy and extravagant mode of giving
encouragement that could be given much better and at
much less cost by bounties or subsidies. If it be wise to
"encourage" American industries, and this we have yet
to examine, the best way of doing so would be to abolish
our tariff entirely and to pay bounties from funds
obtained by direct taxation. In this way the cost could
be distributed with some approach to fairness, and the
citizen who is worth a million times more than another
could have the satisfaction of contributing a million
times as much to the encouragement of American
industry.

I do not forget that, from the bounties given in the
colonial days for the killing of noxious animals to the
subsidies granted to the Pacific railroads, experience has
shown that the bounty system inevitably leads to fraud
and begets corruption, while but poorly accomplishing the
ends sought by it. But these evils are inseparable from

any method of "encouragement," and attach to the protective more than to the bounty system, because its operations are not so clear. If protection has been preferred to bounties it is not that it is a better means of encouragement, but for the same reason that indirect has been preferred to direct taxation—because the people do not so readily realize what is being done. Where a grant of a hundred thousand dollars directly from the treasury would raise an outcry, the imposition of a duty which will enable the appropriation of millions in higher prices excites no comment. Where bounties have been given by our States for the establishment of new industries they have been comparatively small sums, given in a single payment or in a subsidy for a definite term of years. Although the people have in some cases been willing thus to pay bounties to a small extent and for a short time, in no case have they consented to regard them as a settled thing, and to keep on paying them year after year. But protective duties once imposed, the protected industry has always been as clamorous for the continuance of protection as it was in the beginning for the grant of it. And the people not being so conscious of the payment have permitted it to go on.

It is often said by protectionists that free trade is right in theory but wrong in practice. Whatever may be meant by such phrases they involve a contradiction in terms, since a theory that will not agree with facts must be false. But without inquiring into the validity of the protective theory it is clear that no such tariff as it proposes ever has been or ever can be made.

The theory of free trade may be carried into practice to the point of ideal perfection. For to secure free trade we have only to abolish restrictions. But to carry the theory of protection into practice some articles must be taxed and others left untaxed, and, as to the articles taxed, different rates of duty must be imposed. And as the protection given to any industry may be neutralized by protection that enhances the price of its materials, careful discrimination is required, for there are very few articles that can be deemed finished products in relation to all their uses. The finished products of some industries are the materials or tools of other industries. Thus, while the protection of any industry is useless unless sufficient to produce the desired effect, too much protection is likely, even from a protective standpoint, to do harm.

It is not merely that the ideal perfection with which the free-trade theory may be reduced to practice is impossible in the case of protection, but that even a rough approximation to the protective theory is impossible. There never has been a protective tariff that satisfied protectionists, and there never can be. Our present tariff, for instance, is admitted by protectionists to be full of the grossest blunders.* It was adopted only

---

* For instance, to cite only one case, the last Tariff Act, which went into effect in July, 1883, raised the duty on the fabric used in the manufacture of ruching and rufflings from 35 to 125 per cent., while leaving the duty of the finished article at 35 per cent. Previous to this, say the manufacturers of these goods, in a memorial address to the Secretary of the Treasury, they not only supplied the American market, but sold hundreds of thousands of dollars' worth every year to Canada, the West Indies and other countries, the labor-saving machinery which they had in use giving them an advantage which, in spite of the 35-per-cent. tax on their material, enabled them to compete successfully with European factories. But the 125-per-cent. duty has not only cut off this export trade completely, but has led to such an importation of British goods that, as the memorial declares, thousands of hands have lost their employment, and three-fourths of the manufacturers engaged in the business have been utterly ruined. This, of course, was not intended by Congress. The ruffling industry is only one of the many minor industries that were thrown down and trampled upon in the last tariff scramble.

because, after a long wrangle, it was found impossible to agree upon a better one, and it is maintained and defended only because any attempt to amend it would begin a scramble out of which no one can tell what sort of a tariff would come. This has been the case with every former tariff, and must be the case with every future tariff.

To make a protective tariff that would even roughly accord with the protective theory would require in the first place a minute knowledge of all trade and industry, and of the manner in which an effect produced on one industry would act and react on others. This no king, congress or parliament ever can have. But, further than this, absolute disinterestedness is required, for the fixing of protective duties is simply the distribution of pecuniary favors among a crowd of greedy applicants. And even were it possible to obtain for the making of a protective tariff a body of men themselves disinterested and incapable of yielding to bribery, to threats, to friendship or to flattery, they would have to be more than human not to be dazed by the clamor and misled by the representations of selfish interests.

The making of a tariff, instead of being, as the protective theory requires, a careful consideration of the circumstances and needs of each industry, is in practice simply a great "grab" in which the retained advocates of selfish interests bully and beg, bribe and logroll, in the endeavor to get the largest possible protection for themselves without regard for other interests or for the general good. The result is, and always must be, the enactment of a tariff which resembles the theoretical protectionist's idea of what a protective tariff should be about as closely as a bucketful of paint thrown against a wall resembles the fresco of a Raphael.

But this is not all. After a tariff has been enacted, come the interpretations and decisions of treasury officials and courts to unmake and remake it,* and duties are raised or lowered by a printer's placing of a comma or by arbitrary constructions, frequently open to grave suspicion, and which no one can foresee, so that, as Horace Greeley naïvely says ("Political Economy," p. 183):

> The longer a tariff continues the more weak spots are found, the more holes are picked in it, until at last, through the influence of successive evasions, constructions, decisions, its very father could not discern its original features in the transformed bantling that has quietly taken its place.

Under the bounty system, bad as it is, we can come much nearer to doing what we want to, and to knowing what we have done.

---

* The Secretary of the Treasury states that there are now (February, 1886) over 2300 tariff cases pending in the Southern District of New York alone.

CHAPTER X.

THE ENCOURAGEMENT OF INDUSTRY.

WITHOUT questioning the end sought by them we have seen that protective tariffs are to be condemned as a means. Let us now consider their end— the encouragement of home industry.

There can be no difference of opinion as to what encouragement means. To encourage an industry in the protective sense is to secure to those carrying it on larger profits than they could of themselves obtain. Only so far and so long as it does this can any protection encourage an industry.

But when we ask what the industries are that protection proposes to encourage we find a wide difference. Those whom American protectionists have regarded as their ablest advocates have asked protection for the encouragement of "infant industries"— describing the protective system as a means for establishing new industries in countries to which they are adapted.* They

---

* "Whoever will consult Alexander Hamilton's Report on Manufactures, the writings of Matthew Carey, Hezekiah Niles and their compeers, with the speeches of Henry Clay, Thomas Newton, James Tod, Walter Forward, Rollin C. Mallary, and other forensic champions of protection, with the messages of our earlier Presidents, of Governors Simon Snyder, George Clinton, Daniel D. Tompkins, De Witt Clinton, etc., cannot fail to note that they champion not the maintenance, but the creation of home manufactures."—HORACE GREELEY, *Political Economy*, p. 34.

have scouted the idea of attempting to encourage all industry, and declared the encouragement of industries not adapted to a country, or already established, or for a time longer than necessary for their establishment, to be waste and robbery. As it is now popularly advocated and practically applied in the United States the aim of protection, however, is not the encouragement of "infant industries" but the encouragement of "home industry" —that is to say, of all home industries. And what has proved true in our case is generally true. Wherever protection is once begun, the imposition of duties never stops until every home industry of any political strength that can be protected by tariff gets some encouragement. It is only in new countries and in the beginnings of the system that the encouragement of infant industries can be presented as the sole end of protection. European protectionists can hardly ask protection, on the ground of their infancy, for industries that have been carried on since the time of the Romans. And in the United States to ask now the encouragement of such giants as our iron, steel and textile industries as a means for their establishment would, after all these years of high tariffs, be manifestly absurd.

We have thus two distinct propositions to examine— the proposition that new and desirable industries should be encouraged, which still figures in the apologetics of protection, and the proposition popularly urged and which our protectionist legislation attempts to carry into effect—that home industry should be encouraged.

As an abstract proposition it is not, I think, to be denied that there may be industries to which temporary encouragement might profitably be extended. Industries capable, in their development, of much public benefit have often to struggle under great disadvantages in their beginnings, and their development might sometimes be beneficially hastened by judicious encouragement. But there are insuperable difficulties in the way of discovering what industries would repay encouragement. There are, doubtless, in every considerable community some men of exceptional powers who, if provided at public expense with an assured living and left free to investigate, to invent or to think, would make to the public most valuable returns. But it is certain that, under any system yet devised, such livings, if instituted, would not be filled by men of this kind; but by the pushing and influential, by flatterers and dependents of those in power or by respectable nonentities. The very men who would give a good return in such places would, by virtue of their qualities, be the last to get them.

So it is with the encouragement of struggling industries. All experience shows that the policy of encouragement, once begun, leads to a scramble in which it is the strong, not the weak; the unscrupulous, not the deserving, that succeed. What are really infant industries have no more chance in the struggle for governmental encouragement than infant pigs have with full-grown swine about a meal-tub. Not merely is the encouragement likely to go to industries that do not need it, but it is likely to go to industries that can be maintained only in this way, and thus to cause absolute loss to the community by diverting labor and capital from remunerative industries. On the whole, the ability of any industry to establish and sustain itself in a free field is the measure of its public utility, and that "struggle for existence" which drives out unprofitable industries is the best means of determining what industries are needed under existing conditions and what are not. Even promising industries are more apt to be demoralized and stunted than to be aided in healthy growth by encouragement that gives them what they do not earn, just as a young man is more likely to be injured than benefited by being left a fortune. The very difficulties with which new industries must contend not merely serve to determine which are really needed, but also serve to adapt them to surrounding conditions and to develop improvements and inventions that under more prosperous circumstances would never be sought for.

Thus, while it may be abstractly true that there are industries that it would be wise to encourage, the only safe course is to give to all "a fair field and no favor." Where there is a conscious need for the making of some invention or for the establishment of some industry which, though of public utility, would not be commercially profitable, the best way to encourage it is to offer a bounty conditional upon success.

Nothing could better show the futility of attempting to make industries self-supporting by tariff than the confessed inability of the industries that we have so long encouraged to stand alone. In the early days of the American Republic, when the friends of protection were trying to ingraft it upon the Federal revenue system, protection was asked, not for the maintenance of American industry, but for the establishment of "infant industries," which, it was asserted, would, if encouraged for a few years, be able to take care of themselves. The infant boys and girls of that time have grown to maturity, become old men and women, and with rare exceptions have passed away. The nation then fringing the Atlantic seaboard has extended across the continent, and instead of four million now numbers nearly sixty million people. But the "infant industries," for which a little temporary protection was then timidly asked, are still infants in their desire for encouragement. Though they have grown mightily they claim the benefits of the "Baby Act" all the more lustily, declaring that if they cannot have far higher protection than at the beginning they dreamed of asking they must perish outright.

When United States Senator Broderick, shot by Chief-Justice Terry in a duel, died without making a will, a Dublin man wrote to the editor of a San Francisco newspaper claiming to be next of kin. He gave the date of his birth, which showed him forty-seven years of age, and wound up by adjuring the editor to help a poor orphan, who had lost both father and mother. The "infant industry" argument nowadays always reminds me of that orphan.

Protectionist writers have not yet given up the "infant industry" plea, for it is the only ground on which with any semblance of reason protection can be asked; but in the face of the facts they have extended the time in which it is averred that protection can establish an infant industry. The American people used to be told that moderate duties for a few years would enable the protected industries to stand alone and defy foreign competition. But in the latest edition of his "Political Economy" (p. 233), Professor Thompson of the University of Pennsylvania tells us that "it will ordinarily take the lifetime of two generations to acclimatize thoroughly a new manufacture, and to bring the native production up to the native demand."

When we are told that two generations should tax themselves to establish an industry for the third, well may we ask, "What has posterity ever done for us?" Yet even this promise is not borne out by facts. Industries that we have been protecting for more than two generations now need, according to protectionists, more protection than ever.

The popular plea for protection in the United States to-day is not, however, the encouragement of infant industries, but the encouragement of home industry, that is, all home industry.

Now it is manifestly impossible for a protective tariff to encourage all home industry. Duties upon commodities entirely produced at home can, of course, have no effect in encouraging any home industry. It is only when imposed upon commodities partly imported and partly produced at home, or entirely imported, yet capable of being produced at home, that duties can in any way encourage an industry. No tariff which the United States imposed could, for instance, encourage the growth of grain or cotton, the raising of cattle, the production of coal-oil or the mining of gold or silver; for instead of importing these things we not only supply ourselves, but have a surplus which we export. Nor could any import duty encourage any of the many industries which must be carried on where needed, such as building, horseshoeing, the printing of newspapers, and so on. Since these industries that cannot be protected constitute by far the larger part of the industries of every country, the utmost that by a protective tariff can be attempted is the encouragement of only a few of the total industries of a country.

Yet in spite of this obvious fact, protection is never urged for the encouragement of the industries that alone can profit by a tariff. That would be to admit that to some it gave special advantages over others, and so in the popular pleas that are made for it protection is urged for the encouragement of all industry. If we ask how this can be, we are told that the tariff encourages the protected industries, and then the protected industries encourage the unprotected industries; that protection builds up the factory and iron-furnace, and the factory and iron-furnace create a demand for the farmer's productions.

Imagine a village of say a hundred voters. Imagine two of these villagers to make such a proposition as this: "We are desirous, fellow-citizens, of seeing you more

prosperous and to that end propose this plan: Give us
the privilege of collecting a tax of five cents a day from
every one in the village. No one will feel the tax much,
for even to a man with a wife and eight children it will
come only to the paltry sum of fifty cents a day. Yet
this slight tax will give our village two rich citizens who
can afford to spend money. We will at once begin to
live in commensurate style. We will enlarge our houses
and improve our grounds, set up carriages, hire servants,
give parties and buy much more freely at the stores.
This will make trade brisk and cause a greater demand
for labor. This, in turn, will create a greater demand
for agricultural productions, which will enable the neigh-
boring farmers to make a greater demand for store
goods and the labor of mechanics. Thus shall we all
become prosperous."

There is in no country under the sun a village in
which the people would listen to such a proposition.
Yet it is every whit as plausible as the doctrine that
encouraging some industries encourages all industries.

The only way in which we could even attempt to
encourage all industry would be by the bounty or subsidy system. Were we to substitute bounties for duties
as a means of encouraging industry it would not only
become possible for us to encourage other industries
than those now encouraged by tariff, but we should be
forced to do so, for it is not in human nature that the
farmers, the stock-raisers, the builders, the newspaper
publishers and so on, would consent to the payment of
bounties to other industries without demanding them
for their own. Nor could we consistently stop until
every species of industry, to that of the boot-black or rag-
picker, was subsidized. Yet evidently the result of such
encouragement of each would be the discouragement of
all. For as there could be distributed only what was

raised by taxation, less the cost of collection, no one could get back in subsidies, were there any fairness in their distribution, as much as he would be called upon to pay in taxes.

This practical reduction to absurdity is not possible under the protective system, because only a small part of the industries of a country can· thus be "encouraged," while the cost of the encouragement is concealed in prices and is not realized by the masses.   The tax-gatherer does not demand from each citizen a contribution to the encouragement of the favored few.   He sits down in a custom-house and by taxing imports enables the favored producer to collect "encouragement" from his fellow-citizens in higher prices.   Yet it is as true of encouragement by tariff as of encouragement by bounty that the gain to some involves loss to others, and since encouragement by tariff involves far more cost and waste than encouragement by bounty, the proportion which the loss bears to the gain must be greater.   However protection may affect special forms of industry it must necessarily diminish the total return to industry— first, by the waste inseparable from encouragement by tariff, and, second, by the loss due to the transfer of capital and labor from occupations which they would choose for themselves to less profitable occupations which they must be bribed to engage in.   If we do not see this without reflection, it is because our attention is engaged with but a part of the effects of protection.   We see the large smelting-works and the massive mill without realizing that the same taxes which we are told have built them up have made more costly every nail driven and every needleful of thread used throughout the whole country.   Our imaginations are affected as were those of the first Europeans who visited India, and who, impressed by the profusion and magnificence of the

Rajahs, but not noticing the abject poverty of the masses, mistook for the richest country in the world what is really the poorest.

But reflection will show that the claim popularly made for protection, that it encourages home industry (*i.e.*, all home industry), can be true only in one sense—the sense in which Pharaoh encouraged Hebrew industry when he compelled the making of bricks without straw. Protective tariffs make more work, in the sense in which the spilling of grease over her kitchen floor makes more work for the housewife, or as a rain that wets his hay makes more work for the farmer.

CHAPTER XI.

*W*E should keep our own market for our own producers, seems by many to be regarded as the same kind of a proposition as, *We should keep our own pasture for our own cows,* whereas, in truth, it is such a proposition as, *We should keep our own appetites for our own cookery,* or, *We should keep our own transportation for our own legs.*

What is this home market from which protectionists tell us we should so carefully exclude foreign produce? Is it not the home demand—the demand for the satisfaction of our own wants? Hence the proposition that we should keep our home market for home producers is simply the proposition that we should keep our own wants for our own powers of satisfying them. In short, to reduce it to the individual, it is that we ought not to eat a meal cooked by another, since that would deprive us of the pleasure of cooking a meal for ourselves, or make any use of horses or railways because that would deprive our legs of employment.

A short time ago English protectionists (for protection is far from dead in England) were censuring the government for having given large orders for powder to German instead of to English producers. It turned out that the Germans were making a new powder called

103

"cocoa," which in heavy guns gives great velocity with low pressure, and with which all the Continental powers had at once provided themselves. Had the English government refused to buy from foreign producers, English ships, in the event of war, which then seemed imminent, would have been placed at a serious disadvantage.

Now, just as the policy of reserving home markets for home producers would in war put a country which should adhere to it at a great disadvantage—even to the extent, if fully carried out, of restricting the country that does not produce coal to the use of sailing-ships, and compelling the country that yields no iron to fight with bows and arrows—so in all the vocations of peace does this policy involve like disadvantages. Strictly to reserve our home market for home producers would be to exclude ourselves from participation in the advantages which natural conditions or the peculiar skill of their people give to other countries. If bananas will not grow at home we must not eat bananas. If india-rubber is not a home production we must not avail ourselves of its thousand uses. If salt can be obtained in our country only by evaporating sea-water we must continue so to obtain our salt, although in other countries nature has performed this work and provided already crystallized salt in quantities sufficient not only for their people, but for us too. Because we cannot grow the cinchona-tree we must shake with ague and die from malarial diseases, or must writhe in agony under the oculist's knife because the beneficent drug that gives local insensibility is not a home production. And so with all those products in which the peculiar development of industry has enabled the people of various countries to excel. To reserve our home market to home production is to limit the world from which our wants may be supplied to the

bounds of our own country, how little soever that may
be.   And to place any restrictions upon importations is,
in so far as they operate, to deprive ourselves of opportunities to satisfy our wants.

It may be to the interest of a shopkeeper that the
people of his neighborhood should be prohibited from
buying from any one but him, so that they must take
such goods as he chooses to keep, at such prices as he
chooses to charge, but who would contend that this was
to the general advantage?   It might be to the interest of
gas-companies to restrict the number and size of windows, but hardly to the interest of a community.   Broken
limbs bring fees to surgeons, but would it profit a
municipality to prohibit the removal of ice from side-
walks in order to encourage surgery?   Yet it is in such
ways that protective tariffs act.   Economically, what
difference is there between restricting the importation of
iron to benefit iron-producers and restricting sanitary
improvements to benefit undertakers?

To attempt to make a nation prosperous by preventing
it from buying from other nations is as absurd as it
would be to attempt to make a man prosperous by preventing him from buying from other men.   How this
operates in the case of the individual we can see from
that practice which, since its application in the Irish land
agitation, has come to be called "boycotting."   Captain
Boycott, upon whom has been thrust the unenviable
fame of having his name turned into a verb, was in fact
"protected."   He had a protective tariff of the most
efficient kind built around him by a neighborhood decree
more effective than act of Parliament.   No one would
sell him labor, no one would sell him milk or bread or
meat or any service or commodity whatever.   But
instead of growing prosperous, this much-protected man
had to fly from a place where his own market was thus

reserved for his own productions. What protectionists ask us to do to ourselves in reserving our home market for home producers, is in kind what the Land Leaguers did to Captain Boycott. They ask us to boycott ourselves.

In order to convince us that this would be for our benefit, no little ingenuity has been expended. It is asserted (1) that restrictions on foreign trade are beneficial because home trade is more profitable than foreign trade; (2) that even if these restrictions do compel people to pay higher prices for the same commodities, the real cost is no greater, and (3) that even if the cost is greater they get it back again.

Strangely enough, the first of these propositions is fortified by the authority of Adam Smith. In Book II., Chapter V., of "The Wealth of Nations," occurs this passage:

The capital which is employed in purchasing in one part of the country in order to sell in another the produce of the industry of that country, generally replaces by every such operation two distinct capitals that had both been employed in the agriculture or manufactures of that country, and thereby enables them to continue that employment. . . . The capital which sends Scotch manufactures to London, and brings back English corn and manufactures to Edinburgh, necessarily replaces by every such operation two British capitals which had both been employed in the agriculture or manufactures of Great Britain.

The capital employed in purchasing foreign goods for home consumption, when this purchase is made with the produce of domestic industry, replaces, too, by every such operation, two distinct capitals: but one of them only is employed in supporting domestic industry. The capital which sends British goods to Portugal, and brings back Portuguese goods to Great Britain, replaces by every such operation only one British capital. The other is a Portuguese one. Though the returns, therefore, of the foreign trade of consumption should be as quick as those of the home trade, the capital employed in it will give but one-half the encouragement to the industry or productive labor of the country.

This astonishing proposition, of which Adam Smith never seemed to see the significance,* is one of the inconsistencies into which he was led by his abandonment of the solid ground from which labor is regarded as the prime factor in production for that from which capital is so regarded—a confusion of thought which has ever since befogged political economy. This passage is quoted approvingly by protectionist writers, and made by them the basis of assertions even more absurd, if that be possible. Yet the fallacy ought to be seen at a glance. It is of the same nature as the Irishman's division, "Two for you two, and two for me, too," and depends upon the introduction of a term "British," which includes in its meaning two of the terms previously used, "English" and "Scotch." If we substitute for the terms used by Adam Smith other terms of the same relation we may obtain, with equal validity, such propositions as this: If Episcopalians trade with Presbyterians, two profits are made by Protestants; whereas when Presbyterians trade with Catholics only one profit goes to Protestants. Therefore, trade between Protestants is twice as profitable as trade between Protestants and Catholics.

---

* In the next paragraph Adam Smith goes on to carry this proposition to an unconscious *reductio ad absurdum.* He says:

"A capital therefore employed in the home trade will sometimes make twelve operations, or be sent out and returned twelve times, before a capital employed in the foreign trade of consumption has made one. If the capitals are equal, therefore, the one will give four-and-twenty times more encouragement and support to the industry of the country than the other."

This is just such a proposition as that an innkeeper who permits his guests to stay with him only one day can, with equal facilities, furnish twelve times as much entertainment to man and beast as can the innkeeper who permits each guest to stay with him twelve days.

In Adam Smith's illustration there are two quantities of British goods, one in Edinburgh and one in London. In the domestic trade which he supposes, these two quantities of British goods are exchanged; but if the Scotch goods be sent to Portugal instead of to England and Portuguese goods brought back, only one quantity of British goods is exchanged. There will be only one-half the replacement in Great Britain, but there has been only one-half the displacement. The Edinburgh goods which have been sent away have been replaced with Portuguese goods; but the London goods have not been replaced with anything, because they are still there. In the one case twice the amount of British capital is employed as in the other, and consequently double returns show equal profitableness.

The arguments by which it is attempted to prove that it is no hardship to a people to be forced to pay higher prices to home producers for goods they can more cheaply obtain by importation are of no better consistency. The real cost of commodities, it is declared, is not to be measured by their price but by the labor needed to produce them, and hence, as it is put, though higher wages, interest, taxes, etc., may make it impossible to produce certain things for as low a price in one country as in another, their real cost is no greater, if no greater amount of labor is needed for their production, and thus a nation loses nothing by shutting out the cheaper foreign products.

The fallacy is in the assumption that equal amounts of labor always produce equal results. A first-class portrait-painter may be able to do whitewashing with no more labor than a professional whitewasher, but it would nevertheless be a loss to him to take time in which he might earn the wages of a portrait-painter in order to do whitewashing that he might get done for the wages of a whitewasher. Nor would his loss be the less real if he chose to average his income so as to credit himself with as much for whitewashing as for portrait-painting. In the same way, it is not the amount of labor required to produce a thing here or there which determines whether it can be more profitably obtained by home production or by importation, but the relation between what the same labor could produce in that and in other employments. This is shown by price. Though as between different times and places the prices of things do not accurately indicate the relative quantity and quality of labor necessary to obtain them, they do in the same time and place. If at any given time, in any given place, a certain commodity cannot be produced for as low a price as it can be imported for, this is not necessarily proof that it would take more labor to produce it in the given place, but it is proof that labor there and then can be more profitably employed. And when industry is diverted from more profitable to less profitable occupations, though the capital and labor so transferred may be compensated by duties or bounties, there must be a loss to the people as a whole.

The argument that the higher prices which the tariff enables certain home producers to charge involve no loss to those who pay them is thus put by Horace Greeley ("Political Economy," p. 150):

I never made any iron, nor had any other than a public, general interest in making any, while I have bought and used many thousands of dollars' worth, in the shape of power-presses, engines, boilers, building-plates, etc. It is to my interest, you say, to have cheap iron. Certainly; but I buy iron, not (ultimately and really) with money, but with the product of my labor—that is, with newspapers; and I can better afford to pay $70 per ton for iron made by men who can and do buy American newspapers than take it for $50 of those who rarely see and never buy one of my products. The money price of the American iron may be higher, but its real cost to me is less than that of the British iron. And my case is that of the great body of American farmers and other producers of exchangeable wealth.

The fallacy is in the assumption that the ability of certain persons to buy American newspapers depends upon their making of iron, whereas it depends upon their making of something. Newspapers are not bought with iron, nor do newspaper publishers buy iron with newspapers. These transactions are effected with money, which represents no single form of wealth, but value in all forms. If, instead of making iron, the men to whom Mr. Greeley refers had made something else which was exchanged for British iron, Mr. Greeley's purchase of this foreign iron would have been just as truly an exchange of his products for theirs. The $20 per ton additional which the tariff compelled him to pay for iron represented a loss to him which was not a gain to any one else. For on Mr. Greeley's supposition that the tariff was necessary to give American iron-makers the same remuneration such labor could have obtained in other pursuits, its effect was simply to compel the expenditure of $70 worth of labor to obtain what otherwise could have been obtained by $50 worth of labor. To do this was necessarily to lessen the wealth of the country as a whole, and to reduce the fund available for the purchase of newspapers and other articles. This loss is as certain and is of the same kind as if Mr. Greeley had been compelled to employ portrait-painters to do whitewashing.

The more popular forms of this argument that protection costs nothing, hardly need analysis. If, as is asserted, consumers lose nothing in the higher prices the tariff compels them to pay, because these prices are paid to our own people, then producers would lose nothing if compelled to sell to their fellow-citizens below cost. If workmen are necessarily compensated for high-priced goods by the increased demand for their labor, then manufacturers would be compensated for high-priced labor by the increased demand for their goods. In short, on this reasoning it makes no difference to anybody whether the price of anything is high or low. When farmers complain of the high charges of railroads, they are making much ado about nothing; and workmen are taking needless trouble when they demand an increase of wages, while employers are quite as foolish when they try to cut wages down.

CHAPTER XII.

THE aim of protection is to diminish imports, never to diminish exports. On the contrary, the protectionist habit is to regard exports with favor, and to consider the country which exports most and imports least as doing the most profitable trade. When exports exceed imports there is said to be a favorable balance of trade. When imports exceed exports there is said to be an unfavorable balance of trade. In accordance with his idea all protectionist countries afford every facility for sending things away and fine men for bringing things in.

If the things which we thus try to send away and prevent coming in were pests and vermin—things of which all men want as little as possible—this policy would conform to reason. But the things of which exports and imports consist are not things that nature forces on us against our will, and that we have to struggle to rid ourselves of; but things that nature gives only in return for labor, things for which men make exertions and undergo privations. Him who has or can command much of these things we call rich; him who has little we call poor; and when we say that a country increases in wealth we mean that the amount of these things which it contains increases faster than its population. What, then, is more repugnant to reason than the

112

notion that the way to increase the wealth of a country
is to promote the sending of such things away and to
prevent the bringing of them in? Could there be a
queerer inversion of ideas? Should we not think even
a dog had lost his senses that snapped and snarled when
given a bone, and wagged his tail when a bone was taken
from him?

Lawyers may profit by quarrels, doctors by diseases,
rat-catchers by the prevalence of vermin, and so it may
be to the interest of some of the individuals of a nation
to have as much as possible of the good things which we
call "goods" sent away, and as little as possible brought
in. But protectionists claim that it is for the benefit of
a community, as a whole, of a nation considered as one
man, to make it easy to send goods away and difficult to
bring them in.

Let us take a community which we must perforce consider as a whole—that country, with a population of one,
which the genius of De Foe has made familiar not only
to English readers but to the people of all European
tongues.

Robinson Crusoe, we will suppose, is still living alone
on his island. Let us suppose an American protectionist
is the first to break his solitude with the long yearned-for
music of human speech. Crusoe's delight we can well
imagine. But now that he has been there so long he
does not care to leave, the less since his visitor tells him
that the island, having now been discovered, will often be
visited by passing ships. Let us suppose that after having heard Crusoe's story, seen his island, enjoyed such
hospitality as he could offer, told him in return of the
wonderful changes in the great world, and left him books
and papers, our protectionist prepares to depart, but
before going seeks to offer some kindly warning of the
danger Crusoe will be exposed to from the "deluge of

cheap goods" that passing ships will seek to exchange
for fruit and goats.   Imagine him to tell Crusoe just
what protectionists tell larger communities, and to warn
him that, unless he takes measures to make it difficult to
bring these goods ashore, his industry will be entirely
ruined.   "In fact," we may imagine the protectionist to
say, "so cheaply can all the things you require be produced abroad that unless you make it hard to land them
I do not see how you will be able to employ your own
industry at all."

"Will they give me all these things?" Robinson Crusoe
would naturally exclaim.   "Do you mean that I shall get
all these things for nothing and have no work at all to
do?   That will suit me completely.   I shall rest and read
and go fishing for the fun of it.   I am not anxious to
work if without work I can get the things I want."

"No, I don't quite mean that," the protectionist would
be forced to explain.   "They will not give you such
things for nothing.   They will, of course, want something in return.   But they will bring you so much and
will take away so little that your imports will vastly
exceed your exports, and it will soon be difficult for you
to find employment for your labor."

"But I don't want to find employment for my labor,"
Crusoe would naturally reply.   "I did not spend months
in digging out my canoe and weeks in tanning and sew-
ing these goatskins because I wanted employment for
my labor, but because I wanted the things.   If I can get
what I want with less labor, so much the better, and the
more I get and the less I give in the trade you tell me I
am to carry on—or, as you phrase it, the more my
imports exceed my exports—the easier I can live and the
richer I shall be.   I am not afraid of being overwhelmed
with goods.   The more they bring the better it will suit
me."

And so the two might part, for it is certain that no matter how long our protectionist talked the notion that his industry would be ruined by getting things with less labor than before would never frighten Crusoe.

Yet, are these arguments for protection a whit more absurd when addressed to one man living on an island than when addressed to sixty millions living on a continent? What would be true in the case of Robinson Crusoe is true in the case of Brother Jonathan. If foreigners will bring us goods cheaper than we can make them ourselves, we shall be the gainers. The more we get in imports as compared with what we have to give in exports, the better the trade for us. And since foreigners are not liberal enough to give us their productions, but will only let us have them in return for our own productions, how can they ruin our industry? The only way they could ruin our industry would be by bringing us for nothing all we want, so as to save us the necessity for work. If this were possible, ought it seem very dreadful?

Consider this matter in another way: To impose taxes on exports in order that home consumers might get the advantage of lower prices would be quite as just as to impose taxes on imports in order that home producers may get the advantage of higher prices, and it would be far more conformable to the principle of "the greatest good of the greatest number," since all of us are consumers, while only a few of us are producers of the things that can be raised in price by taxes on imports. And since the wealthy country is the country that in proportion to its population contains the largest quantities of the things of which exports and imports consist, it would be a far more plausible method of national enrichment to keep such things from going out than to keep them from coming in.

Now, supposing it were seriously proposed, as a means for enriching the United States, to put restrictive duties on the carrying out of wealth instead of the bringing in of wealth. It is certain that this would be opposed by protectionists. But what objection could they make?

The objection they would make would be in substance this: "The sending away of things in trade from one country to another does not involve a loss to the country from which they are sent, but a gain, since other things of more value are brought back in return for them. Therefore, to place any restriction upon the sending away of things would be to lessen instead of to increase the wealth of a country." This is true. But to say this, is to say that to restrict exports would be injurious because it would diminish imports. Yet, to diminish imports is the direct aim and effect of protective tariffs.

Exports and imports, so far as they are induced by trade, are correlative. Each is the cause and complement of the other, and to impose any restrictions on the one is necessarily to lessen the other. And so far from its being the mark of a profitable commerce that the value of a nation's exports exceeds her imports, the reverse of this is true.

In a profitable international trade the value of imports will always exceed the value of the exports that pay for them, just as in a profitable trading voyage the return cargo must exceed in value the cargo carried out. This is possible to all the nations that are parties to commerce, for in a normal trade commodities are carried from places where they are relatively cheap to places where they are relatively dear, and their value is thus increased by the transportation, so that a cargo arrived at its destination has a higher value than on leaving the port of its exportation. But on the theory that a trade is profitable only when exports exceed imports, the only way for all countries to trade profitably with one another would be to carry commodities from places where they are relatively dear to places where they are relatively cheap. An international trade made up of such transactions as the exportation of manufactured ice from the West Indies to New England, and the exportation of hothouse fruits from New England to the West Indies, would enable all countries to export much larger values than they imported. On the same theory the more ships sunk at sea the better for the commercial world. To have all the ships that left each country sunk before they could reach any other country would, upon protectionist principles, be the quickest means of enriching the whole world, since all countries could then enjoy the maximum of exports with the minimum of imports.

It must, however, be borne in mind that all exporting and importing are not the exchanging of products. This, however, is a fact which puts in still stronger light, if that be possible, the absurdity of the notion that an excess of exports over imports shows increasing wealth. When Rome was mistress of the world, Sicily, Spain, Africa, Egypt, and Britain exported to Italy far more than they imported from Italy. But so far from this excess of their exports over their imports indicating their enrichment, it indicated their impoverishment. It meant that the wealth produced in the provinces was being drained to Rome in taxes and tribute and rent, for which no return was made. The tribute exacted by Germany from France in 1871 caused a large excess of French exports over imports. So in India the "home charges" of an alien government and the remittances of alien officials secure a permanent excess of exports over imports. So the foreign debt which has been fastened upon Egypt requires large amounts of the produce of that country to be sent away for which there is no return in imports. And so for many years the exports from Ireland have largely exceeded the imports into Ireland, owing to the rent drain of absentee landlords. The Irish landlords who live abroad do not directly draw produce for their rent, nor yet do they draw money. Irish cattle, hogs, sheep, butter, linen and other productions are exported as if in the regular course of trade, but their proceeds, instead of coming back to Ireland as imports, are, through the medium of bank and mercantile exchanges, placed to the credit of the absent landlords, and used up by them. This drain of commodities in return for which no commodities are imported, would be greater yet were it not for the fact that thousands of Irishmen cross the Channel every summer to help get in the English harvests, and then return home, and that from those who have permanently emigrated to other countries there is a constant stream of remittances to relatives left behind.*

The last time I crossed to England I sat at the steamer table by two young Englishmen, who drank much champagne and in other ways showed they had plenty of money. As we became acquainted I learned that they were younger sons of English "county families," graduates of a sort of school which has been established in

---

* In Dublin in 1882 I several times met the secretary of one of the great banking institutions whose branches ramify through Ireland. Each time he asked my opinion of the crop prospects in the United States, as though that were uppermost in his mind whenever he met an American. Finally I said to him, "I suppose poor crops in the United States would be to your advantage, as they would increase the value of the agricultural products that Ireland exports." "Oh, no," he replied ; "we are greatly interested in having the American crops good. Good crops mean good times, and good times in the United States mean large remittances from the Irish in America to their families at home, and these remittances are more important to business here than the prices we get for our own products."

Iowa for wealthy young Englishmen who wish to become
"gentlemen farmers" or "estate-owners" in the United
States. Each had got him a considerable tract of new
land, had cut it up into farms, erected on each farm a
board house and barn, and then rented these farms to
tenants for half the crops. They liked America, they
said; it was a good country to have an estate in. The
land laws were very good, and if a tenant did not pay
promptly you could get rid of him without long formality. But they preferred to live in England, and were
going back to enjoy their incomes there, having put their
affairs in the hands of an agent, to whom the tenants
were required to give notice when they wished to reap
their crops, and who saw that the landlord's half was
properly rendered. Thus in this case half the crop (less
commissions) of certain Iowa farmers must annually be
exported without any return in imports. And this tide
of exports for which no imports come back is only
commencing to flow. Many Englishmen already own
American land by the hundred thousand, and even by
the million acres, and are only beginning to draw rent
and royalties. *Punch* recently had a ponderous joke, the
point of which was that the British House of Lords had
much greater landed interests in the United States than
in Great Britain. If not true already, it will not under
present conditions be many years before the English
aristocracy will draw far larger incomes from their
American estates than from their home estates—incomes
to supply which we must export without any return in
imports.*

---

* The *Chicago Tribune* of January 25, 1886, contains a long account
of the American estates of an Irish landlord, William Scully. This
Scully, who was one of the most notorious of the rack-renting and
evicting Irish landlords, owns from 75,000 to 90,000 acres of the
richest land in Illinois, besides large tracts in other States. His

In the commerce which goes on between the United States and Europe there are thus other elements than the exchange of productions. The sums borrowed of Europe by the sale of railway and other bonds, the sums paid by Europeans for land in the United States or invested in industrial enterprises here, capital brought by emigrants, what is spent by Europeans traveling here, and some small amounts of the nature of gifts, legacies, and successions tend to swell our imports or reduce our exports.

On the other hand, not only do we pay in exports to Europe for our imports from Brazil, India, and such countries, but interest on bonds and other obligations, profits on capital invested here, rent for American land owned abroad, remittances from immigrants to relatives at home, property passing by will or inheritance to people abroad, payments for ocean transportation formerly carried on by our own vessels but now carried on by foreign vessels, the sums spent by American tourists who every year visit Europe, and by the increasing number of rich Americans who live in Europe, all contribute to swell our exports and reduce our imports.

---

estates are cut up into farms and rented to tenants who are obliged to pay all taxes and make all improvements, and who are not permitted to sell their crops until the rent is paid. A "spy system" is maintained, and tenants are required to doff their hats when they enter the "estate office." The *Tribune* describes them as reduced to a condition of absolute serfdom. The houses in which they live are the poorest shanties, consisting generally of a room and a half, and the whole district is described as blighted. Scully got most of his land at nominal prices, ranging as low as seventy-five cents per acre. He lives in London, and is said to draw from his American estates a net income of $400,000 a year, which means, of course, that American produce to that value is exported every year without any imports coming back. The *Tribune* closes its long account by saying: "Not content with acquiring land himself, Scully has induced a number of his relatives to become American landlords, and their system is patterned on his own."

The annual balance against us on these accounts is already very large and is steadily growing larger. Were we to prevent importations absolutely we should still have to export largely in order to pay our rents, to meet interest, and to provide for the increasing number of rich Americans who travel or reside abroad. But the fact that our exports must now thus exceed our imports instead of being what protectionists take it for, an evidence of increasing prosperity, is simply the evidence of a drain upon national wealth like that which has so impoverished Ireland.

But this drain is not to be stopped by tariffs. It proceeds from a deeper cause than any tariff can touch, and is but part of a general drift. Our internal commerce also involves the flow from country to city, and from West to East, of commodities for which there is no return. Our large mine-owners, ranch-owners, land speculators, and many of our large farmers, live in the great cities. Our small farmers have had in large part to buy their farms on mortgage of men who live in cities to the east of them; the bonds of the national, State, county, and municipal governments are largely so held, as are the stocks and bonds of railway and other companies—the result being that the country has to send to the cities, the West to the East, more than is returned. This flow is increasing, and, no matter what be our tariff legislation, must continue steadily to increase, for it springs from the most fundamental of our social adjustments, that which makes land private property. As the land in Illinois, or Iowa, or Oregon, or New Mexico owned by a resident of New York or Boston increases in value, people who live in those States must send more and more of their produce to the New Yorker or Bostonian. They may work hard, but grow relatively poorer; he may not work at all, but grow relatively richer, so that when they need capital for building railroads or any other purpose, they must borrow and pay interest, while he can lend and get interest. The tendency of the time is thus to the ownership of the whole country by residents of cities, and it makes no difference to the people of the country districts whether those cities are in America or Europe.

CHAPTER XIII.

THERE is no one who in exchanging his own productions for the productions of another would think
that the more he gave and the less he got the better off
he would be. Yet to many men nothing seems clearer
than that the more of its own productions a nation sends
away, and the less of the productions of other nations it
receives in return, the more profitable its trade. So
wide-spread is this belief that to-day nearly all civilized
nations endeavor to discourage the bringing in of the
productions of other nations while regarding with satisfaction the sending away of their own.

What is the reason of this? Men are not apt to apply
to the transactions of nations principles opposite to those
they apply to individual transactions. On the contrary,
the natural tendency is to personify nations, and to
think and speak of them as actuated by the same motives
and governed by the same laws as the human beings of
whom they are made up. Nor have we to look far to see
that the preposterous notion that a nation gains by
exporting and loses by importing actually arises from
the application to the commerce between nations of ideas
to which individual transactions accustom civilized men.
What men dispose of to others we term their sales; what
they obtain from others we term their purchases. Hence
we become accustomed to think of exports as sales, and

of imports as purchases. And as in daily life we habitually think that the greater the value of a man's sales and
the less the value of his purchases the better his business; so, if we do not stop to fix the meaning of the
words we use, it seems a matter of course that the more
a nation exports and the less it imports the richer it will
become.

It is significant of its origin that such a notion is
unknown among savages. Nor could it have arisen
among civilized men if they were accustomed to trade as
savages do. Not long ago a class of traders called
" soap-fat men " used to go from house to house exchanging soap for the refuse fat accumulated by housewives.
In this petty commerce, carried on in this primitive
manner, the habit of thinking that in a profitable trade
the value of sales must exceed the value of purchases
could never have arisen, it being clearly to the interest of
each party that the value of what he sold (or exported)
should be as little as possible, and the value of what he
bought (or imported) as great as possible. But in civilized society this is only the exceptional form of trade.
Buying and selling, as our daily life familiarizes us with
them, are not the exchange of commodities for commodities, but the exchange of money for commodities, or of
commodities for money.

It is to confusions of thought growing out of this use
of money that we may trace the belief that a nation
profits by exporting and loses by importing—a belief to
which countless lives and incalculable wealth have been
sacrificed in bloody wars, and which to-day molds the
policy of nearly all civilized nations and interposes artificial barriers to the commerce of the world.

The primary form of trade is barter—the exchange of
commodities for commodities. But just as when we
begin to think and speak of length, weight or bulk, it is

necessary to adopt measures or standards by which these qualities can be expressed, so when trade begins there arises a need for some common standard by which the value of different articles can be apprehended.   The difficulties attending barter soon lead, also, to the adoption by common consent of some commodity as a medium of exchange, by means of which he who wishes to exchange a thing for one or more other things is no longer obliged to find some one with exactly reciprocal desires, but is enabled to divide the complete exchange into stages or steps, which can be made with different persons, to the enormous saving of time and trouble.

In primitive society, cattle, skins, shells and many other things have in a rude way fulfilled these functions. But the precious metals are so peculiarly adapted to this use that wherever they have become known mankind has been led to adopt them as money.   They are at first used by weight, but a great step in advance is taken when they are coined into pieces of definite weight and purity, so that no one who receives them needs to take the trouble of weighing and testing them.   As civilization advances, as society becomes more settled and orderly, and exchanges more numerous and regular, gold and silver are gradually superseded as mediums of exchange by credit in various forms.   By means of accounts current, one purchase is made to balance another purchase and one debt to cancel another debt.   Individuals or associations of recognized solvency issue bills of exchange, letters of credit, notes and drafts, which largely take the place of coin; banks transfer credits between individuals, and clearing-houses transfer credits between banks, so that immense transactions are carried on with a very small actual use of money; and finally, credits of convenient denominations, printed upon paper, and adapted to transference from hand to hand without indorsement or formality, being cheaper and more convenient, take in part or in whole the place of gold or silver in the country where they are issued.

This is, in brief, the history of that labor-saving instrument which ranges in its forms from the cowries of the African or the wampum of the red Indian to the banknote or greenback, and which does so much to facilitate trade that without it civilization would be impossible. The part which it plays in social life and intercourse is so necessary, its use is so common in thought and speech and actual transaction, that certain confusions with regard to it are apt to grow up. It is not needful to speak of the delusion that interest grows out of the use of money, or that increase of money is increase of wealth, or that paper money cannot properly fulfil its functions unless an equivalent of coin is buried somewhere, but only of such confusions of thought as have a relation to international trade.

I was present yesterday when one farmer gave another farmer a horse and four pigs for a mare. Both seemed pleased with the transaction, but neither said, "Thank you." Yet when money is given for anything else it is usual for the person who receives the money to say, "Thank you," or in some other way to indicate that he is more obliged in receiving the money than the other party is in receiving the thing the money is given for. This custom is one of the indications of a habit of thought which (although it is clear that a dollar cannot be more valuable than a dollar's worth) attaches the idea of benefit more to the giving of money for commodities than to the giving of commodities for money.

The main reason of this I take to be that difficulties of exchange are most felt on the side of reduction to the medium of exchange. To exchange anything for money it is necessary to find some one who wants that particular thing, but, this exchange effected, the exchange of money for other things is generally easier, since all who have anything to exchange are willing to take money for it. This, and the fact that the value of money is more certain and definite than the value of things measured by it, and the further fact that the sale or conversion of commodities into money completes those transactions upon which we usually estimate profit, easily lead us to look upon the getting of money as the object and end of trade, and upon selling as more profitable than buying.

Further than this, money, being the medium of exchange—the thing that can be most quickly and easily exchanged for other things—is, therefore, the most convenient in contingencies. In ruder times, before the organization of credit had reached such development as now, when the world was cut up into small states constantly warring with each other, when order was less well preserved, property far more insecure and the exhibition of riches often led to extortion; when pirates infested the sea and robbers the land; when fires were frequent and insurance had not been devised; when prisoners were held to ransom and captured cities given up to sack, the contingencies in which it is important to have wealth in the form in which it can be most conveniently carried, readily concealed and speedily exchanged, were far more numerous than now, and every one strove to keep some part of his wealth in the precious metals. The peasant buried his savings, the merchant kept his money in his strong box, the miser gloated over his golden hoard and the prince sought to lay up a great treasure for time of sudden need. Thus gold and silver were even more striking symbols of wealth than now, and the habit of thinking of them as the only real wealth was formed.

This habit of thought gave ready support to the protective policy. When the growth of commerce made it possible to raise large revenues by indirect taxation, kings and their ministers soon discovered how easily the people could thus be made to pay an amount of taxes that they would have resisted if levied directly. Import taxes were first levied to obtain revenue, but not only was it found to be exceedingly convenient to tax goods in the seaport towns from whence they were distributed through the country, but the taxation of imported goods met with the warm support of such home producers as were thus protected from competition. An interest was thus created in favor of "protection," which availed itself of national prejudices and popular habits of thought, and a system was by degrees elaborated, which for centuries swayed the policy of European nations.

This system, which Adam Smith attacked under the name of the mercantile system of political economy, regarded nations as merchants competing with each other for the money of the world, and aimed at enriching a country by bringing into it as much gold and silver as possible, and permitting as little as possible to flow out. To do this it was sought not only to prohibit the carrying of precious metals out of the country, but to encourage the domestic production of goods that could be sold abroad, and to throw every obstacle in the way of similar foreign or colonial industries. Not only were heavy import duties or absolute prohibitions placed on such products of foreign industry as might come into competition with home industry, but the exports of such raw materials as foreign industries might require were burdened with export duties or entirely prohibited under savage penalties of death or mutilation. Skilled workmen were forbidden to leave the country lest they might teach foreigners their art; domestic industries were encouraged by bounties, by patents of monopoly and by the creation of artificial markets—sometimes by premiums paid on exports, and sometimes by laws which compelled the use of their products. One instance of this was the act of Parliament which required every corpse to be buried in a woolen shroud, a piece of stupidity only paralleled by the laws under which the American people are taxed to bury in underground safes $2,000,000 of coined silver every month, and keep a hundred millions of gold lying idle in the treasury.

But to attempt to increase the supply of gold and silver by such methods is both foolish and useless. Though the value of the precious metals is high their utility is low; their principal use, next to that of money, being in ostentation. And just as a farmer would become poorer, not richer, by selling his breeding-stock and seed-grain to obtain gold to hoard and silver to put on his table, or as a manufacturer would lessen his income by selling a useful machine and keeping in his safe the money he got for it, so must a nation lessen its productive power by stimulating its exports or reducing its imports of things that could be productively used, in order to accumulate gold and silver for which it has no productive use. Such amounts of the precious metals as are needed for use as money will come to every nation that participates in the trade of the world, by virtue of a tendency that sets at naught all endeavors artificially to enhance supply, a tendency as constant as the tendency of water to seek a level. Wherever trade exists all commodities capable of transportation tend to flow from wherever their value is relatively low to wherever their value is relatively high. This tendency is checked by the difficulties of transportation, which vary with different things as their bulk, weight and liability to injury compare with their value. The precious metals do not suffer from transportation, and having (especially gold) little weight and bulk as compared with their value, are so portable that a very slight change in their relative value is sufficient to cause their flow. So easily can they be carried and concealed that legal restrictions, backed by coast-guards and custom-house officials, have never been able to prevent them from finding their way out of a country where their value was relatively low and into a country where their value was relatively high. The attempts of her despotic monarchs to keep in Spain the precious metals she drew from America were like trying to hold water in a sieve.

The effect of artificially increasing the supply of precious metals in any country must be to lower their value as compared with that of other commodities. The moment, therefore, that restrictions by which it is attempted to attract and retain the precious metals, begin so to operate as to increase the supply of those metals, a tendency to their outflowing is set up, increasing in force as the efforts to attract and retain them. become more strenuous. Thus all efforts artificially to increase the gold and silver of a country have had no result save to hamper industry and to make the country that engaged in them poorer instead of richer. This, experience has taught civilized nations, and few of them now make any direct efforts to attract or retain the precious metals, save by uselessly hoarding them in burglar-proof vaults as we do.

But the notion that gold and silver are the only true money, and that as such they have a peculiar value, still underlies protectionist arguments,* and the habit of asso-

---

* For instance, Professor Thompson writing where and when, save for subsidiary tokens, paper money was exclusively used, and so conscious of its ability to perform all the functions of money that he declares it to be as much superior to coin as the railway is to the

ciating incomes with sales, and expenditure with purchases, which is formed in the thought and speech of every-day life, still disposes men to accept a policy which aims at restricting imports by protective tariffs. Being accustomed to measure the profits of business men by the excess of their sales over their purchases, the assumption that the exports of a nation are equivalent to the sales of a merchant, and its imports to his purchases, leads easily to the conclusion that the greater the amount of exports and the less the amount of imports, the more profit a nation gets by its trade.*

Yet it needs only attention to see that this assumption involves a confusion of ideas. When we say that a merchant is doing a profitable business because his sales exceed his purchases, what we are really thinking of as sales is not the goods he sends out, but the money that we infer he takes in in exchange for them; what we are really thinking of as purchases is not the goods he takes in, but the money we infer he pays out. We mean, in short, that he is growing richer because his income exceeds his outgo. We become so used in ordinary affairs to this transposition of terms by inference, that when we think of a nation's exports as its sales and of its imports as its purchases, habit leads us to attach to these words the

---

stage-coach ("Political Economy," p. 152), goes on subsequently (p. 223) to contend that protective duties are necessary to prevent the poorer country being drained of its money by the richer country, thus tacitly assuming that gold and silver alone are money—since neither he nor any one else would pretend that one country could drain another of its paper money.

* A conclusion frequently carried by protectionists to the most ridiculous lengths, as, for instance, in the recent declaration of a protectionist Senator (William M. Evarts of New York), that he would be ready for free trade "when protection had so far developed all our industries that the United States could sell in competition with all the world, and at the same time be free from the necessity of buying anything from all the world."

same inferential meaning, and thus unconsciously to give to a word expressive of outgoing, the significance of incoming; and to a word expressive of incoming, the significance of outgoing. But, manifestly, when we compare the trade of a merchant carried on in the usual way with the trade of a nation, it is not the goods that a merchant sells, but the money that he pays out, that is analogous to the exports of a country; not the goods that he buys, but the money he takes in, that is analogous to imports. It is only where the trade of a merchant is carried on by the exchange of commodities for commodities, that the commodities he sells are analogous to the exports, and the commodities he buys are analogous to the imports of a nation. And the village dealer who exchanges groceries and dry-goods for eggs, poultry and farm produce, or the Indian trader who exchanges manufactured goods for furs, is manifestly doing the more profitable business the more the value of the commodities he takes in (his imports) exceeds the value of the goods he gives out (his exports).

The fact is, that all trade in the last analysis is simply what it is in its primitive form of barter, the exchange of commodities for commodities. The carrying on of trade by the use of money does not change its essential character, but merely permits the various exchanges of which trade is made up to be divided into parts or steps, and thus more easily effected. When commodities are exchanged for money, but half a full exchange is completed. When a man sells a thing for money it is to use the money in buying some other thing—and it is only as money has this power that any one wants or will take it. Our common use of the word "money" is largely metaphorical. We speak of a wealthy man as a moneyed man, and in talking of his wealth say that he has so much "money," whereas the fact probably is, that though he may be worth millions, he never has at any one time more than a few dollars, or at most a few hundred dollars, in his possession. His possessions really consist of houses, lands, goods, stocks, or of bonds or other obligations to pay money. The possession of these things we speak of as the possession of money because we habitually estimate their value in money. If we habitually estimated value in shells, sugar or cattle, we would speak of rich men as having much of these, just as the use of postage-stamps as currency at the beginning of our civil war led to speaking of rich men in the slang of the day, as those who had plenty of "stamps." And so, when a merchant is doing a profitable business, though we speak of him as making or accumulating money, the fact is, save in very rare cases, that he is putting out money as fast as he gets it in. The shrewd business man does not stow away money. On the contrary, with the money he obtains from his sales he hastens to make other purchases. If he does not buy commodities for use in his business, or commodities or services for personal gratification, he buys lands, houses, stocks, bonds, mortgages or other things from which he expects a profitable return.

The trade between nations, made up as it is of numerous individual transactions which separately are but parts or steps in a complete exchange, is in the aggregate, like the primitive form of trade, the exchange of commodities for commodities. Money plays no part in international trade, and the world has yet to reach that stage of civilization which will give us international money. The paper currency which in all civilized nations now constitutes the larger part of their money, is never exported to settle balances, and when gold or silver coin is exported or imported it is as a commodity, and its value is estimated at that of the bullion contained. What each nation imports is paid for in the commodities which it exports, unless received as loans or investments, or as interest, rent or tribute. Before commerce had reached its present refinement of division and sub-division this was in many individual cases clear enough. A vessel sailed from New York, Philadelphia or Boston carrying, on account of owner or shipper, a cargo of flour, lumber and staves to the West Indies, where it was sold, and the proceeds invested in sugar, rum and molasses, which were brought back, or which, perhaps, were carried to Europe, there sold, and the proceeds invested in European goods, which were brought home. At present the exporter and importer are usually different persons, but the bills of exchange drawn by the one against goods exported are bought by the other, and used to pay for goods imported. So far as the country is concerned, the transaction is the same as though importers and exporters were the same persons, and that imports exceed exports in value is no more proof of a losing trade than that in the old times a trading ship brought home a cargo worth more than that she carried out was proof of an unprofitable voyage.

CHAPTER XIV.

DO HIGH WAGES NECESSITATE PROTECTION?

IN the United States, at present, protection derives strong support from the belief that the products of the lower-paid labor of other countries could undersell the products of our higher-paid labor if free competition were permitted. This belief not only leads working-men to imagine protection necessary to keep up wages—a matter of which I shall speak hereafter; but it also induces the belief that protection is necessary to the interests of the country at large—a matter which now falls in our way.

And further than concerns the tariff this belief has important bearings. It enables employers to persuade themselves that they are serving general interests in reducing wages or resisting their increase, and greatly strengthens the opposition to the efforts of working-men to improve their condition, by setting against them a body of opinion that otherwise would be neutral, if not strongly in their favor. This is clearly seen in the case of the eight-hour system. Much of the opposition to this great reform arises from the belief that the increase of wages to which such a reduction of working-hours would be equivalent, would place the United States at a great disadvantage in production as compared with other countries.

It is evident that even those who most vociferously assert that we need a protective tariff on account of our higher standard of wages do not really believe it themselves. For if protection be needed against countries of lower wages, it must be most needed against countries of lowest wages and least needed against countries of highest wages. Now, against what country is it that American protectionists most demand protection? If we could have a protective tariff against only one country in the whole world, what country is it that American protectionists would select to be protected against? Unquestionably it is Great Britain. But Great Britain, instead of being the country of lowest wages, is, next to the United States and the British colonies, the country of highest wages.

"It is a poor rule that will not work both ways." If we require a protective tariff because of our high wages, then countries of low wages require free trade—or, at the very least, have nothing to fear from free trade. How is it, then, that we find the protectionists of France, Germany and other low-wage countries protesting that their industries will be ruined by the free competition of the higher-wage industries of Great Britain and the United States just as vehemently as our protectionists protest that our industries would be ruined if exposed to free competition with the products of the "pauper labor" of Europe?

As popularly put, the argument that the country of high wages needs a protective tariff runs in this way: "Wages are higher here than elsewhere; therefore, if the produce of cheaper foreign labor were freely admitted it would drive the produce of our dearer domestic labor out of the market." But the conclusion does not follow from the premise. To make it valid two intermediate propositions must be assumed: first, that low wages mean low cost of production; and second, that production is determined solely by cost—or, to put it in another way, that trade being free, everything will be produced where it can be produced at least cost. Let us examine these two propositions separately.

If the country of low wages can undersell the country of high wages, how is it that though the American farmhand receives double the wages of the English agricultural laborer, yet American grain undersells English grain? How is it that while the general level of wages is higher here than anywhere else in the world we nevertheless do export the products of our high-priced labor to countries of lower-priced labor?

The protectionist answer is that American grain undersells English grain, in spite of the difference of wages, because of our natural advantages for the production of grain; and that the bulk of our exports consists of those crude productions in which wages are not so important an element of cost, since they do not embody so much labor as the more elaborate productions called manufactures.

But the first part of this answer is an admission that the rate of wages is *not* the determining element in the cost of production, and that the country of low wages does not necessarily produce more cheaply than the country of high wages; while, as for the distinction drawn between the cruder and the more elaborate productions, it is evident that this is founded on the comparison of such things by bulk or weight, whereas the only measure of embodied labor is value. A pound of cloth embodies more labor than a pound of cotton, but this is not true of a dollar's worth. That a small weight of cloth will exchange for a large weight of cotton, or a small bulk of watches for a large bulk of wheat, means simply that equal amounts of labor will produce larger

weights or bulks of the one thing than of the other; and
in the same way the exportation of a certain value of
grain, ore, stone or timber means the exportation of
exactly as much of the produce of labor as would the
exportation of the same value of lace or fancy goods.

Looking further, we see in every direction that it is
not the fact that low-priced labor gives advantage in
production.   If this is the fact how was it that the
development of industry in the slave States of the American Union was not more rapid than in the free States?
How is it that Mexico, where peon labor can be had for
from four to six dollars a month, does not undersell the
products of our more highly paid labor?   How is it that
China and India and Japan are not "flooding the world"
with the products of their cheap labor?   How is it that
England, where labor is better paid than on the Continent, leads the whole of Europe in commerce and manufactures?   The truth is, that a low rate of wages does
not mean a low cost of production, but the reverse.   The
universal and obvious truth is, that the country where
wages are highest can produce with the greatest economy, because workmen have there the most intelligence,
the most spirit and the most ability; because invention
and discovery are there most quickly made and most
readily utilized.   The great inventions and discoveries
which so enormously increase the power of human labor
to produce wealth have all been made in countries where
wages are comparatively high.

That low wages mean inefficient labor may be seen
wherever we look.   Half a dozen Bengalese carpenters
are needed to do a job that one American carpenter can
do in less time.   American residents in China get
servants for almost nothing, but find that so many are
required that servants cost more than in the United
States; yet the Chinese who are largely employed in

domestic service in California, and get wages that they would not have dreamed of in China, are efficient workers. Go to High Bridge, and you will see a great engine attended by a few men, exerting the power of thousands of horses in pumping up a small river for the supply of New York city, while on the Nile you may see Egyptian fellahs raising water by buckets and tread-wheels. In Mexico, with labor at four or five dollars a month, silver ore has for centuries been carried to the surface on the backs of men who climbed rude ladders, but when silver-mining began in Nevada, where labor could not be had for less than five or six dollars a day, steam-power was employed. In Russia, where wages are very low, grain is still reaped by the sickle and threshed with the flail or by the hoofs of horses, while in our Western States, where labor is very high as compared with the Russian standard, grain is reaped, threshed and sacked by machinery.

If it were true that equal amounts of labor always produced equal results, then cheap labor might mean cheap production. But this is obviously untrue. The power of human muscle is, indeed, much the same everywhere, and if his wages be sufficient to keep him in good bodily health the poorly paid laborer can, perhaps, exert as much physical force as the highly paid laborer. But the power of human muscles, though necessary to all production, is not the primary and efficient force in production. That force is human intelligence, and human muscles are merely the agency by which that intelligence makes connection with and takes hold of external things, so as to utilize natural forces and mold matter to conformity with its desires. A race of intelligent pygmies with muscles no stronger than those of the grasshopper could produce far more wealth than a race of stupid giants with muscles as strong as those of the elephant.

Now, intelligence varies with the standard of comfort, and the standard of comfort varies with wages. Wherever men are condemned to a poor, hard and precarious living their mental qualities sink toward the level of the brute. Wherever easier conditions prevail the qualities that raise man above the brute and give him power to master and compel external nature develop and expand. And so it is that the efficiency of labor is greatest where laborers get the best living and have the most leisure— that is to say, where wages are highest.

How then, in the face of these obvious facts, can we account for the prevalence of the belief that the low-wage country has an advantage in production over the high-wage country? It cannot be charged to the teaching of protection. This is one of the fallacies which protectionism avails itself of, rather than one for which it is responsible. Men do not hold it because they are protectionists, but become protectionists because they hold it. And it seems to be as firmly held, and on occasion as energetically preached, by so-called free traders as by protectionists. Witness the predictions of free-trade economists that trades-unions, if successful in raising wages and shortening hours, would destroy England's ability to sell her goods to other nations, and the similar objections by so-called free traders to similar movements on the part of working-men in the United States.

The truth is that the notion that low wages give a country an advantage in production is a careless inference from the every-day fact that it is an advantage to an individual producer to obtain labor at low wages.

It is true that an individual producer gains an advantage when he can force down the wages of his employees below the ordinary level, or can import laborers who will work for him for less, and that he may by this means be enabled to undersell his competitors, while the employer who continues to pay higher wages than other employers about him will, before long, be driven out of business. But it by no means follows that the country where wages are low can undersell the country where wages are high. For the efficiency of labor, though it may somewhat vary with the particular wages paid, is in greater degree determined by the general standard of comfort and intelligence, and the prevailing habits and methods which grow out of them. When a single employer manages to get labor for less than the rate of wages prevailing around him, the efficiency of the labor he gets is still largely fixed by that rate. But a country where the general rate of wages is low does not have a similar advantage over other countries, because there the general efficiency of labor must also be low.

The contention that industry can be more largely carried on where wages are low than where wages are high, another form of the same fallacy, may readily be seen to spring from a confusion of thought. For instance, in the earlier days of California it was often said that the lowering of wages would be a great benefit to the State, as lower wages would enable capitalists to work deposits of low-grade quartz that it would not pay to work at the then existing rate of wages. But it is evident that a mere reduction of wages would not have resulted in the working of poorer mines, since it could not have increased the amount of labor or capital available for the working of mines, and what existed would still have been devoted to the working of the richer in preference to the poorer mines, no matter how much wages were reduced. It might, however, have been said that the effect would be to increase the profits of capital and thus bring in more capital. But, to say nothing of the deterrent effect upon the coming in of labor, a moment's reflection will show that such a reduction of wages would not add to the profits of capital. It would add to the profits of mine-owners, and mines would bring higher prices. Eliminating improvements in methods, or changes in the value of the product, lower wages and the working of poorer mines come, of course, together, but this is not because the lower wages cause the working of poorer mines, but the reverse. As the richer natural opportunities are taken up and production is forced to devote itself to natural opportunities that will yield less to the same exertion, wages fall. There is, however, no gain to capital; and under such circumstances we do not see interest increase. The gain accrues to those who have possessed themselves of natural opportunities, and what we see is that the value of land increases.

The immediate effect of a general reduction of wages in any country would be merely to alter the distribution of wealth. Of the amount produced less would go to the laborers and more to those who share in the results of production without contributing to it. Some changes in exports and imports would probably follow a general reduction of wages, owing to changes in relative demand. The working-classes, getting less than before, would have to reduce their luxuries, and perhaps live on cheaper food. Other classes, finding their incomes increased, might use more costly food and demand more of the costlier luxuries, and larger numbers of them might go abroad and use up in foreign countries the produce of exports, by which, of course, imports would be diminished. But except as to such changes the foreign commerce of a country would be unaffected. The country as a whole would have no more to sell and could buy no more than before. And in a little while the inevitable effect of the degradation of labor involved in the reduction of wages would begin to tell in the reduced power of production, and both exports and imports would fall off.

So if in any country there were a general increase of wages, the immediate effect would only be so to alter the distribution of wealth that more of the aggregate product would go to the laboring-classes and less to those who live on the labor of others. The result would be that more of the cheaper luxuries would be called for and less of the more costly luxuries. But productive power would in no wise be lessened; there would be no less to export than before and no less ability to pay for imports. On the contrary, some of the idle classes would find their incomes so reduced that they would have to go to work and thus increase production, while as soon as an increase in wages began to tell on the habits of the people and on industrial methods productive power would increase.

CHAPTER XV.

OF ADVANTAGES AND DISADVANTAGES AS REASONS
FOR PROTECTION.

WE have seen that low wages do not mean low cost of production, and that a high standard of wages, instead of putting a country at a disadvantage in production, is really an advantage. This disposes of the claim that protection is rendered necessary by high wages, by showing the invalidity of the first assumption upon which it is based. But it is worth while to examine the second assumption in this claim — that production is determined by cost, so that a country of less advantages cannot produce if the free competition of a country of greater advantages be permitted. For while we are sometimes told that a country needs protection because of great natural advantages that ought to be developed, we are at other times told that protection is needed because of the sparseness of population, the want of capital or machinery or skill, or because of high taxes or a high rate of interest,* or other conditions which, it may be, involve real disadvantage.

---

* The higher rate of interest in the United States than in Great Britain has until recently been one of the stock reasons of American protectionists for demanding a high tariff. We do not hear so much of this now that the rate in New York is as low as in London, if not lower, but we hear no less of the need for protection. It is hardly necessary in this discussion to treat of the nature and law of inter-

But without reference to the reality of the alleged advantage or disadvantage, all these special pleas for protection are met when it is shown, as it can be shown, that whatever be its advantages or disadvantages for production a country can always increase its wealth by foreign trade.

If we suppose two countries each of which is, for any reason, at a decided disadvantage in some branch of production in which the other has a decided advantage, it is evident that the free exchange of commodities between them will be mutually beneficial, by enabling each to make up for its own disadvantage by availing itself of the advantage of the other, just as the blind man and the lame man did in the familiar story. Trade between them will give to each country a greater amount of all things than it could otherwise obtain with the same quantity of labor. Such a case resembles that of two workmen, each having as to some things skill superior to the other, and who, by working together, each devoting himself to that part for which he is the better fitted, can accomplish more than twice as much as if each worked separately.

But let us suppose two countries, one of which has advantages superior to the other for all the productions of which both are capable. Trade between them being free, would one country do all the exporting and the other all the importing? That, of course, would be preposterous. Would trade, then, be impossible? Certainly

---

est, a subject which I have gone over in "Progress and Poverty." It may, however, be worth while to say that a high rate of interest where it does not proceed from insecurity, is not to be regarded as a disadvantage, but rather as evidence of the large returns to the active factors of production, labor and capital—returns which diminish as rent rises and the landowner gets a larger share of their produce for permitting labor and capital to work.

not. Unless the people of the country of less advantages transferred themselves bodily to the country of greater advantages, trade would go on with mutual benefit. The people of the country of greater advantages would import from the country of less advantages those prod· ucts as to which the difference of advantage between the two countries was least, and would export in return those products as to which the difference was greatest. By this exchange both peoples would gain. The people of the country of poorest advantages would gain by it some part of the advantages of the other country, and the people of the country of greatest advantages would also gain, since, by being saved the necessity of producing the things as to which their advantage was least, they could concentrate their energies upon the production of things in which their advantage was greatest. This case would resemble that of two workmen of different degrees of skill in all parts of their trade, or that of a skilled workman and an unskilled helper. Though the workman might be able to perform all parts of the work in less time than the helper, yet there would be some parts in which the advantage of his superior skill would be less than in others; and as by leaving these to the helper he could devote more time to those parts in which superior skill would be most effective, there would be, as in the former case, a mutual gain in their working together.

Thus it is that neither advantages nor disadvantages afford any reason for restraining trade.* Trade is

---

* In point of fact there is no country which as to all branches of production can be said to have superior advantages. The conditions which make one part of the habitable globe better fitted for some productions, unfit it for others, and what is disadvantage for some kinds of production, is generally advantage for other kinds. Even the lack of rain which makes some parts of the globe useless to man,

always to the benefit of both parties. If it were not there would be no disposition to carry it on.

And thus we see again the fallacy of the protectionist contention that if it takes no more labor to produce a thing in our country than elsewhere, we shall lose nothing by shutting out the foreign product, even though we have to pay a higher price for the home product. The interchange of the products of labor does not depend upon differences of absolute cost, but of comparative cost. Goods may profitably be sent from places where they cost more labor to places where they cost less labor, provided (and this is the only case in which they ever will be so sent) that a still greater difference in labor-cost exists as to other things which the first country desires to obtain. Thus tea, which Horace Greeley was fond of referring to as a production that might advantageously be naturalized in the United States by a heavy duty, could undoubtedly be produced in the United States at less cost of labor than in China, for in transportation to the seaboard, packing, etc., we could save upon Chinese methods. But there are other things, such as the mining of silver, the refining of oil, the weaving of cloth, the making of clocks and watches, as to which our advantage over the Chinese is enormously greater than in the growing of tea. Hence, by producing these things and exchanging them directly **or** indirectly for

---

may, if invention ever succeeds in directly utilizing the power of the sun's rays, be found to be especially advantageous for certain parts of production. The advantages and disadvantages that come from the varying density of population, the special development of certain forms of industry, etc., are also largely relative. The most positive of all advantages in production—that which most certainly gives superiority in all branches, is that which arises from that general intelligence which increases with the increase of the comfort and leisure of the masses of the people, that is to say, with the increase of wages.

Chinese tea, we obtain, in spite of the long carriage, more tea for the same labor than we could get by growing our own tea.

Consider how this principle, that the interchange of commodities is governed by the comparative, not the absolute, cost of production, applies to the plea that protective duties are required on account of home taxation. It is of course true that a special tax placed upon any branch of production puts it at a disadvantage unless a like tax is placed upon the importation of similar productions. But this is not true of such general taxation as falls on all branches of industry alike. As such taxation does not alter the comparative profitableness of industries it does not diminish the relative inducement to carry any of them on, and to protect any particular industry from foreign competition on account of such general taxation is simply to enable those engaged in it to throw off their share of a general burden.

A favorite assumption of American protectionists is, or rather has been (for we once heard much more of it than now), that free trade is a good thing for rich countries but a bad thing for poor countries—that it enables a country of better-developed industries to prevent the development of industry in other countries, and to make such countries tributary to itself. But it follows from the principle which, as we have seen, causes and governs international exchanges, that for any country to impose restrictions on its foreign commerce on account of its own disadvantages in production is to prevent such amelioration of those disadvantages as foreign trade would bring. Free trade is voluntary trade. It cannot go on unless to the advantage of both parties, and, as between the two, free trade is relatively more advantageous to the poor and undeveloped country than to the rich and prosperous country. The opening up of trade between a Robinson Crusoe and the rest of the world would be to the advantage of both parties. But relatively the advantage would be far greater to Robinson Crusoe than to the rest of the world.

There is a certain class of American protectionists who concede that free trade is good in itself, but who say that we cannot safely adopt it until all other nations have adopted it, or until all other nations have come up to our standard of civilization; or, as it is sometimes phrased, until the millennium has come and men have ceased to struggle for their own interests as opposed to the interests of others. And so British protectionists have now assumed the name of "Fair Traders." They have ceased to deny the essential goodness of free trade, but contend that so long as other countries maintain protective tariffs Great Britain, in self-defense, should maintain a protective tariff too, at least against countries that refuse to admit British productions free.

The fallacy underlying most of these American excuses for protection is that considered in the previous chapter —the fallacy that the country of low wages can undersell the country of high wages; but there is also mixed with this the notion to which the British fair traders appeal— the notion that the abolition of duties by any country is to the advantage, not of the people of that country, but of the people of the other countries that are thus given free access to its markets. "Is not the fact that British manufacturers desire the abolition of our protective tariff a proof that we ought to continue it?" ask American protectionists. "Is it not a suicidal policy to give foreigners free access to our markets while they refuse us access to theirs?" cry British fair traders.

All these notions are forms of the delusion that to export is more profitable than to import, but so wide-

spread and influential are they that it may be well to
devote a few words to them. The direct effect of a tariff
is to restrain the people of the country that imposes
it. It curtails the freedom of foreigners to trade only
through its operation in curtailing the freedom of
citizens to trade. So far as foreigners are concerned it
only indirectly affects their freedom to trade with that
particular country, while to citizens of that country it is
a direct curtailment of the freedom to trade with all the
world. Since trade involves mutual benefit, it is true
that any restriction that prevents one party from trading
must operate in some degree to the injury of another
party. But the indirect injury which a protective tariff
inflicts upon other countries is diffused and slight, as
compared with the injury it inflicts directly upon the
nation that imposes it.

To illustrate : The tariff which we have so long maintained upon iron to prevent our people from exchanging
their products for British iron has unquestionably
lessened our trade with Great Britain. But the effect
upon the United States has been very much more injurious than the effect upon Great Britain. While it has
lessened our trade absolutely, it has lessened the trade of
Great Britain only with us. What Great Britain has
lost in this curtailment of her trade with us she has
largely made up in the consequent extension of her trade
elsewhere. For the effect of duties on iron and iron ore,
and of the system of which they are part, has been so to
increase the cost of American productions as to give to
Great Britain the greater part of the carrying trade of
the world, for which we were her principal competitor,
and to hand over to her the trade of South America and
of other countries, of which, but for this, we should have
had the largest share.

And in the same way, for any nation to restrict the freedom of its own citizens to trade, because other nations so restrict the freedom of their citizens, is a policy of the "biting off one's nose to spite one's face" order. Other nations may injure us by the imposition of taxes which tend to impoverish their own citizens, for as denizens of the world it is to our real interest that all other denizens of the world should be prosperous. But no other nation can thus injure us so much as we shall injure ourselves if we impose similar taxes upon our own citizens by way of retaliation.

Suppose that a farmer who has an improved variety of potatoes learns that a neighbor has wheat of such superior kind that it will yield many more bushels to the acre than that he has been sowing. He might naturally go to his neighbor and offer to exchange seed-potatoes for seed-wheat. But if the neighbor while willing to sell the wheat should refuse to buy the potatoes, would not our farmer be a fool to declare, "Since you will not buy my superior potatoes I will not buy your superior wheat!" Would it not be very stupid retaliation for him to go on planting poorer seed and getting poorer crops?

Or, suppose, isolated from the rest of mankind, half a dozen men so situated and so engaged that mutual convenience constantly prompts them to exchange productions with one another. Suppose five of these six to be under the dominion of some curious superstition which leads them when they receive anything in exchange to burn one-half of it up before carrying home the other half. This would indirectly be to the injury of the sixth man, because by thus lessening their own wealth his five neighbors would lessen their ability to exchange with him. But, would he better himself if he were to say:

"Since these fools will insist upon burning half of all they get in exchange I must, in self-defense, follow their example and burn half of all I get"?

The constitution and scheme of things in this world in which we find ourselves for a few years is such that no one can do either good or evil for himself alone. No one can release himself from the influence of his surroundings, and say, "What others do is nothing to me;" nor yet can any one say, "What I do is nothing to others." Nevertheless it is in the tendency of things that he who does good most profits by it, and he who does evil injures, most of all, himself. And those who say that a nation should adopt a policy essentially bad because other nations have embraced it are as unwise as those who say, Lie, because others are false; Be idle, because others are lazy; Refuse knowledge, because others are ignorant.

CHAPTER XVI.

ENGLISH protectionists, during the present century at least, struggled for the protection of agriculture, and the repeal of the corn-laws in 1846 was their Waterloo. On the Continent, also, it is largely agriculture that is held to need protection, and special efforts have been made to protect the German hog, even to the extent of shutting out its American competitor. But in the United States the favorite plea for protection has been that it is necessary to the establishment of manufactures; and the prevalent American idea of protection is that it is a scheme for fostering manufactures.

As a matter of fact, American protection has not been confined to manufactures, nor has there been any hesitation in imposing duties which by raising the cost of materials are the very reverse of encouraging to manufactures. In the scramble which the protective system has induced, every interest capable of being protected and powerful enough to compel consideration in Congressional log-rolling has secured a greater or less share of protection—a share not based upon any standard of needs or merits, but upon the number of votes it could command. Thus wool, the production of which is one of the most primitive of industries, preceding even the tilling of the soil, has been protected by high duties, although certain grades of foreign wool are necessary to

153

American woolen-manufacturers, who have by these duties been put at a disadvantage in competing with foreign manufacturers. Thus iron ore has been protected despite the fact that American steel-makers need foreign ore to mix with American ore, and are obliged to import it even under the high duty. Thus copper ore has been protected, to the disadvantage of American smelters, as well as of all the many branches of manufacture into which copper enters. Thus salt has been protected, though it is an article of prime necessity, used in large quantities in such important industries as the curing of meats and fish, and entering into many branches of manufacture. Thus lumber has been protected in spite of its importance in manufacturing as well as of the protests of all who have inquired into the consequences of the rapid clearing of our natural woodlands. Thus coal has been protected, though to many branches of manufacturing cheap fuel is of first importance. And so on, through the list.

Protection of this kind is direct discouragement of manufactures. Nor yet is it encouragement of any industry, since its effect is, not to make production of any kind more profitable, but to raise the price of lands or mines from which these crude products are obtained.

Yet in spite of all this discouragement of manufactures, of which the instances I have given are but samples, protection is still advocated as necessary to manufactures, and the growth of American manufactures is claimed as its result.

So long and so loudly has this claim been made that to-day many of our people believe, what protectionist writers and speakers constantly assume, that but for protection there would not now be a manufacture of any importance carried on in the United States, and that were protection abolished the sole industry that this great country could carry on would be the raising of agricultural products for exportation to Europe.

That so many believe this is a striking instance of our readiness to accept anything that is persistently dinned into our ears. For that manufactures grow up without protection, and that the effect of our protective tariff is to stunt and injure them, can be conclusively shown from general principles and from common facts.

But first, let me call attention to a confusion of thought which gives plausibility to the notion that manufactures should be "encouraged." Manufactures grow up as population increases and capital accumulates, and, in the natural order of industry, are best developed in countries of dense population and accumulated wealth. Seeing this connection, it is easy to mistake for cause what is really effect, and to imagine that manufacturing brings population and wealth. Here, in substance, is the argument which has been addressed to the people of the United States from the time when we became a nation to the present day:

Manufacturing countries are always rich countries. Countries that produce only raw materials are always poor. Therefore, if we would be rich we must have manufactures, and in order to get manufactures we must encourage them.

To many this argument seems plausible, especially as the taxes for the "encouragement" of the protected industries are levied in such a way that their payment is not realized. But I could make as good an argument to the people of the little town of Jamaica, near which I am now living, in support of a subsidy to a theater. I could say to them:

"All large cities have theaters, and the more theaters it has, the larger the city. Look at New York! New York has more theaters than any other city in America, and is consequently the greatest city in America. Philadelphia ranks next to New York in the number and size of its theaters, and therefore comes next to New York in population and wealth. So, throughout the country, wherever you find large, well-appointed theaters, you will find large and prosperous towns, while where there are no theaters the towns are small. Is it any wonder that Jamaica is so small and grows so slowly when it has no theaters at all? People do not like to settle in a place where they cannot occasionally go to the theater. If you want Jamaica to thrive you must take steps to build a fine theater, which will attract a large population. Look at Brooklyn! Brooklyn was only a small riverside village before its people had the enterprise to start a theater, and see now, since they began to build theaters, how large a city Brooklyn has become."

Modeling my argument on that addressed to American voters by the Presidential candidate of the Republican party in 1884, I might then drop into "statistics" and point to the fact that when theatrical representations first began in this country its population did not amount to a million; that it was totally destitute of railroads and without a single mile of telegraph-wire. Such has been our progress since theaters were introduced that the census of 1880 showed that we had 50,155,783 people, 97,907 miles of railroad and $291,212_{\frac{9}{10}}$ miles of telegraph-wires. Or I might go into greater detail, as some protectionist "statisticians" are accustomed to do. I might take the date of the building of each of the New York theaters, give the population and wealth of the city at that time, and then, by presenting the statistics of population and wealth a few years later, show that the building of each theater had been followed by a marked increase in population and wealth. I might point out that San Francisco had not a theater until the Americans came there, and was consequently but a straggling village; that the new-comers immediately set up theaters and maintained them more generously than any other similar population in the world, and that the consequence was the marvelous growth of San Francisco. I might show that Chicago and Denver and Kansas City, all remarkably good theater towns, have also been remarkable for their rapid growth, and, as in the case of New York, prove statistically that the building of each theater these cities contain has been followed by an increase of population and wealth.

Then, stretching out after protectionist fashion into the historical argument, I might refer to the fact that Nineveh and Babylon had no theaters that we know of, and so went to utter ruin; dilate upon the fondness of the ancient Greeks for theatrical entertainments conducted at public expense, and their consequent greatness in arts and arms; point out how the Romans went even further than the Greeks in their encouragement of the theater, and built at public cost the largest theater in the world, and how Rome became the mistress of the nations. And, to embellish and give point to the argument, I might perhaps drop into poetry, recalling Byron's lines:

> When falls the Colosseum, Rome shall fall;
> And when Rome falls—the world!

Recovering from this, I might cite the fact that in every province they conquered the Romans established theaters, as explaining the remarkable facility with which they extended their civilization and made the conquered provinces integral parts of their great empire; point out that the decline of these theaters and the decay of Roman power and civilization went on together; and that the extinction of the theater brought on the night of the Dark Ages. Dwelling then a moment upon the rudeness and ignorance of that time when there were no theaters, I might triumphantly point to the beginning of modern civilization as contemporaneous with the revival of theatrical entertainments in miracle-plays and court masks. And showing how these plays and masks were always supported by monasteries, municipalities or princes, and how places where they began became sites of great cities, I could laud the wisdom of "encouraging infant theatricals." Then, in the fact that English actors, until recently, styled themselves her Majesty's servants and that the Lord Chamberlain still has authority over the English boards, and must license plays before they can be acted, I could trace to a national system of subsidizing infant theatricals the foundation of England's greatness. Coming back to our own times, I could call attention to the fact that Paris, where theaters are still subsidized and actors still draw their salaries from the public treasury, is the world's metropolis of fashion and art, steadily growing in population and wealth, though other parts of the same country which do not enjoy subsidized theaters are either at a standstill or declining. And finally I could point to the astuteness of the Mormon leaders, who early in the settlement of Salt Lake built a spacious theater, and whose little village in the sage-brush, then hardly as large as Jamaica, has since the building of this theater grown to be a populous and beautiful city, and indignantly ask whether the virtuous people of Jamaica should allow themselves to be outdone by wicked polygamists.

If such an argument would not induce the Jamaicans to tax themselves to "encourage" a theater, would it not at least be as logical as arguments that have induced the American people to tax themselves to encourage manufactures?

The truth is that manufactures, like theaters, are the result, not the cause, of the growth of population and wealth.

If we take a watch, a book, a steam-engine, a piece of dry-goods, or the product of any of the industries which we class as manufactures, and trace the steps by which the material of which it is composed has been brought from the condition in which it is afforded by nature into finished form, we will see that to the carrying on of any manufacturing industry many other industries are necessary. That an industry of this kind shall be able to avail itself freely of the products of other industries is a prime condition of its successful prosecution. Hardly less important is the existence of related industries, which aid in economizing material and utilizing waste, or make easier the procurement of supplies or services, or the sale and distribution of products. This is the reason why the more elaborate industries tend within certain limits to localization, so that we find a particular district, without any assignable reason of soil, climate, material productions, or character of the people, become noted for a particular manufacture, while different places within that district become noted for different branches. Thus, in those parts of Massachusetts where the manufacture of boots and shoes is largely carried on, distinctions such as those between pegged and sewed goods, men's and women's wear, coarse and fine, will be found to characterize the industry of different towns. And in any considerable city we may see the disposition of various industries, with their related industries, to cluster together.

But with this tendency to localization there is also a tendency which causes industries to arise in their order wherever population increases. This tendency is due not only to the difficulty and cost of transportation, but to differences in taste and to the individuality of demands. For instance, it will be much more convenient and satisfactory to me, if I wish to have a boat built, to have it built where I can talk with the builder and

watch its construction; or to have a coat made where I
can try it on; or to have a book printed where I can
readily read the proofs and consult with the printer.
Further than this, that relation of industries which
makes the existence of certain industries conduce to the
economy with which others can be carried on, not merely
causes the growth of one industry to prepare the way for
others, but to promote their establishment.

Thus the development of industry is of the nature of
an evolution, which goes on with the increase of population
and the progress of society, the simpler industries coming
first and forming a basis for the more elaborate ones.

The reason that newly settled countries do not manufacture is that they can get manufactured goods cheaper
—that is to say, with less expenditure of labor—than by
manufacturing them.   Just as the farmer, though he
may have ash and hickory growing on his place, finds it
cheaper to buy a wagon than to make one, or to take his
wagon to the wheelwright's when it wants repairing,
rather than attempt the job himself, so in a new and
sparsely settled country it may take less labor to obtain
goods from long distances than to manufacture them,
even when every natural condition for their manufacture exists.   The conditions for profitably carrying on
any manufacturing industry are not merely natural conditions.   Even more important than climate, soil and
mineral deposits are the existence of subsidiary industries
and of a large demand.   Manufacturing involves the
production of large quantities of the same thing.   The
development of skill, the use of machinery and of
improved processes, become possible only as large quantities of the same product are required.   If the small
quantities of all the various things needed must be produced for itself by each small community, they can be
produced only by rude and wasteful methods.   But if

trade permits these things to be produced in large quantities the same labor becomes much more effective, and all the various wants can be much better supplied.

The rude methods of savages are due less to ignorance than to isolation. A gun and ammunition will enable a man to kill more game than a bow and arrows, but a man who had to make his own weapons from the materials furnished by nature, could hardly make himself a gun in a lifetime, even if he understood gun-making. Unless there is a large number of men to be supplied with guns and ammunition, and the materials of which these are made can be produced with the economy that comes with the production of large quantities, the most effective weapons, taking into account the labor of producing them, are bows and arrows, not firearms. With a steel ax a tree may be felled with much less labor than with a stone ax. But a man who must make his own ax would be able to fell many trees with a stone ax in the time he would spend trying to make a steel ax from the ore. We smile at the savages who for a sheath-knife or copper kettle gladly give many rich furs. Such articles are with us of little value, because being made in large quantities the expenditure of labor required for each is very small, but if made in small quantities, as the savage would have to make them, the expenditure of labor would far exceed that needed to obtain the furs. Even if they had the fullest knowledge of the tools and methods of civilized industry, men isolated as savages are isolated, would be forced to resort to the rude tools and methods of savages. The great advantage which civilized men have over savages in settling among them, is in the possession of tools and weapons made in that state of society in which alone it is possible to manufacture them, and that by keeping up communication with the denser populations they have left behind them, the settlers are able by means of trade to avail themselves of the manufacturing advantages of a more fully developed society. If the first American colonists had been unable to import from Europe the goods they required, and thus to avail themselves of the fuller development of European industry, they must soon have been reduced to savage tools and weapons. And this would have happened to all new settlements in the westward march of our people had they been cut off from trade with larger populations.

In new countries the industries that yield the largest comparative returns are the primary or extractive industries which obtain food and the raw materials of manufacture from nature. The reason of this is that in these primary industries there are not required such costly tools and appliances, nor the coöperation of so many other industries, nor yet is production in large quantities so important. The people of new countries can therefore get the largest return for their labor by applying it to the primary or extractive industries, and exchanging their products for those of the more elaborate industries that can best be carried on where population is denser.

As population increases, the conditions under which the secondary or any more elaborate industries can be carried on gradually arise, and such industries will be established—those for which natural conditions are peculiarly favorable, and those whose products are in most general demand and will least bear transportation, coming first. Thus in a country having fine forests, manufactures of wood will arise before manufactures for which there is no special advantage. The making of bricks will precede the making of china, the manufacture of plowshares that of cutlery, window-glass will be made before telescope lenses, and the coarser grades of cloth before the finer.

But while we may describe in a general way the conditions which determine the natural order of industry, yet so many are these conditions and so complex are their actions and reactions upon one another that no one can predict with any exactness what in any given community this natural order of development will be, or say when it becomes more profitable to manufacture a thing than to import it. Legislative interference, therefore, is sure to prove hurtful, and such questions should be left to the unfettered play of individual enterprise, which is to the community what the unconscious vital activities are to the man. If the time has come for the establishment of an industry for which proper natural conditions exist, restrictions upon importation in order to promote its establishment are needless. If the time has not come, such restrictions can only divert labor and capital from industries in which the return is greater, to others in which it must be less, and thus reduce the aggregate production of wealth. Just as it is evident that to prevent the people of a new colony from importing from countries of fuller industrial development would deprive them of many things they could not possibly make for themselves, so it is evident that to restrict importations must retard the symmetrical development of domestic industries. It may be that protection applied to one or to a few industries may sometimes hasten their development at the expense of the general industrial growth; but when protection is indiscriminately given to every industry capable of protection, as it is in the United States, and as is the inevitable tendency wherever protection is begun, the result must be to check not merely the general development of industry, but even the development of the very industries for whose benefit the system of protection is most advocated, by making more costly the products which they must use and repressing the correlative industries with which they interlace.

To assume, as protectionists do, that economy must necessarily result from bringing producer and consumer together in point of space,* is to assume that things can be produced as well in one place as in another, and that difficulties in exchange are to be measured solely by distance. The truth is, that commodities can often be produced in one place with so much greater facility than in another that it involves a less expenditure of labor to bring them long distances than to produce them on the spot, while two points a hundred miles apart may be commercially nearer each other than two points ten miles apart. To bring the producer to the consumer in point of distance, is, if it increases the cost of production, not economy but waste.

But this is not to deny that trade as it is carried on to-day does involve much unnecessary transportation, and that producer and consumer are in many cases needlessly separated. Protectionists are right when they point to the wholesale exportation of the elements of fertility of our soil, in the great stream of breadstuffs and meats which pours across the Atlantic, as reckless profligacy, and fair traders are right when they deplore the waste involved in English importations of food while English fields are going out of cultivation. Both are right in saying that one country ought not to be made a "draw farm" for another, and that a true economy of the powers of nature would bring factory and field closer together. But they are wrong in attributing these evils to the freedom of trade, or in supposing that the remedy

---

* Protectionist arguments frequently involve the additional assumption that the "home producer" and "home consumer" are necessarily close together in point of space, whereas, as in the United States, they may be thousands of miles apart.

lies in protection. That tariffs are powerless to remedy these evils may be seen in the fact that this exhausting exportation goes on in spite of our high protective tariff, and that internal trade exhibits the same features. Everywhere that modern civilization extends, and with greatest rapidity where its influences are most strongly felt, population and wealth are concentrating in huge towns and an exhausting commerce flows from country to city. But this ominous tendency is not natural, and does not arise from too much freedom; it is unnatural, and arises from restrictions. It may be clearly traced to monopolies, of which the monopoly of material opportunities is the first and most important. In a word, the Roman system of landownership, which in our modern civilization has displaced that of our Celtic and Teutonic ancestors, is producing the same effect that it did in the Roman world—the engorgement of the centers and the impoverishment of the extremities. While London and New York grow faster than Rome ever did, English fields are passing out of cultivation as did the fields of Latium, and in Iowa and Dakota goes on the exhausting culture that impoverished the provinces of Africa. The same disease which rotted the old civilization is exhibiting its symptoms in the new. That disease cannot be cured by protective tariffs.

CHAPTER XVII.

PROTECTION AND PRODUCERS.

THE primary purpose of protection is to encourage producers*—that is to say, to increase the profits of capital engaged in certain branches of industry.

The protective theory is that the increase a protective duty causes in the price at which an imported commodity can be sold within the country, *protects* the home producer (*i.e.*, the man on whose account commodities are produced for sale) from foreign competition, so as to *encourage* him by larger profits than he could otherwise get to engage in or increase production. All the beneficial effects claimed for protection depend upon its effect in thus encouraging the employing producer, just as all the effects produced by the motion of an engine upon the complicated machinery of a factory are dependent upon its effect in turning the main driving-wheel. The main driving-wheel (so to speak) of the protective theory is that protection increases the profits of the protected producer.

But when, assuming this, the opponents of protection represent the whole class of protected producers as grow-

---

* For want of a better term I have here used the word "producers" in that limited sense in which it is applied to those who control capital and employ labor engaged in production. The industries protected by our tariff are (with perhaps some nominal exceptions) of the kind carried on in this way.

ing rich at the expense of their fellow-citizens, they are contradicted by obvious facts. Business men well know that in our long-protected industries the margin of profit is as small and the chances of failure as great as in any others—if, in fact, those protected industries are not harder to win success in by reason of the more trying fluctuations to which they are subject.

The reason why protection in most cases thus fails to encourage is not difficult to see.

The cost of any protective duty to the people at large is (1), the tax collected upon imported goods, plus the profits upon the tax, plus the expense and profits of smuggling in all its forms; plus the expense of sometimes trying smugglers of the coarser sort, and occasionally sending a poor and friendless one to the penitentiary; plus bribes and moieties received by government officers; and (2), the additional prices that must be paid for the products of the protected home industry.

It is from this second part alone that the protected industry can get its encouragement. But only a part of this part of what the people at large pay is real encouragement. In the first place, it is true of protective duties, as it is true of direct subsidies, that they cannot be had for nothing. Just as the Pacific Mail Steamship Company and the various land- and bond-grant railways had to expend large sums to secure representation at Washington, and had to divide handsomely with the Washington lobby, so the cost of securing Congressional "recognition" for an infant industry, or fighting off threatened reductions in its "encouragement," and looking after every new tariff bill, is a considerable item. But still more important is the absolute loss in carrying on industries so unprofitable in themselves that they can be maintained only by subsidies. And to this loss must be added the waste that seems inseparable from governmental fosterage, for just in proportion as industries are sheltered from competition are they slow to avail themselves of improvements in machinery and methods.* Out of the encouragement which the tariff beneficiaries receive in higher prices, much must thus be consumed, so that the net encouragement is only a small fraction of what consumers pay. Taking encouraged producers and taxed consumers together there is an enormous loss. Hence in all cases in which duties are imposed for the benefit of any particular industry the discouragement to industry in general must be greater than the encouragement of the particular industry. So long, however, as the one is spread over a large surface and the other over a small surface, the encouragement is more marked than the discouragement, and the disadvantage imposed on all industry does not much affect the few subsidized industries.

But to introduce a tariff bill into a congress or parliament is like throwing a banana into a cage of monkeys. No sooner is it proposed to protect one industry than all the industries that are capable of protection begin to screech and scramble for it. They are, in fact, forced to do so, for to be left out of the encouraged ring is necessarily to be discouraged. The result is, as we see in the

---

* This disposition is, of course, largely augmented by the greater cost of machinery under our protective tariff, which not only increases the capital required to begin, but makes the constant discarding of old machinery and purchase of new, required to keep up with the march of invention, a much more serious matter. Cases have occurred in which British manufacturers, compelled by competition to adopt the latest improvements, have actually sold their discarded machinery to be shipped to the United States and used by protected Americans. It was his coming across a case of this kind that led David A. Wells, when he visited Europe as Special Commissioner of Revenue, to begin to question the usefulness of our tariff in promoting American industry.

United States, that they all get protected, some more and some less, according to the money they can spend and the political influence they can exert. Now every tax that raises prices for the encouragement of one industry must operate to discourage all other industries into which the products of that industry enter. Thus a duty that raises the price of lumber necessarily discourages the industries which make use of lumber, from those connected with the building of houses and ships to those engaged in the making of matches and wooden toothpicks; a duty that raises the price of iron discourages the innumerable industries into which iron enters; a duty that raises the price of salt discourages the dairyman and the fisherman; a duty that raises the price of sugar discourages the fruit-preserver, the maker of syrups and cordials, and so on. Thus it is evident that every additional industry protected lessens the encouragement of those already protected. And since the net encouragement that tariff beneficiaries can receive as a whole is very much less than the aggregate addition to prices required to secure it, it is evident that the point at which protection will cease to give any advantage to the protected must be much short of that at which every one is protected. To illustrate: Say that the total number of industries is one hundred, of which one-half are capable of protection. Let us say that of what the protection costs, one-fourth is realized by the protected industries. Then (presuming equality), as soon as twenty-five industries obtain protection, the protection can be of no benefit even to them, while, of course, involving a heavy discouragement to all the rest.

I use this illustration merely to show that there is a point at which protection must cease to benefit even the industries it strives to encourage, not that I think it possible to give numerical exactness to such matters.

But that there is such a point is certain, and that in the
United States it has been reached and passed is also certain. That is to say, not only is our protective tariff a
dead-weight upon industry generally, but it is a dead-
weight upon the very industries it is intended to stimulate.

If there are producers who permanently profit by protective duties, it is only because they are in some other
way protected from domestic competition, and hence the
profit which comes to them by reason of the duties does not
come to them as producers but as monopolists. That is
to say, *the only cases in which protection can more than
temporarily benefit any class of producers are cases in which
it cannot stimulate industry.* For that neither duties nor
subsidies can give any permanent advantage in any business open to home competition results from the tendency
of profits to a common level. The risk to which protected industries are exposed from changes in the tariff
may at times keep profits in them somewhat above the
ordinary rate; but this represents not advantage, but the
necessity for increased insurance, and though it may
constitute a tax upon consumers does not operate to
extend the industry. This element of insurance eliminated, profits in protected industries can be kept above
those of unprotected industries only by some sort of
monopoly which shields them from home competition as
the tariff does from foreign competition. The first effect
of a protective duty is to increase profits in the protected
industry. But unless that industry be in some way
protected from the influx of competitors which such
increased profits must attract, this influx must soon
bring these profits to the general level. A monopoly,
more or less complete, which may thus enable certain
producers to retain for themselves the increased profits
which it is the first effect of a protective duty to give,

may arise from the possession of advantages of different kinds.

It may arise, in the first place, from the possession of some peculiar natural advantage. For instance, the only chrome-mines yet discovered in the United States, belonging to a single family, that family have been much encouraged by the higher prices which the protective duty on chrome has enabled them to charge home consumers. In the same way, until the discovery of new and rich copper deposits in Arizona and Montana the owners of the Lake Superior copper-mines were enabled to make enormous dividends by the protective duty on copper, which, so long as home competition was impossible, shut out the only competition that could reduce their profits, and enabled them to get three or four cents more per pound for the copper they sold in the United States than for the copper they shipped to Europe.

Or a similar monopoly may be obtained by the possession of exclusive privileges given by the patent laws. For instance, the combination based on patents for making steel have, since home competition with them was thus shut out, been enabled, by the enormous duty on imported steel, to add most encouragingly to their dividends, and the owners of the patented process used in making paper from wood have been similarly encouraged by the duty on wood-pulp.

Or again, a similar monopoly may be secured by the concentration of a business requiring large capital and special knowledge, or by the combination of producers in a "ring" or "pool" so as to limit home production and crush home competition. For instance, the protective duty on quinine, until its abolition in 1879, resulted to the sole benefit of three houses, while a combination of quarry-owners—the Producers' Marble Company—have

succeeded in preventing any home competition in the production of marble, and are thus enabled to retain to
themselves the higher profits which the protective duty
on foreign marble makes possible, and largely to concentrate in their own hands the business of working up
marble.

But the higher profits thus obtained in no way encourage the extension of such industries. On the contrary,
they result from the very conditions natural or artificial
which prevent the extension of these industries. They
are, in fact, not the profits of capital engaged in industry,
but the profits of ownership of natural opportunities, of
patent rights, or of organization or combination, and
they increase the value of ownership in these opportunities, rights and monopolistic combinations, not the
returns of capital engaged in production. Though they
may go to individuals or companies who are producers,
they do not go to them *as* producers; though they may
increase the income of persons who are capitalists, they
do not go to them by virtue of their employment of capital, but by virtue of their ownership of special privileges.

Of the monopolies which thus get the benefit of profits
erroneously supposed to go to producers, the most important are those arising from the private ownership of
land. That what goes to the landowner in no wise
benefits the producer we may readily see.

The two primary factors of production, without which
nothing whatever can be produced, are land and labor.
To these essential factors is added, when production
passes beyond primitive forms, a third factor, capital—
which consists of the product of land and labor (wealth)
used for the purpose of facilitating the production of
more wealth. Thus to production as it goes on in civilized societies the three factors are land, labor and
capital, and since land is in modern civilization made a

subject of private ownership, the proceeds of production are divided between the landowner, the labor-owner, and the capital-owner.

But between these factors of production there exists an essential difference. Land is the purely passive factor; labor and capital are the active factors—the factors by whose application and according to whose application wealth is brought forth. Therefore, it is only that part of the produce which goes to labor and capital that constitutes the reward of producers and stimulates production. The landowner is in no sense a producer—he adds nothing whatever to the sum of productive forces, and that portion of the proceeds of production which he receives for the use of natural opportunities no more rewards and stimulates production than does that portion of their crops which superstitious savages might burn up before an idol in thank-offering for the sunlight that had ripened them. There can be no labor until there is a man; there can be no capital until man has worked and saved; but land was here before man came. To the production of commodities the laborer furnishes human exertion; the capitalist furnishes the results of human exertion embodied in forms that may be used to aid further exertion; but the landowner furnishes—what? The superficies of the earth? the latent powers of the soil? the ores beneath it? the rain? the sunshine? gravitation? the chemical affinities? *What* does the landowner furnish that involves any contribution *from him* to the exertion required in production? The answer must be, nothing! And hence it is that what goes to the landowner out of the results of production is not the reward of producers and does not stimulate production, but is merely a toll which producers are compelled to pay to one whom our laws permit to treat as his own what Nature furnishes.

Now, keeping these principles in mind, let us turn to the effects of protection. Let us suppose that England were to do as the English agriculturist landlords are very anxious to have her do—go back to the protective policy and impose a high duty on grain. This would much increase the price of grain in England, and its first effect would be, while seriously injuring other industries, to give much larger profits to English farmers. This increase of profits would cause a rush into the business of farming, and the increased competition for the use of agricultural land would raise agricultural rents, so that the result would be, when industry had readjusted itself, that though the people of England would have to pay more for grain, the profits of grain-producing would not be larger than profits in any other occupation. The only class that would derive any benefit from the increased price that the people of England would have to pay for their food would be the agricultural landowners, who are not producers at all.

Protection cannot add to the value of the land of a country as a whole, any more than it can stimulate industry as a whole; on the contrary, its tendency is to check the general increase of land values by checking the production of wealth; but by stimulating a particular form of industry it may increase the value of a particular kind of land. And it is instructive to observe this, for it largely explains the motive in urging protection, and where its benefits go.

For instance, the duty on lumber has not been asked for and lobbied for by the producers of lumber—that is to say, the men engaged in cutting down and sawing up trees, and who derive their profits solely from that source—nor has it added to their profits. The parties who have really lobbied and logrolled for the imposition and maintenance of the lumber duty are the owners of timber lands, and its effect has been to increase the price of "stumpage," the royalty which the producer of lumber must pay to the owner of timber land for the privilege of cutting down trees. A certain class of forestallers have made a business of getting possession of timber lands by all the various "land-grabbing" devices as soon as the progress of population promised to make them available. Constituting a compact and therefore powerful interest (three parties in Detroit, for instance, are said to own $\frac{99}{100}$ of the timber lands in the great timber State of Michigan), they have been able to secure a duty on lumber, which, nominally imposed for the encouragement of the lumber producer, has really encouraged only the timber-land forestaller, who, instead of being a producer at all, is merely a blackmailer of production.*

So it is with many other duties. The effect of the sugar duty, for instance, is to increase the value of sugar lands in Louisiana, and our treaty with the Hawaiian Islands, by which Hawaiian sugar is admitted free of this duty, being equivalent (since the production of Hawaiian sugar is not sufficient to supply the United States) to the payment of a heavy bounty to Hawaiian sugar-growers, has enormously increased the value of sugar lands in the Hawaiian Islands. So with the duty on copper and copper ore, which for a long time enabled American copper companies to keep up the price of copper in the United States while they were shipping

---

* When, after the great fire in Chicago, a bill was introduced in Congress permitting the importation free of duty of materials intended for use in the rebuilding of that city, the Michigan timber-land barons went to Washington in a special car and induced the committee to omit lumber from the bill.

copper to Europe and selling it there at a considerably lower price.* The benefit of these duties went to companies engaged in producing copper, but it went to them not as producers of copper but as owners of copper-mines. If, as is largely the case in coal- and iron-mining, the work had been carried on by operators who paid a royalty to the mine-owners, the enormous dividends would have gone to the mine-owners and not to the operators.

Horace Greeley used to think that he conclusively disproved the assertion that the duties on iron were enriching a few at the expense of the many, when he declared that our laws gave to no one any special privilege of making iron, and asked why, if the tariff gave such enormous profits to iron producers as the free traders said it did, these free traders did not go to work and make iron. So far as concerned those producers who derived no special advantage from patent rights or combinations, Mr. Greeley was right enough—the fact that there was no special rush to get into the business proving that iron producers as producers were making on the average no more than ordinary profits. And could iron be made from air, this fact would have shown what Mr. Greeley seems to have imagined it did, though it would not have

---

* A striking illustration of the way American industry has been encouraged by a duty which enabled the stockholders in a couple of copper-mines to pay dividends of over a hundred per cent. is afforded by the following case : Some years ago a Dutch ship arrived at Boston having in her hold a quantity of copper with which her master proposed to have her resheathed in Boston. But learning that in this "land of liberty" he would not be permitted to take the copper from the inside of his ship and employ American mechanics to nail it on the outside, without paying a duty of forty-five per cent. on the new copper put on, as well as a duty of four cents per pound on the old copper taken off, he found it cheaper to sail in ballast to Halifax, get his ship re-coppered by Canadian workmen, and then come back to Boston for his return cargo.

shown that the nation was not losing greatly by the duty. But iron cannot be made from air; it can only be made from iron ore. And though Nature, especially in the United States, has provided abundant supplies of iron ore, she has not distributed them equally, but has stored them in large deposits in particular places. If inclined to take Horace Greeley's advice to go and make iron, should I think its price too high, I must obtain access to one of these deposits, and that a deposit sufficiently near to other materials and to centers of population. I may find plenty of such deposits which no one is using, but where can I find such a deposit that is free to be used by me?

The laws of my country do not forbid me from making iron, but they do allow individuals to forbid me from making use of the natural material from which alone iron can be made—they do allow individuals to take possession of these deposits of ore which Nature has provided for the making of iron, and to treat and hold them as though they were their own private property, placed there by themselves and not by God. Consequently these deposits of iron ore are appropriated as soon as there is any prospect that any one will want to use them, and when I find one that will suit my purpose I find that it is in the possession of some owner who will not let me use it until I pay him down in a purchase price, or agree to pay him in a royalty of so much per ton, nearly, if not quite, all I can make above the ordinary return to capital in producing iron. Thus, while the duty which raises the price of iron may not benefit producers, it does benefit the dogs in the manger whom our laws permit to claim as their own the stores which eons before man appeared were accumulated by Nature for the use of the millions who would one day be called into being—enabling the monopolists of our iron land to levy heavy taxes on their fellow-citizens long before they could otherwise have done so.* So with the duty on coal. It adds nothing to the profits of the coal operator who buys the right to take coal out of the earth, but it does enable a ring of coal-land- and railway-owners to levy in many places an additional blackmail upon the use of Nature's bounty.

The motive and effect of many of our duties are well illustrated by the import duty we levy on borax and boracic acid. We had no duties on borax and boracic acid (which have important uses in many branches of manufacture) until it was discovered that in the State of Nevada Nature had provided a deposit of nearly pure borax for the use of the people of this continent. This free gift of the Almighty having been reduced to private ownership, in accordance with the laws of the United States for such cases made and provided, the enterprising forestallers at once applied to Congress for (and of course secured) the imposition of a duty which would

---

* The royalty paid by iron-miners for the privilege of taking the ore out of the earth in many cases equals and in some cases exceeds the cost of mining it. The royalties of the Pratt Iron and Coal Company of Alabama are said to run as high as $10,000 per acre. In the *Chicago Inter-Ocean*, a stanch protectionist paper, of October 11, 1885, I find a description of the Colby Iron-Mine at Bessemer, Mich. This mine, it is said, is owned by parties who got it for $1.25 per acre. They lease the privilege of taking out ore on a royalty of 40 cents per ton to the Colbys, who sub-lease it to Morse & Co. for 52½ cents per ton royalty, who have a contract with Captain Sellwood to put the ore on the cars for 87½ cents per ton. Sellwood sub-lets this contract for 12½ cents per ton, and the sub-contractors are said to make a profit of 2½ cents per ton, as the work is done by a steam-shovel. Deducting transportation, etc., the ore brings $2.80 per ton, as mined, of which only 12½ cents goes to the firm who do the actual work of production. The output is 1200 tons per day, which, according to the *Inter-Ocean* correspondent, gives to the owners a net profit of $480 per day; to the Colbys, $150 per day; Morse & Co., $1680; Captain Sellwood, $90 per day; and

make borax artificially dear and increase the profits of this monopoly of a natural advantage.

While our manufacturers and other producers have been caught readily enough with the delusive promise that protection would increase their profits, and have used their influence to institute and maintain protective duties, I am inclined to think that the most efficient interest on the side of protection in the United States has been that of those who have possessed themselves of lands or other natural advantages which they hoped protection would make more valuable. For it has been not merely the owners of coal, iron, timber, sugar, orange, or wine lands, of salt-springs, borax lakes, or copper deposits, who have seen in the shutting out of foreign competition a quicker demand and higher value for their lands, but the same feeling has had its influence upon the holders of city and village real estate, who, realizing that the establishment of factories or the working of mines in their vicinity would give value to their

---

the sub-contractors who do the work of mining, $30 per day, "a total net profit from the mine, over and above what profit there may be in the labor, of $2430 per day." The account concludes by saying: "As the product will be at least doubled during the coming year, you see there will be some fortunes made out of the Colby mine." To these fortunes our protective duty on foreign ore undoubtedly contributes, but how much does it in this case encourage production?

In Lebanon County, Pennsylvania, is a hill of magnetic iron ore nearly pure, which has merely to be quarried out. It is owned by the Coleman heirs, and has made them so enormously wealthy that these are said by some to be the richest people in the United States. They are producers of iron, smelting their own ore, as well as railway-owners and farmers, owning and cultivating by superintendents great tracts of valuable land. They, doubtless, have been much encouraged by the duty on iron which we have maintained for "the protection of American labor," but this encouragement comes to them as owners of this rich gift of Nature to—Mr. Coleman's heirs. The deposit of iron ore would be worked were there no duty, and was worked, I believe, before any duty on iron was imposed.

lots, have been disposed to support a policy which had
for its avowed object the transfer of such industries
from other countries to our own.

To repeat: It is only at first that a protective duty
can stimulate an industry. When the forces of production have had time to readjust themselves, profits in the
protected industry, unless kept up by obstacles which
prevent further extension of the industry, must sink to
the ordinary level, and the duty losing its power of
further stimulation ceases to yield any advantage to
producers unprotected against home competition. This
is the situation of the greater part of "protected"
American producers. They feel the general injury of
the system without really participating in its special
benefits.

How, then, it may be asked, is it that even these producers who are not sheltered by any home protection are
in general so strongly in favor of a protective tariff?
The true reason is to be found in the causes I will hereafter speak of, which predispose the common mind to an
acceptance of protective ideas. And, while keen enough
as to their individual interests, these producers are as
blind to social interests as any other class. They have
so long heard and been accustomed to repeat, that free
trade would ruin American industry, that it never occurs
to them to doubt it; and the effect of duties upon so
many other products being to enhance the cost of their
own productions, they see, without apprehending the
cause, that were it not for the particular duty that protects them they could be undersold by foreign products,
and so they cling to the system. Protection *is* necessary
to them in many cases, because of the protection of other
industries. But were the whole system abolished there
can be no doubt that American industry would spring
forward with new vigor.

CHAPTER XVIII.

EFFECTS OF PROTECTION ON AMERICAN INDUSTRY.

IF there is one country in the world where the assumption that protection is necessary to the development of manufactures and the "diversification of industry" is conclusively disproved by the most obvious facts, that country is the United States. The first settlers in America devoted themselves to trade with the Indians and to those extractive industries which a sparse population always finds most profitable, the produce of the forest, of the soil, and of the fisheries, constituting their staples, while even bricks and tiles were at first imported from the mother country. But without any protection and in spite of British regulations intended to prevent the growth of manufactures in the colonies, one industry after another took root, as population increased, until at the time of the first Tariff Act, in 1789, all the more important manufactures, including those of iron and textiles, had become firmly established. As up to this time they had grown without any tariff, so must they have continued to grow with the increase of population, even if we had never had a tariff.

But the American who contends that protection is necessary to the diversification of industry must not merely ignore the history of his country during that long period before the first tariff of any kind was instituted, but he must ignore what has been going on ever since, and is still going on under his eyes.

We need look no further back than the formation of the Union to see that if it were true that manufacturing could not grow up in new countries without the protection of tariffs the manufacturing industries of the United States would to-day be confined to a narrow belt along the Atlantic seaboard. Philadelphia, New York and Boston were considerable cities, and manufactures had taken a firm root along the Atlantic, when Western New York and Western Pennsylvania were covered with forests, when Indiana and Illinois were buffalo-ranges, when Detroit and St. Louis were trading-posts, Chicago undreamed of, and the continent beyond the Mississippi as little known as the interior of Africa is now. In the United States, the East has had over the West all the advantages which protectionists say make it impossible ⁴or a new country to build up its manufacturing industries against the competition of an older country—larger capital, longer experience, and cheaper labor. Yet without any protective tariff between the West and the East, manufacturing has steadily moved westward with the movement of population, and is moving westward still. This is a fact that of itself conclusively disproves the protective theory.

The protectionist assumption that manufactures have increased in the United States *because* of protective tariffs is even more unfounded than the assumption that the growth of New York after the building of each new theater was because of the building of the theater. It is as if one should tow a bucket behind a boat and insist that it helped the boat along because she still moved forward. Manufacturing has increased in the United States because of the growth of population and the development of the country ; not because of tariffs, but in spite of them.

That protective tariffs have injured instead of helped American manufactures is shown by the fact that our manufactures are much less than they ought to be, considering our population and development — much less relatively than they were in the beginning of the century. Had we continued the policy of free trade our manufactures would have grown up in natural hardihood and vigor, and we should now not only be exporting manufactured goods to Mexico and the West Indies, South America and Australia, as Ohio is exporting manufactured goods to Kansas, Nebraska, Colorado and Dakota, but we should be exporting manufactured goods to Great Britain, just as Ohio is to-day exporting manufactured goods to Pennsylvania and New York, where manufactures began before Ohio was settled. But so heavily are our manufactures weighted by a tariff which increases the cost of all their materials and appliances, that, in spite of our natural advantages and the inventiveness of our people, our sales are confined to our protected market, and we can nowhere compete with the manufactures of other countries. In spite of the increase of duties with which we have attempted to keep out foreign importations and build up our own manufacturing industries, the great bulk of our importations to-day are of manufactured goods, while all but a trivial percentage of our exports consist of raw materials. Even where we import largely from such countries as Brazil, which have almost no manufactures of their own, we cannot send them in return the manufactured goods they want, but to pay for what we buy of them must send our raw materials to Europe.

This is not a natural condition of trade. The United States have long passed the stage of growth in which raw materials constitute the only natural exports. We have now a population of nearly sixty millions, and consume more manufactured goods than any other nation. We possess unrivaled advantages for manufacturing. In extent and accessibility our coal deposits far surpass those of any other civilized country, while we have reservoirs of natural gas that supply fuel almost without labor. Moreover, we are the first of civilized nations in the invention and use of machinery, and in the economy of material and labor. But all these advantages are neutralized by the wall of protection we have built along our coasts.

For as long as I can remember, the protectionist press has been from time to time chronicling the fact that considerable orders for this, that or the other American manufacture had been received from abroad, as proving that protection was at last beginning to bring about the results promised for it, and that American manufacturing industry, so safely guarded during its infancy by a protective tariff, was now about to enter the markets of the world. The statements that have been made the basis of these congratulations have generally been true, but the predictions founded upon them have never been verified, and, while our population has doubled, our exports of manufactured articles have relatively declined. The explanation is this: The higher rates of wages that have prevailed in the United States, and the consequent higher standard of general intelligence, have stimulated American invention, and we are constantly making improvements upon the tools, methods and patterns elsewhere in use. These improvements are constantly starting a foreign demand for American manufactures which seems to promise large increase. But before this increase takes place the improvements are adopted in countries where manufacturing is not so heavily burdened by taxes on material, and what should have been peculiarly an American manufacture is transferred to a foreign country.

Every American who has visited London has doubtless noticed, opposite the Parliament House at Westminster, a shop devoted to the sale of "American notions." There are a number of such shops in London, and they are also to be found in every town of any size in the three kingdoms. These shops must sell in the aggregate quite an amount of American tools and contrivances, which in part accounts for the fact that we still export some manufactures. But the American will be deluded who, from the number of these shops and the interest taken by the people who are constantly looking in the windows or examining the goods, imagines that American manufactures are beginning to gain a foothold in the Old World. These shops are in fact curiosity-shops, just as are the Chinese and Japanese shops that we find in the larger American cities, and people go to them to see the ingenious things the Americans are getting up. But no sooner do these shops so far popularize an "American notion" that a considerable demand for it arises, than some English manufacturer at once begins to make it, or the American inventor, if he holds an English patent, finds more profit in manufacturing it abroad. Not having the discouragements of American protection to contend with, he can make it in Great Britain cheaper than in the United States, and the consequence of the introduction of an American "notion" is that, instead of its importation from America increasing, it comes to an end.

This illustrates the history of American manufactures abroad. One article after another which has been invented or improved in the United States has seemed to get a foothold in foreign markets only to lose it when fairly introduced. We have sent locomotives to Russia, arms to Turkey and Germany, agricultural implements to England, river steamers to China, sewing-machines to all parts of the world, but have never been able to hold the trade our inventiveness should have secured.

But it is on the high seas and in an industry in which we once led the world that the effect of our protective policy can be most clearly seen.

Thirty years ago ship-building had reached such a pitch of excellence in this country that we built not only for ourselves but for other nations. American ships were the fastest sailers, the largest carriers, and everywhere got the quickest despatch and the highest freights. The registered tonnage of the United States almost equaled that of Great Britain, and a few years promised to give us the unquestionable supremacy of the ocean.

The abolition of the more important British protective duties in 1846 was followed in 1854 by the repeal of the Navigation Laws, and from thenceforth not only were British subjects free to buy or build ships wherever they pleased, but the coasting trade of the British Isles was thrown open to foreigners. Dire were the predictions of British protectionists as to the utter ruin that was thus prepared for British commerce. The Yankees were to sweep the ocean, and "half-starved Swedes and Norwegians" were to drive the "ruddy, beef-eating English tar" from his own seas and channels.

While one great commercial nation thus abandoned protection, the other redoubled it. The breaking out of our civil war was the golden opportunity of protection, and the unselfish ardor of a people ready to make any sacrifice to prevent the dismemberment of their country was taken advantage of to pile protective taxes upon them. The ravages of Confederate cruisers and the consequent high rate of insurance on American ships would under any circumstances have diminished our deep-sea commerce; yet this effect was only temporary, and but for our protective policy we should at the end of the war have quickly resumed our place in the carrying trade of the world and moved forward to the lead with more vigor than ever.

But crushed by a policy which prevents Americans from building, and forbids them to buy ships, our commerce, ever since the war, has steadily shrunk, until American ships, which, when we were a nation of twenty-five millions, plowed every sea of the globe, are now, when we number nearly sixty millions, seldom seen on blue water. In Liverpool docks, where once it seemed as if every other vessel was American, you must search the forests of masts to find one. In San Francisco Bay you may count English ship, and English ship, and English ship, before you come to an American, while five-sixths of the foreign commerce of New York is carried on in foreign bottoms. Once no American dreamed of crossing the Atlantic save on an American ship; to-day no one thinks of taking one. It is the French and the Germans who compete with the British in carrying Americans to Europe and bringing them back. Once our ships were the finest on the ocean. To-day there is not a first-class ocean carrier under the American flag, and but for the fact that foreign vessels are absolutely prohibited from carrying between American ports, ship-building, in which we once led the world, would now be with us a lost art. As it is, we have utterly lost our place. When I was a boy we confidently believed that American war-ships could outsail, when they could not outfight, anything that floated, and in the event of war with a commercial nation we knew that every sea of the globe would swarm with swift American privateers. To-day, the ships on which we have wasted millions are, for purposes of modern warfare, as antiquated as Roman galleys. Compared with the vessels of other nations they can neither fight nor run; while, as for privateers or chartered vessels, Great Britain could take from those greyhounds of the sea which American travel and trade support, enough fleet ships to snap up any vessel that ventured out of an American port.

I do not complain of the inefficiency of our navy. The maintenance of a navy in time of peace is unworthy of the dignity of the Great Republic and of the place she should aspire to among the nations, and to my mind the hundreds of millions that during the last twenty years we have spent upon our navy would have been as truly wasted had they secured us good ships. But I do complain of the decadence in our ability to build ships. Our misfortune is not that we have no navy, but that we lack the swift merchant fleet, the great foundries and ship-yards, the skilled engineers and seamen and mechanics, in which, and not in navies, true power upon the seas consists. A people in whose veins runs the blood of Vikings have been driven off the ocean by—themselves.

Of course the selfish interests that profit, or imagine they profit, by the policy which has swept the American flag from the ocean as no foreign enemy could have done, ascribe this effect to every cause but the right one. They say, for instance, that we cannot compete with other nations in ocean commerce, because they have an advantage in lower wages and cheaper capital, in wilful disregard of the fact that when the difference in wages and interest between the two sides of the Atlantic was far greater than now we not only carried for ourselves but for other nations, and were rapidly rising to the position of the greatest of ocean carriers. The truth is, that if wages are higher with us this is really to our advantage, while not only can capital now be had as cheaply in New York as in London, but American capital is actually being used to run vessels under foreign flags, because of the taxes which make it unprofitable to build or run American vessels.

De Tocqueville, fifty years ago, was struck with the fact that nine-tenths of the commerce between the United States and Europe and three-fourths of the commerce of the New World with Europe was carried in American ships; that these ships filled the docks of Havre and Liverpool, while but few English and French vessels were to be seen at New York. This, he saw, could only be explained by the fact that "vessels of the United States can cross the seas at a cheaper rate than any other vessels in the world." But, he continues:

It is difficult to say for what reason the American can trade at a lower rate than other nations; and one is at first sight led to attribute this circumstance to the physical or natural advantages which are within their reach; but this supposition is erroneous. The American vessels cost almost as much as our own; they are not better built, and they generally last for a shorter time, while the pay of the American sailor is more considerable than the pay on board European ships. I am of opinion that the true cause of their superiority must not be sought for in physical advantages but that it is wholly attributable to their moral and intellectual qualities.

. . . The European sailor navigates with prudence; he only sets sail when the weather is favorable; if an unforeseen accident befalls him, he puts into port; at night he furls a portion of his canvas; and when the whitening billows intimate the vicinity of land, he checks his way and takes an observation of the sea. But the American neglects these precautions, and braves these dangers. He weighs anchor in the midst of tempestuous gales; by night and by day he spreads his sheets to the wind; he repairs as he goes along such damages as his vessel may have sustained from the storm; and when at last he approaches the term of his voyage he darts onward to the shore as if he already descried a port. The Americans are often shipwrecked, but no trader crosses the sea so rapidly, and, as they perform the same distance in a shorter time, they can perform it at a cheaper rate.

I cannot better explain my meaning than by saying that the American affects a sort of heroism in his manner of trading, in which he follows not only a calculation of his gain, but an impulse of his nature.

What the observant Frenchman describes in somewhat
extravagant language was a real advantage—an advantage that attached not merely to the sailing of ships, but
to their designing, their building, and everything connected with them. And what gave this advantage was
not anything in American nature that differed from
other human nature, but the fact that higher wages and
the resulting higher standard of comfort and better
opportunities developed a greater power of adapting
means to ends. In short, the secret of our success upon
the ocean (as of all our other successes) lay in the very
things that according to the exponents of protectionism
now shut us out from the ocean.*

Again, it is said that it is the substitution of steam for
canvas and iron for wood that has led to the decay of

---

* By way of consolation for the manner in which protectionism
has driven American ships from the ocean, Professor Thompson
("Political Economy," p. 216) says:

"If there were no other reason for the policy that seeks to reduce
foreign commerce to a minimum, a sufficient one would be found in
its effect upon the human material it employs. Bentham thought
the worst possible use that could be made of a man was to hang
him; a worse still is to make a common sailor of him. The life and
the manly character of the sailor has been so admired in song and
prose, and the real excellences of individuals of the profession have
been made so prominent, that we forget what the mass of this class
of men are, and what representatives of our civilization and Christianity we send out to all lands in the tenants of the forecastle."

There is some truth in this, but what there is is due to protectionism in its broader sense. There is no reason in the nature of his
vocation why the sailor should not be as well fed, well paid and well
treated, as intelligent and self-respecting, as any mechanic. That
he is not is at bottom due to the paternal interference of maritime
law with the relations of employer and employed. The law does not
specifically enforce contracts for services on shore, and for any
breach of contract by an employee the employer has only a civil
remedy. He cannot restrain the employed of his liberty, coerce
him by violence or duress, or, should he quit work, call on the law

American shipping. This is no more a reason for the decay of American shipping than is the substitution of the double topsail-yard for the single topsail-yard. River steamers were first developed here; it was an American steamship that first crossed from New York to Liverpool, and thirty years ago American steamers were making the "crack" passages. The same skill, the same energy, the same facility of adapting means to ends which enabled our mechanics to build wooden ships would have enabled them to continue to build ships no matter what the change in material. With free trade we should not merely have kept abreast of the change from wood to iron, we should have led it. This we should have done even though not a pound of iron could have been produced on the whole continent. In the glorious days of American ship-building Donald McKay

---

to bring him back, and thus the personal relations of employer and employed are left to the free play of mutual interest. For services requiring vigilance and sobriety, and where great loss or danger would result from a sudden refusal to go on with the work, the employer must look to the character of the men he employs, and must so pay and treat them that there will be no danger of their wishing to leave him. But what on shore is thus left to the self-regulative principle of freedom is, as to services to be performed on shipboard, attempted to be regulated on the paternal principle of protectionism. Here the law steps in to compel the specific performance of contracts, and not only gives the employer or his representative the right to restrain the employed of his personal liberty, and by violence or duress to compel his performance of services he has contracted for, but if the employed leave the ship the law may be invoked to arrest, imprison, and force him back. The result has been on the one hand largely to destroy the incentive to proper treatment of their crews on the part of owners and masters of ships, and on the other to degrade the character of seamen. Crews have been largely obtained by a system of virtual impressment or kidnapping called in longshore vernacular "shanghaing," by which men are put on board ship when drunk or even by force, for the sake of their advance wages or a bonus called "blood-

of Boston and William H. Webb of New York drew the
materials for their white-winged racers from forests that
were practically almost as far from those cities as they
were from the Clyde, the Humber, or the Thames. Had
our ship-builders been as free as their English rivals to
get their materials wherever they could buy them best
and cheapest, they could as easily have built ships with
iron brought from England as they did build them with
knees from Florida, and planks from Maine and North
Carolina, and spars from Oregon. Ireland produces
neither iron nor coal, but Belfast has become noted for
iron ship-building, and iron can be carried across the
Atlantic almost as cheaply as across the Irish Sea.

But so far from its being necessary to bring iron from
Great Britain, our deposits of iron and coal are larger,
better, and more easily worked than those of Great Britain, and before the Revolution we were actually exporting iron to that country. Had we never embraced the

---

money," which the power of keeping the men on board and compelling them to work enables the ship-owners safely to pay. The
power that must be intrusted to the master of a ship, on whose skill
and judgment depends the safety of all on board, is necessarily
despotic, but while the abuse of this power has, under a system
which enables a brutal captain to get crews with as much or almost
as much facility as a humane one, been little checked by motives of
self-interest, it has been stimulated by the degradation which such
a system inevitably produces in the character of the crews. Various
attempts have been made to remedy this state of things; but nothing
can avail much that does not go to the root of the difficulty and lead
the sailor, no matter what contract he may have signed or what
advances have been paid to or for him, as free to quit a vessel as
any mechanic on shore is free to quit his employment. Theoret-
ically the law may guard the rights of one party to a contract as
well as those of the other; but practically the poor and uninfluential
are always at a disadvantage in appealing to the law. This is a vice
which inheres in all forms of protectionism, from that of absolute
monarchy to that of protective duties.

policy of protection we should to-day have been the first of iron producers. The advantage that Great Britain has over us is simply that she has abandoned the repressive system of protection, while we have increased it. This difference in policy, while it has enabled the British producer to avail himself of the advantages of all the world, has handicapped the American producer and restricted him to the market of his own country. The ores of Spain and Africa which, for some purposes, it is necessary to mix with our own ores, have been burdened with a heavy duty; a heavy duty has enabled a great steel combination to keep steel at a monopoly price; a heavy duty on copper has enabled another combination to get a high price for American copper at home, while exporting it to Great Britain for a low price; and to encourage a single bunting factory the very ensign of an American ship has been subjected to a duty of 150 per cent. From keelson to truck, from the wire in her stays to the brass in her taffrail log, everything that goes to the building, the fitting or the storing of a ship is burdened with heavy taxes. Even should she be repaired abroad she must pay taxes for it on her return home. Thus has protection strangled an industry in which with free trade we might still have led the world. And the injury we have done ourselves has been, in some degree at least, an injury to mankind. Who can doubt that ocean steamers would to-day have been swifter and better had American builders been free to compete with English builders?

Though our Navigation Laws, which forbid the carrying of a pound of freight or a single passenger from American port to American port on any other than an American-built vessel, obscure the effects of protection in our coasting trade, they are just as truly felt as in our ocean trade. The increased cost of building and running vessels has, especially as to steamers, operated to stunt the growth of our coasting trade, and to check by higher freights the development of other industries. And how restriction strengthens monopoly is seen in the manner in which the effect of protection upon our coastwise trade has been to make easier the extortions of railway syndicates. For instance, the Pacific Railway pool has for years paid the Pacific Mail Steamship Company $85,000 a month to keep up its rates of fare and freight between New York and San Francisco. It would have been impossible for the railway ring thus to prevent competition had the trade between the Atlantic and Pacific been open to foreign vessels.

CHAPTER XIX.

PROTECTION AND WAGES.

WE have sufficiently seen the effect of protection on the production of wealth. Let us now inquire as to its effect on wages. This is a question of the distribution of wealth.

Discussions of the tariff question seldom go further than the point we have now reached, for though much is said, in the United States at least, of the effect of protection on wages, it is as a deduction from what is asserted of its effect on the production of wealth. Its advocates claim that protection raises wages; but in so far as they attempt to prove this it is only by arguments, such as we have examined, that protection increases the prosperity of a country as a whole, from which it is assumed that it must increase wages. Or when the claim that protection raises wages is put in the negative form (a favorite method with American protectionists) and it is asserted that protection prevents wages from falling to the lower level of other countries, this assertion is always based on the assumption that protection is necessary to enable production to be carried on at the higher level of wages, and that if it were withdrawn production would so decline, by reason of the underselling of home producers by foreign producers, that wages must also decline.*

---

* Here, for instance, taken from the *New York Tribune* during the last Presidential campaign (1884), is a sample of the arguments

But although its whole basis has already been over-thrown, let us (since this is the most important part of the question) examine directly and independently the claim that protection raises (or maintains) wages. Though the question of wages is primarily a question of the distribution of wealth, no protectionist writer that I know of ventures to treat it as such, and free traders generally stop where protectionists stop, arguing that protection must diminish the production of wealth, and (so far as they treat the matter of wages) from this inferring that protection must reduce wages. For purposes of controversy this is logically sufficient, since, free trade being natural trade, the onus of proof must lie upon those who would restrict it. But as my purpose is more than that of controversy, I cannot be contented with showing merely the unsoundness of the arguments for protection. A true proposition may be supported by a bad argument, and to satisfy ourselves thoroughly as to the effect of protection we must trace its influence on the distribution, as well as on the production of wealth. Error often arises from the assumption that what benefits or injures the whole must in like manner affect all its

for protection which are manufactured about election-times for the consumption of "the intelligent and highly paid American working-man":

"All workers know that labor in other countries is not paid as well as it is here. But this difference could not exist if the products of 50-cent labor in England or Germany or Canada could be sold freely in our market, instead of the production of $1 labor here. Hence, this country compels the employers of the 50-cent labor abroad to pay duty for the privilege of selling their goods in this market. That duty is called a tariff. If it is made high enough to fit the difference in rate of wages, so that labor in this country cannot be degraded toward the level of similar labor in other countries, it is called a protective tariff. Such a tariff is a defense of American industry against direct competition with the underpaid labor of other countries."

parts. Causes which increase or decrease aggregate wealth often produce the reverse effect on classes or individuals. The resort to salt instead of kelp for obtaining soda increased the production of wealth in Great Britain, but lessened the income of many Highland landlords. The introduction of railways, greatly as they have added to aggregate wealth, ruined the business of many small villages. Out of wars, destructive to national wealth though they be, great fortunes arise. Fires, floods and famines, while disastrous to the community, may prove profitable to individuals, and he who has a contract to fill, or who has speculated in stocks for a fall, may be enriched by hard times.

As, however, those who live by their labor constitute in all countries the large majority of the people, there is a strong presumption that no matter who else is benefited, anything that reduces the aggregate income of the community must be injurious to working-men. But that we may leave nothing to presumption, however strong, let us examine directly the effect of protective tariffs on wages.

Whatever affects the production of wealth may at the same time affect distribution. It is also possible that increase or decrease in the production of wealth may, under certain circumstances, alter the proportions of distribution. But it is only with the first of these questions that we have now to deal, since the second goes beyond the question of tariff, and if it shall become necessary to open it, that will not be until after we have satisfied ourselves as to the tendencies of protection.

Trade, as we have seen, is a mode of production, and the tendency of tariff restrictions on trade is to lessen the production of wealth. But protective tariffs also operate to alter the distribution of wealth, by imposing higher prices on some citizens and giving extra profits to

others. This alteration of distribution in their favor is
the impelling motive with those most active in procuring
the imposition of protective duties and in warning workmen of the dire calamities that will come on them if such
duties are repealed. But in what way can protective
tariffs affect the distribution of wealth in favor of labor?
The direct object and effect of protective tariffs is to
raise the price of commodities. But men who work for
wages are not sellers of commodities; they are sellers of
labor. They sell labor in order that they may buy commodities. How can increase in the price of commodities
benefit them?

I speak of price in conformity to the custom of com-
paring other values by that of money. But money is
only a medium of exchange and a measure of the comparative values of other things. Money itself rises and
falls in value as compared with other things, varying
between time and time, and place and place. In reality
the only true and final standard of values is labor—the
real value of anything being the amount of labor it will
command in exchange. To speak exactly, therefore, the
effect of a protective tariff is to increase the amount of
labor for which certain commodities will exchange.
Hence it reduces the value of labor just as it increases
the value of commodities.

Imagine a tariff that prevented the coming in of
laborers, but placed no restriction on the coming in of
commodities. Would those who have commodities to sell
deem such a tariff for their benefit? Yet to say this
would be as reasonable as to say that a tariff upon commodities is for the benefit of those who have labor to sell.

It is not true that the products of lower-priced labor
will drive the products of higher-priced labor out of any
market in which they can be freely sold, since, as we
have already seen, low-priced labor does not mean cheap

production, and it is the comparative, not the absolute, cost of production that determines exchanges. And we have but to look around to see that even in the same occupation, wages paid for labor whose products sell freely together are generally higher in large cities than in small towns, in some districts than in others.

It is true that there is a constant tendency of all wages to a common level, and that this tendency arises from competition. But this competition is not the competition of the goods-market; it is the competition of the labor-market. The differences between the wages paid in the production of goods that sell freely in the same market cannot arise from checks on the competition of goods for sale; but manifestly arises from checks on the competition of labor for employment. As the competition of labor varies between employment and employment, or between place and place, so do wages vary. The cost of living being greater in large cities than in small towns, the higher wages in the one are not more attractive than the lower wages in the other, while the differing rates of wages in different districts are manifestly maintained by the inertia and friction which retard the flow of population, or by causes, physical or social, which produce differences in the intensity of competition in the labor-market.

The tendency of wages to a common level is quickest in the same occupation, because the transference of labor is easiest. There cannot be, in the same place, such differences in wages in the same industry as may exist between different industries, since labor in the same industry can transfer itself from employer to employer with far less difficulty than is involved in changing an occupation. There are times when we see one employer reducing wages and others following his example, but this occurs too quickly to be caused by the competition of the

goods-market. It occurs at times when there is great
competition in the labor-market, and the same conditions
which enable one employer to reduce wages enable others
to do the same. If it were the competition of the goods-
market that brought wages to a level, they could not be
raised in one establishment or in one locality unless at
the same time raised in others that supplied the same
market; whereas, at the times when wages go up, we see
workmen in one establishment or in one locality first
demanding an increase, and then, if they are successful,
workmen in other establishments or localities following
their example.

If we pass now to a comparison of occupation with
occupation, we see that although there is a tendency to a
common level, which maintains between wages in different occupations a certain relation, there are, in the same
time and place, great differences of wages. These differences are not inconsistent with this tendency, but are
due to it, just as the rising of a balloon and the falling
of a stone exemplify the same physical law. While the
competition of the labor-market tends to bring wages in
all occupations to a common level, there are differences
between occupations (which may be summed up as differences in attraction and differences in the difficulty of
access) that check in various degrees the competition of
labor and produce different relative levels of wages.
Though these differences exist, wages in different occupations are nevertheless held in a certain relation to each
other by the tendency to a common level, so that a
reduction of wages in one trade tends to bring about a
reduction in others, not through the competition of the
goods-market, but through that of the labor-market.
Thus cabinet-makers, for instance, could not long get $2
where workmen in other trades as easily learned and
practised were only getting $1, since the superior wages

would so attract labor to cabinet-making as to increase
competition and bring wages down. But if the cabinet-
makers possessed a union strong enough strictly to limit
the number of new workmen entering the trade, is it not
clear that they could continue to get $2 while in other
trades similar labor was getting only $1? As a matter
of fact, trades-unions, by checking the competition of
labor, have considerably raised wages in many occupations, and have even brought about differences between
the wages of union and non-union men in the same occupation. And what limits the possibility of thus raising
wages is clearly not the free sale of commodities, but the
difficulty of restricting the competition of labor.

Do not these facts show that what American workmen
have to fear is not the sale in our goods-market of the
products of "cheap foreign labor," but the transference
to our labor-market of that labor itself? Under the conditions existing over the greater part of the civilized
world, the minimum of wages is fixed by what economists call the "standard of comfort"—that is to say, the
poorer the mode of life to which laborers are accustomed
the lower are their wages and the greater is their ability
to compel a reduction in any labor-market they enter.
What, then, shall we say of that sort of "protection of
American working-men" which, while imposing duties
upon goods, under the pretense that they are made by
"pauper labor," freely admits the "pauper laborer"
himself?

The incoming of the products of cheap labor is a very
different thing from the incoming of cheap labor. The
effect of the one is upon the production of wealth,
increasing the aggregate amount to be distributed; the
effect of the other is upon the distribution of wealth,
decreasing the proportion which goes to the working-
classes. We might permit the free importation of

Chinese commodities without in the slightest degree affecting wages; but, under our present conditions, the free immigration of Chinese laborers would lessen wages.

Let us imagine under the general conditions of modern civilization, one country of comparatively high wages, and another country of comparatively low wages. Let us, in imagination, bring these countries side by side, separating them only by a wall which permits the free transmission of commodities, but is impassable for human beings. Can we imagine, as protectionist notions require, that the high-wage country would do all the importing and the low-wage country all the exporting, until the demand for labor so lessened in the one country that wages would fall to the level of the other? That would be to imagine that the former country would go on pushing its commodities through this wall and getting back nothing in return. Clearly the one country would export no more than it got a return for, and the other could import no more than it gave a return for. What would go on between the two countries is the exchange of their respective productions, and, as previously pointed out, what commodities passed each way in this exchange would be determined, not by the difference in wages between the two countries, nor yet by differences between them in cost of production, but by differences in each country in the comparative cost of producing different things. This exchange of commodities would go on to the mutual advantage of both countries, increasing the amount which each obtained, but no matter to what dimensions it grew, how could it lessen the demand for labor or have any effect in reducing wages?

Now let us change the supposition and imagine such a barrier between the two countries as would prevent the passage of commodities, while permitting the free passage of men. No goods produced by the lower-paid labor of the one country could now be brought into the other; but would this prevent the reduction of wages? Manifestly not. Employers in the higher-wage country, being enabled to get in laborers willing to work for less, could quickly lower wages.

What we may thus see by aid of the imagination accords with what we do see as a matter of fact. In spite of the high duties which shut out commodities on the pretense of protecting American labor, American workmen in all trades are being forced into combinations to protect themselves by checking the competition of the labor-market. Our protective tariff on commodities raises the price of commodities, but what raising there is of wages has been accomplished by trades-unions and the Knights of Labor. Break up these organizations and what would the tariff do to prevent the forcing down of wages in all the now organized trades?

A scheme really intended for the protection of working-men from the competition of cheap labor would not merely prohibit the importation of cheap labor under contract, but would prohibit the landing of any laborer who had not sufficient means to raise him above the necessity of competing for wages, or who did not give bonds to join some trades-union and abide by its rules. And if, under such a scheme, any duties on commodities were imposed, they would be imposed, in preference, on such commodities as could be produced with small capital, not on those which require large capital—that is to say, the effort would be to protect industries in which workmen can readily engage on their own account, rather than those in which the mere workman can never hope to become his own employer.

Our tariff, like all protective tariffs, aims at nothing of this kind. It shields the employing producer from competition, but in no way attempts to lessen competition

among those who must sell him their labor; and the
industries it aims to protect are those in which the mere
workman, or even the workman with a small capital, is
helpless—those which cannot be carried on without large
establishments, costly machinery, great amounts of capi
tal, or the ownership of natural opportunities which bear
a high price.

It is manifest that the aim of protection is to lessen
competition in the selling of commodities, not in the
selling of labor.   In no case, save in the peculiar and
exceptional cases I shall hereafter speak of, can a tariff
on commodities benefit those who have labor, not commodities, to sell.   Nor is there in our tariff any provision
that aims at compelling such employers as it benefits to
share their benefits with their workmen.   While it gives
these employers protection in the goods-market it leaves
them free trade in the labor-market, and for any protection they need workmen have to organize.

I am not saying that any tariff could raise wages.   I
am merely pointing out that in our protective tariff there
is no attempt, however inefficient, to do this—that the
whole aim and spirit of protection is not the protection
of the sellers of labor but the protection of the buyers of
labor, not the maintaining of wages but the maintaining
of profits.   The very class that profess anxiety to protect American labor by raising the price of what they
themselves have to sell, notoriously buy labor as cheap
as they can and fiercely oppose any combination of workmen to raise wages.   The cry of "protection for American labor" comes most vociferously from newspapers
that lie under the ban of the printers' unions; from coal
and iron lords who, importing "pauper labor" by
wholesale, have bitterly fought every effort of their men
to claim anything like decent wages; and from factory-
owners who claim the right to dictate the votes of men.

The whole spirit of protection is against the rights of labor.

This is so obvious as hardly to need illustration, but there is a case in which it is so clearly to be seen as to tempt me to reference.

There is one kind of labor in which capital has no advantage, and that a kind which has been held from remote antiquity to redound to the true greatness and glory of a country—the labor of the author, a species of labor hard in itself, requiring long preparation, and in the vast majority of cases extremely meager in its pecuniary returns. What protection have the protectionist majorities that have so long held sway in Congress given to this kind of labor? While the American manufacturer of books—the employing capitalist who puts them on the market—has been carefully protected from the competition of foreign manufacturers, the American author has not only *not* been protected from the competition of foreign authors, but has been exposed to the competition of labor for which nothing whatever is paid. He has never asked for any protection save that of common justice, but this has been steadily refused. Foreign-made books have been saddled with a high protective duty, a force of customs examiners is maintained in the post-office, and an American is not even allowed to accept the present of a book from a friend abroad without paying a tax for it.* But this is not to protect the

---

* Although a great sum is raised in the United States every year to send the Bible to the heathen in foreign parts, we impose for the protection of the home "Bible manufacturer" a heavy tax upon the bringing of Bibles into our country. There have recently been complaints of the smuggling of Bibles across our northern frontier, which have doubtless inspired our custom-house officers to renewed vigilance, since, according to an official advertisement, the following property seized for violation of the United States revenue laws was

American author, who as an author is a mere laborer, but to protect the American publisher, who is a capitalist. And this capitalist, so carefully protected as to what he has to sell, has been permitted to compel the American author to compete with stolen labor. Congress, which year after year has been maintaining a heavy tariff, on the hypocritical plea of protecting American labor, has steadily refused the bare justice of acceding to an international copyright which would prevent American publishers from stealing the work of foreign authors, and enable American authors not only to meet foreign authors on fair terms at home, but to get payment for their books when reprinted in foreign countries. An international copyright, demanded as it is by honor, by morals and by every dictate of patriotic policy, has always been opposed by the protective interest.* Could anything more clearly show that the real motive of protection is always the profit of the employing capitalist, never the benefit of labor?

What would be thought of the Congressman who should propose, as a "working-man's measure," to divide the surplus in the treasury between two or three railway kings, and who should gravely argue that to do this would be to raise wages in all occupations, since the railway kings, finding themselves so much richer, would at once raise the wages of their employees; which would lead to the raising of wages on all railways, and this again to the raising of wages in all occupations? Yet the

---

sold at public auction in front of the Custom-House, Detroit, on Saturday, February 6, 1886, at 12 o'clock noon : 1 set silver jewelry, 3 bottles of brandy, 7 yards astrakhan, 1 silk tidy, 7 books, 1 shawl, 1 sealskin cloak, 4 rosaries, 1 woolen shirt, 2 pairs of mittens, 1 pair of stockings, 1 bottle of gin, 1 Bible.

* An exception is to be made in favor of Horace Greeley, who, though a protectionist, did advocate an international copyright.

contention that protective duties on goods raise wages involves just such assumptions.

It is claimed that protection raises the wages of labor —that is to say, of labor generally. It is not merely contended that it raises wages in the special industries protected by the tariff. That would be to confess that the benefits of protection are distributed with partiality, a thing which its advocates are ever anxious to deny. It is always assumed by protectionists that the benefits of protection are felt in all industries, and even the wages of farm-laborers (in an industry which in the United States is not and cannot be protected by the tariff) are pointed to as showing the results of protection.

The scheme of protection is, by checking importation to increase the price of protected commodities so as to enable the home producers of these commodities to make larger profits. It is only as it does this, and so long as it does this, that protection can have any encouraging effect at all, and whatever effect it has upon wages must be derived from this.

I have already shown that protection cannot, except temporarily, increase the profits of producers as producers, but without regard to this it is clear that the contention that protection raises wages involves two assumptions : (1) that increase in the profits of employers means increase in the wages of their workmen ; and (2) that increase of wages in the protected occupations involves increase of wages in all occupations.

To state these assumptions is to show their absurdity. Is there any one who really supposes that because an employer makes larger profits he therefore pays higher wages ?

I rode not long since on the platform of a Brooklyn horse-car and talked with the driver. He told me, bitterly and despairingly, of his long hours, hard work

and poor pay—how he was chained to that car, a verier
slave than the horses he drove; and how by turning
himself into this kind of a horse-driving machine he
could barely keep wife and children, laying by nothing for
a "rainy day."

I said to him, "Would it not be a good thing if the
Legislature were to pass a law allowing the companies to
raise the fare from five to six cents, so as to enable them
to raise the wages of their drivers and conductors?"

The driver measured me with a quick glance, and then
exclaimed: "They give us more, because they made
more! You might raise the fare to six cents or to sixty
cents, and they would not pay us a penny more. No
matter how much *they* made, we would get no more, so
long as there are hundreds of men waiting and anxious
to take our places. The company would pay higher dividends or water the stock; not raise our pay."

Was not the driver right? Buyers of labor, like buyers
of other things, pay, not according to what they can, but
according to what they must. There are occasional
exceptions, it is true; but these exceptions are referable
to motives of benevolence, which the shrewd business
man keeps out of his business, no matter how much he
may otherwise indulge them. Whether you raise the
profits of a horse-car company or of a manufacturer,
neither will on that account pay any higher wages.
Employers never give the increase of their profits as a
reason for raising the wages of their workmen, though
they frequently assign decreased profits as a reason for
reducing wages. But this is an excuse, not a reason.
The true reason is that the dull times which diminish
their profits increase the competition of workmen for
employment. Such excuses are given only when employers feel that if they reduce wages their employees will be
compelled to submit to the reduction, since others will

be glad to step into their places. And where trades-unions succeed in checking this competition they are enabled to raise wages. Since my talk with the driver, the horse-car employees of New York and Brooklyn, organized into assemblies of the Knights of Labor and supported by that association, have succeeded in somewhat raising their pay and shortening their hours, thus gaining what no increase in the profits of the companies would have had the slightest tendency to give them.

No matter how much a protective duty may increase the profits of employers, it will have no effect in raising wages unless it so acts upon competition as to give workmen power to compel an increase of wages.

There are cases in which a protective duty may have this effect, but only to a small extent and for a short time. When a duty, by increasing the demand for a certain domestic production, suddenly increases the demand for a certain kind of skilled labor, the wages of such labor may be temporarily increased, to an extent and for a time determined by the difficulties of obtaining skilled laborers from other countries or of the acquirement by new laborers of the needed skill.

But in any industry it is only the few workmen of peculiar skill who can thus be affected, and even when by these few such an advantage is gained, it can be maintained only by trades-unions that limit entrance to the craft. The cases are, I think, few indeed in which any increase of wages has thus been gained by even that small class of workmen who in any protected industry require such exceptional skill that their ranks cannot easily be swelled; and the cases are fewer still, if they exist at all, in which the difficulties of bringing workmen from abroad, or of teaching new workmen, have long sufficed to maintain such increase. As for the great mass of those engaged in the protected industries, their labor can hardly be called skilled. Much of it can be performed by ordinary unskilled laborers, and much of it does not need even the physical strength of the adult man, but consists of the mere tending of machinery, or of manipulations which can be learned by boys and girls in a few weeks, a few days, or even a few hours. As to all this labor, which constitutes by far the greater part of the labor required in the industries we most carefully protect, any temporary effect which a tariff might have to increase wages in the way pointed out would be so quickly lost that it could hardly be said to come into operation. For an increase in the wages of such occupations would at once be counteracted by the flow of labor from other occupations. And it must be remembered that the effect of "encouraging" any industry by taxation is necessarily to discourage other industries, and thus to force labor into the protected industries by driving it out of others.

Nor could wages be raised if the bounty which the tariff aims to give employing producers were given directly to their workmen. If, instead of laws intended to add to the profits of the employing producers in certain industries, we were to make laws by which so much should be added to the wages of the workmen, the increased competition which the bounty would cause would soon bring wages plus the bounty to the rate at which wages stood without the bounty. The result would be what it was in England when, during the early part of this century, it was attempted to improve the miserable condition of agricultural laborers by "grants in aid of wages" from parish rates. Just as these grants were made, so did the wages paid by the farmers sink.

The car-driver was right. Nothing could raise his wages that did not lessen the competition of those who stood ready to take his place for the wages he was getting. If we were to enact that every car-driver should be paid a dollar a day additional from public funds, the result would simply be that the men who are anxious to get places as car-drivers for the wages now paid would be as anxious to get them at one dollar less. If we were to give every car-driver two dollars a day, the companies would be able to get men without paying them anything, just as where restaurant waiters are customarily feed by the patrons, they get little or no wages, and in some cases even pay a bonus for their places.

But if it be preposterous to imagine that any effect a tariff may have to raise profits in the protected industries can raise wages in those industries, what shall we say of the notion that such raising of wages in the protected industries would raise wages in all industries? This is like saying that to dam the Hudson River would raise the level of New York Harbor and consequently that of the Atlantic Ocean. Wages, like water, tend to a level, and unless raised in the lowest and widest occupations can be raised in any particular occupation only as it is walled in from competition.

The general rate of wages in every country is manifestly determined by the rate in the occupations which require least special skill, and to which the man who has nothing but his labor can most easily resort. As they engage the greater body of labor these occupations constitute the base of the industrial organization, and are to other occupations what the ocean is to its bays. The rate of wages in the higher occupations can be raised above the rate prevailing in the lower, only as the higher occupations are shut off from the inflow of labor by their greater risk or uncertainty, by their requirement of superior skill, education or natural ability, or by restrictions such as those imposed by trades-unions. And to secure anything like a general rise of wages, or even to secure a rise of wages in any occupation upon ingress to which restrictions are not at the same time placed, it is necessary to raise wages in the lower and wider occupations. That is to say, to return to our former illustration, the level of the bays and harbors that open into it cannot be raised until the level of the ocean is raised.

If it were evident in no other way, the recognition of this general principle would suffice to make it clear that duties on imports can never raise the general rate of wages. For import duties can only "protect" occupations in which there is not sufficient labor employed to produce the supply we need. The labor thus engaged can never be more than a fraction of the labor engaged in producing commodities of which we not only provide the home supply but have a surplus for export, and the labor engaged in work that must be done on the spot.

No matter what the shape or size of an iceberg, the mass above the water must be very much less than the mass below the water. So no matter what be the conditions of a country or what the peculiarities of its industry, that part of its labor engaged in occupations that can be "protected" by import duties must always be small as compared with that engaged in occupations that cannot be protected. In the United States, where protection has been carried to the utmost, the census returns show that not more than one-twentieth of the labor of the country is engaged in protected industries.

In the United States, as in the world at large, the lowest and widest occupations are those in which men apply their labor directly to nature, and of these agriculture is the most important. How quickly the rise of wages in these occupations will increase wages in all occupations was shown in the early days of California, as afterwards in Australia. Had anything happened in California to increase the demand for cooks or carpenters or painters, the rise in such wages would have been quickly met by the inflow of labor from other occupations, and in this way retarded and finally neutralized. But the discovery of the placer-mines, which greatly raised the wages of unskilled labor, raised wages in all occupations.

The difference of wages between the United States and European countries is itself an illustration of this principle. During our colonial days, before we had any protective tariff, ordinary wages were higher here than in Europe. The reason is clear. Land being easy to obtain, the laborer could readily employ himself, and wages in agriculture being thus maintained at a higher level, the general rate of wages was higher. And since up to the present time it has been easier to obtain land here than in Europe, the higher rate of wages in agriculture has kept up a higher general rate.

To raise the general rate of wages in the United States the wages of agricultural labor must be raised. But our tariff does not and cannot raise even the price of agricultural produce, of which we are exporters, not importers. Yet, even had we as dense a population in proportion to our available land as Great Britain, and were we, like her, importers not exporters of agricultural productions, a protective tariff upon such productions could not increase agricultural wages, still less could it increase wages in other occupations, which would then have become the widest. This we may see by the effect of the corn-laws in Great Britain, which was to increase, not the wages of the agricultural laborer, nor even the profits of the farmer, but the rent of the agricultural landlord. And even if the differentiation between landowner, farmer and laborer had, under the conditions I speak of, not become as clear here as in Great Britain, nothing which benefited the farmer would have the slightest tendency to raise wages, save as it benefited him, not as an owner of land or an owner of capital, but as a laborer.

We thus see from theory that protection cannot raise wages. That it does not, facts show conclusively. This has been seen in Spain, in France, in Mexico, in England during protection times, and everywhere that protection has been tried. In countries where the working-classes have little or no influence upon government it is never even pretended that protection raises wages. It is only in countries like the United States, where it is necessary to cajole the working-class, that such a preposterous plea is made. And here the failure of protection to raise wages is shown by the most evident facts.

Wages in the United States are higher than in other countries, not because of protection, but because we have had much vacant land to overrun. Before we had any tariff, wages were higher here than in Europe, and far higher, relatively to the productiveness of labor, than they are now after our years of protection. In spite of all our protection—and, for the last twenty-four years at least, protectionists have had it all their own way—the condition of the laboring-classes of the United States has been slowly but steadily sinking to that of the "pauper labor" of Europe. It does not follow that this is because of protection, but it is certain that protection has proved powerless to prevent it.

To discover whether protection has or has not benefited the working-classes of the United States it is not necessary to array tables of figures which only an expert can verify and examine. The determining facts are notorious. It is a matter of common knowledge that those to whom we have given power to tax the American people "for the protection of American industry" pay their employees as little as they can, and make no scruple of importing the very foreign labor against whose products the tariff is maintained. It is notorious that wages in the protected industries are, if anything, lower than in the unprotected industries, and that, though the protected industries do not employ more than a twentieth of the working population of the United States, there occur in them more strikes, more lockouts, more attempts to reduce wages, than in all other industries. In the highly protected industries of Massachusetts, official reports declare that the operative cannot get a living without the work of wife and children. In the highly protected industries of New Jersey, many of the "protected" laborers are children whose parents are driven by their necessities to find employment for them by misrepresenting their age so as to evade the State law. In the highly protected industries of Pennsylvania, laborers, for whose sake we are told this high protection is imposed, are working for sixty-five cents a day, and half-clad women are feeding furnace fires. "Pluck-me stores," company tenements and boarding-houses, Pinkerton detectives and mercenaries, and all the forms and evidences of the oppression and degradation of labor are, throughout the country, characteristic of the protected industries.

The greater degradation and unrest of labor in the protected than in the unprotected industries may in part be accounted for by the fact that the protected employers have been the largest importers of "foreign pauper labor." But, in some part at least, it is due to the greater fluctuations to which the protected industries are exposed. Being shut off from foreign markets, scarcity of their productions cannot be so quickly met by importation, nor surplus relieved by exportation, and so with them for much of the time it is either "a feast or a famine." These violent fluctuations tend to bring workmen into a state of dependence, if not of actual peonage, and to depress wages below the general standard. But whatever be the reason, the fact is that so far is protection from raising wages in the protected industries, that the capitalists who carry them on would soon "enjoy" even lower-priced labor than now, were it not that wages in them are kept up by the rate of wages in the unprotected industries.

CHAPTER XX.

THE ABOLITION OF PROTECTION.

OUR inquiry has sufficiently shown the futility and absurdity of protection. It only remains to consider the plea that is always set up for protection when other excuses fail—the plea that since capital has been invested and industry organized upon the basis of protection it would be unjust and injurious to abolish protective duties at once, and that their reduction must be gradual and slow. This plea for delay, though accepted and even urged by many of those who up to this time have been the most conspicuous opponents of protection, will not bear examination. If protection be unjust, if it be an infringement of equal rights that gives certain citizens the power to tax other citizens, then anything short of its complete and immediate abolition involves a continuance of injustice. No one can acquire a vested right in a wrong; no one can claim property in a privilege. To admit that privileges which have no other basis than a legislative Act cannot at any time be taken away by legislative Act, is to commit ourselves to the absurd doctrine that has been carried to such a length in Great Britain, where it is held that a sinecure cannot be abolished without buying out the incumbent, and that because a man's ancestors have enjoyed the privilege of living on other people, he and his descendants, to the

217

remotest time, have acquired a sacred right to live upon other people. The true doctrine—of which we ought never, on any pretense, to yield one iota—is that enunciated in our Declaration of Independence, the self-evident doctrine that men are endowed by their Creator with equal and unalienable rights, and that any law or institution that denies or impairs this natural equality may at any time be altered or abolished. And no more salutary lesson could to-day be taught to capitalists throughout the world than that justice is an element in the safety of investments, and that the man who trades upon the ignorance or the enslavement of a people does so at his own risk. A few such lessons, and every throne in Europe would topple, and every great standing army melt away.

Moreover, abolition at once is the only way in which the industries now protected could be treated with any fairness. The gradual abolition of protection would give rise to the same scrambling and pipe-laying and log-rolling which every tariff change brings about, and the stronger would save themselves at the expense of the weaker.

But further than this, the gradual abolition of protection would not only continue for a long time, though in a diminishing degree, the waste, loss and injustice inseparable from the system, but during all this period the anticipation of coming changes and the uncertainty in regard to them would continue to inspire insecurity and depress business; whereas, were protection abolished at once, the shock, whatever it might be, would soon be over, and exchange and industry could at once reorganize upon a sure basis. Even on the theory that the abolition of protection involves temporary disaster, immediate abolition is as preferable to gradual abolition as amputation at one operation is to amputation by inches.

And to the working-classes—the classes for whom those who deplore sudden change profess to have most concern—the difference would be greater still. It is always to the relative advantage of the poorer classes that any change involving disaster should be as sudden as possible, since the effect of delay is simply to give the richer classes opportunity to avoid it at the expense of the poorer.

If there is to be a certain loss to any community, whether by flood, by fire, by invasion, by pestilence, or by commercial convulsion, that loss will fall more lightly on the poor and more heavily on the rich the shorter the time in which it is concentrated. If the currency of a country slowly depreciates, the depreciating currency will be forced into the hands of those least able to protect themselves, the price of commodities will advance in anticipation of the depreciation, while the price of labor will lag along after it; capitalists will have opportunity to make secure their loans and to speculate in advancing prices, and the loss will thus fall with far greater relative severity upon the poor than upon the rich. In the same way, if a depreciated currency be slowly restored to par, the price of labor falls more quickly than the price of commodities; debtors struggle along in the endeavor to pay their obligations in an appreciating currency, and those who have the most means are best able to avoid the disadvantages and avail themselves of the speculative opportunities brought about by the change. But the more suddenly any given change in the value of currency takes place the more equal will be its effects.

So it is with the imposition of public burdens. It is manifestly to the advantage of the poorer class that any great public expense be met at once rather than spread over years by means of public debts. Thus, if the expenses of our civil war had been met by taxation levied at the time, such taxation must have fallen heavily upon the rich. But by the device of a public debt—a twin invention to that of indirect taxation—the cost of the war was not, as was pretended, shifted from present time to future time (for that would have been possible only had the means to carry on the war been borrowed from abroad, which was not the case), but taxation, which otherwise must have fallen upon individuals in proportion to their wealth, was changed into taxation spread over a long series of years and falling upon individuals in proportion, not to their means, but to their consumption, thus imposing upon the poor far greater relative burdens than upon the rich. Whether the rich would have had the patriotism to support a war which thus called upon them for sacrifices more commensurate with those of the poor, who in all wars furnish the far greater portion of " the food for powder," is another matter ; but it is certain that the spreading of the war taxation over years has not only made the cost of the war many times greater, but has been to the advantage of the rich and to the disadvantage of the working-classes.

If the abolition of protection is, as protectionists predict, certain to disorganize trade and industry, then it is better for all, and especially is it better for the working-classes, that the change should be sharp and short. If the return to a natural condition of trade and production must temporarily throw men out of employment, then it is better that they should be thrown out at once and have done with it, than that the same loss of employment should be spread over a series of years with a constant depressing effect upon the labor-market. In a sharp but short period of depression the public purse could, without serious consequences, be drawn upon to relieve distress, but any attempt to relieve in that way

the less general but more protracted distress incident to
a long period of depression, would tend to create an
army of habitual paupers.

But, in truth, the talk about the commercial convul-
sions and industrial distress that would follow the abolition of protection is as baseless as the story with which
Southern slaveholders during the war attempted to keep
their chattels from running away—that the Northern
armies would sell them to Cuba; as baseless as the predictions of Republican politicians that the election of a
Democratic President would mean the assumption of the
Confederate debt, if not the revival of the "Lost Cause."

The real fear that underlies all this talk of the disastrous effects of the sudden abolition of protection was
well exemplified in a conversation a friend of mine had
awhile ago with a large manufacturer, who belongs to a
combination which prevents competition at home while
the tariff prevents competition from abroad. The manufacturer was inveighing against any meddling with the
tariff, and dilating upon the ruin that would be brought
upon the country by free trade.

"Yes," said my friend, who had been listening with an
air of sympathetic attention, "I suppose, if the tariff
were abolished, you would have to shut up your works."

"Well, no; not quite that," said the manufacturer.
"We could go ahead, even with free trade; but then—we
couldn't get the same profit."

The notion that our manufactures would be suspended
and our iron-works closed and our coal-mines shut down
by the abolition of protection is a notion akin to that of
"the tail wagging the dog." Where are the goods to
come from which are thus to deluge our markets, and
how are they to be paid for? There is not productive
power enough in Europe to supply them, nor are there
ships to transport them, to say nothing of the effect

upon European prices of the demands of sixty millions of people, who, head for head, consume more than any other people in the world. And since other countries are not going to deluge us with the products of their labor without demanding the products of our own labor in payment, any increase in our imports from the abolition of protection would involve a corresponding increase in exports.

The truth is that the change would be not only beneficial to our industries at large—four-fifths of which, at least, are not brought into competition with imported commodities, but it would be beneficial even to the "protected" industries. In those that are sheltered by home monopolies, profits would be reduced; in those in which the tariff permits the use of inferior machinery and slovenly methods, better machinery would have to be provided and better methods introduced; but in the great bulk of our manufacturing industries, the effect would be only beneficial, the reduction in the cost of material far more than compensating for the reduction in prices. And with a lower cost of production foreign markets from which our manufacturers are now shut out would be opened. If any industry would be "crushed" it could only be some industry now carried on at national loss.

The increased power which the removal of restrictions upon trade would give in the production of wealth would be felt in all directions. Instead of a collapse there would be a revivification of industry. Rings would be broken up, and where profits are now excessive they would come down; but production would go on under healthier conditions and with greater energy. American manufacturers would begin to find markets the whole world over. American ships would again sail the high seas. The Delaware would ring like the Clyde with the clash of riveting hammers, and the United States would rapidly take that first place in the industrial and commercial world to which her population and her natural resources entitle her, but which is now occupied by England, while legislation and administration would be relieved of a great cause of corruption, and all governmental reforms would be made easier.

CHAPTER XXI.

THE point we have now reached is that at which discussions of the tariff question usually end—the extreme limit to which the avowed champions of the opposing policies carry their controversy.

We have, in fact, reached the legitimate end of our inquiry so far as it relates to the respective merits of protection and free trade. The stream, whose course our examination has been following, here blends with other streams, and though it still flows on, it is as part of a wider and deeper river. As he who would trace the waters of the Ohio to their final union with the ocean cannot stop when the Ohio ends, but must still follow on that mighty Mississippi which unites streams from far different sources, so, as I said in the beginning, really to understand the tariff question we must go beyond the tariff question. This we may now see.

So far as relates to questions usually debated between protectionists and free traders our inquiry is now complete and conclusive. We have seen the absurdity of protection as a general principle and the fallacy of the special pleas that are made for it. We have seen that protective duties cannot increase the aggregate wealth of the country that enforces them, and have no tendency to give a greater proportion of that wealth to the working-

224

class. We have seen that their tendencies, on the contrary, are to lessen aggregate wealth, and to foster monopolies at the expense of the masses of the people.

But although we have directly or inferentially disproved every argument that is made for protection, although we have seen conclusively that protection is in its nature inimical to general interests, and that free trade is in its nature promotive of general interests, yet if our inquiry were to stop here we should not have accomplished the purpose with which we set out. For my part, did it end here, I should deem the labor I have so far spent in writing this book little better than wasted. For all that we have seen has, with more or less coherence and clearness, been shown again and again. Yet protection still retains its hold on the popular mind. And until something more is shown, protection will retain this hold.

In exposing the fallacies of protection I have endeavored in each case to show what has made the fallacy plausible, but it still remains to explain why such exposures produce so little effect. The very conclusiveness with which our examination has disproved the claims of protection will suggest that there must be something more to be said, and may well prompt the question, "If the protective theory is really so incongruous with the nature of things and so inconsistent with itself, how is it that after so many years of discussion it still obtains such wide and strong support?"

Free traders usually attribute the persistence of the belief in protection to popular ignorance, played upon by special interests. But this explanation will hardly satisfy an unbiased mind. Vitality inheres in truth, not in error. Though accepted error has always the strength of habit and authority, and the battle against it must always be hard at first, yet the tendency of discussion in

which error is confronted with truth is to make the truth
steadily clearer. That a theory which seems wholly false
holds its ground in popular belief despite wide and long
discussion, should prompt its opponents to inquire
whether their arguments have really gone to the roots of
popular belief, and whether this belief does not derive
support from truths they have not considered, or from
errors not yet exposed, which still pass for truths—
rather than to attribute its vitality to popular incapacity
to recognize truth.

I shall hereafter show that the protective idea does
indeed derive support from doctrines that have been
actively taught and zealously defended by the very
economists who have assailed it (who, so to speak, have
been vigorously defending protection with the right hand
while raining blows upon it with the left), and from
habits of thought which the opponents no less than the
advocates of protection have failed to call in question.
But what I now wish to point out is the inadequacy of
the arguments which free traders usually rely on to
convince working-men that the abolition of protection is
for their interest.

In our examination we have gone as far, and in certain respects somewhat further than free traders usually
go. But what have we proved as to the main issue?
Merely that it is the *tendency* of free trade to increase the
production of wealth, and thus to *permit* of the increase
of wages, and that it is the *tendency* of protection to
decrease the production of wealth and foster certain
monopolies. But from this it does not follow that the
abolition of protection would be of any benefit to the
working-class. The tendency of a brick pushed off a
chimney-top is to fall to the surface of the ground. But
it will *not* fall to the surface of the ground if its fall be
intercepted by the roof of a house. The tendency of

anything that increases the productive power of labor is to augment wages. But it will *not* augment wages under conditions in which laborers are forced by competition to offer their services for a mere living.

In the United States, as in all countries where political power is in the hands of the masses, the vital point in the tariff controversy is as to its effect upon the earnings of "the poor people who have to work." *

But this point lies beyond the limit to which free traders are accustomed to confine their reasoning. They *prove* that the tendency of protection is to reduce the production of wealth and to increase the price of commodities, and from this they *assume* that the effect of the abolition of protection would be to increase the earnings of labor. But not merely is such an assumption logically invalid until it is shown that there is nothing in existing conditions to prevent the working-classes from getting the benefit of this tendency; but, although in itself a natural assumption, it is in the minds of "the poor people who have to work" contradicted by obvious facts.

In this is the invalidity of the free-trade argument, and here, and not in the ignorance of the masses, is the reason why all attempts to convert working-men to the free-tradeism which would substitute a revenue tariff for a protective tariff must, save under such conditions as existed in England forty years ago, utterly fail.

While both sides have shown the same indisposition to go to the heart of the controversy, there can be no question that so far as issue is joined between protectionists and free traders, in current discussion, the free traders have the best of the argument.

---

* I find this suggestive phrase in a protectionist newspaper. But it well expresses the attitude toward labor of many of the free-trade writers also.

But that the belief in protection has survived long and wide discussion, that it seems to spring up again when beaten down and to arise with apparent spontaneity in communities such as the United States, Canada and Australia, that have grown up without tariffs, and where the system lacks the advantage of inertia and of enlisted interests, proves that beyond the discussion there must be something which strongly commends protection to the popular mind.

This may also be inferred from what protectionists themselves say. Beaten in argument, the protectionist usually falls back upon some declaration which implies that the real grounds of his belief have been untouched, and which generally takes the form of an assertion that though free trade may be true in theory it fails in practice. In such form the assertion is untenable. A theory is but an explanation of the relation of facts, and nothing can be true in theory that is not true in practice. But free traders really beg the question when they answer by merely pointing this out. The real question is, whether the reasoning on which free traders rely takes into account all existing conditions? What the protectionist means, or at least the perception that he appeals to, when he talks in this way of the difference between theory and fact, is, that the free-trade theory does not take into account all existing facts. And this is true.

As the tariff question is presented, there are indeed, under existing social conditions, two sides to the shield, so that men who look only at one side, closing their eyes to the other, may continue, with equal confidence, to hold opposite opinions. And that the distinction between them may, with not entire inaptness, be described as that of exclusively regarding theory and that of exclusively regarding facts, we shall see when we have developed a theory which will embrace all the facts, and which will explain not only why it is that honest men have so diametrically differed upon the question of protection *vs.* free trade, but why the advocates of neither policy have been inclined to press on to that point where honest differences may be reconciled.   For we have reached the place where the Ohio of the tariff question flows into the Mississippi of the great social question.   It need not surprise us that both parties to the controversy, as it has hitherto been conducted, should stop here, for it would be as rational to expect any thorough treatment of the social question from the well-to-do class represented in the English Cobden Club or the American Iron and Steel Association, or from their apologists in professorial chairs, as it would be to look for any thorough treatment of the subject of personal liberty in the controversies of the slave-holding Whigs and slave-holding Democrats of forty years ago, or in the sermons of the preachers whose salaries were paid by them.

CHAPTER XXII.

THE REAL WEAKNESS OF FREE TRADE.

HOW the abolition of protection would stimulate production, weaken monopolies and relieve government of a great cause of corruption, we have seen.

"But what," it will be asked, "would be the gain to working-men? Will wages increase?"

For some time, and to some extent, yes. For the spring of industrial energy consequent upon the removal of the dead-weight of the tariff would for a time make the demand for labor brisker and employment steadier, and in occupations where they can combine, working-men would have better opportunity to reduce their hours and increase their wages, as, since the abolition of the protective tariff in England, many trades there have done. But even from the total abolition of protection, it is impossible to predict any general and permanent increase of wages or any general and permanent improvement in the condition of the working-classes. The effect of the abolition of protection, great and beneficial though it must be, would in nature be similar to that of the inventions and discoveries which in our time have so greatly increased the production of wealth, yet have nowhere really raised wages or of themselves improved the condition of the working-classes.

Here is the weakness of free trade as it is generally advocated and understood.

The working-man asks the free trader: "How will the change you propose benefit me?"

The free trader can only answer: "It will increase wealth and reduce the cost of commodities."

But in our own time the working-man has seen wealth enormously increased without feeling himself a sharer in the gain. He has seen the cost of commodities greatly reduced without finding it any easier to live. He looks to England, where a revenue tariff has for some time taken the place of a protective tariff, and there he finds labor degraded and underpaid, a general standard of wages lower than that which prevails here, while such improvements as have been made in the condition of the working-classes since the abolition of protection are clearly not traceable to that, but to trades-unions, to temperance and beneficial societies, to emigration, to education, and to such acts as those regulating the labor of women and children, and the sanitary conditions of factories and mines.

And seeing this, the working-man, even though he may realize with more or less clearness the hypocrisy of the rings and combinations which demand tariff duties for "the protection of American labor," accepts the fallacies of protection, or at least makes no effort to throw them off, not because of their strength so much as of the weakness of the appeal which free trade makes to him. A considerable proportion, at least, of the most intelligent and influential of American working-men are fully conscious that "protection" does nothing for labor, but neither do they see what free trade could do. And so they regard the tariff question as one of no practical concern to working-men—an attitude hardly less satisfactory to the protected interests than a thorough belief in protection. For when an interest is already intrenched in law and habit of thought, those who are not against it are for it.

To prove that the abolition of protection would tend to increase the aggregate wealth is not of itself enough to evoke the strength necessary to overthrow protection. To do that, it must be proved that the abolition of protection would mean improvement in the condition of the masses.

It is, as I have said, natural to assume that increased production of wealth would be for the benefit of all, and to a child, a savage, or a civilized man who lived in his study and did not read the daily papers, this would doubtless seem a necessary assumption. Yet, to the majority of men in civilized society, so far is this assumption from seeming necessary, that current explanations of the most important social phenomena involve the reverse.

Without question the most important social phenomena of our time arise from that partial paralysis of industry which in all highly civilized countries is in some degree chronic, and which at recurring periods becomes intensified in wide-spread and long-continued industrial depressions. What is the current explanation of these phenomena? Is it not that which attributes them to over-production?

This explanation is positively or negatively supported even by men who attribute to popular ignorance the failure of the masses to appreciate the benefits of substituting a revenue tariff for a protective tariff. But so long as conditions which bring racking anxiety and bitter privation to millions are commonly attributed to the over-production of wealth, is it any wonder that a reform which is urged on the ground that it would still further increase the production of wealth should fail to arouse popular enthusiasm?

If, indeed, it be popular ignorance that gives persistence to the belief in protection, it is an ignorance that extends to questions far more important and pressing than any question of tariff—an ignorance that the advocates of free trade have done nothing to enlighten, and that they can do nothing to enlighten until they explain why it is that in spite of the enormous increase of productive power that has been going on with accelerating rapidity all this century it is yet so hard for the mere laborer to get a living.

In this great fact, that increase in wealth and in the power of producing wealth does not bring any general benefit in which all classes share—does not for the great masses lessen the intensity of the struggle to live, lies the explanation of the popular weakness of free trade. It is owing to the increasing appreciation of this fact, and not to accidental causes, that all over the civilized world the free-trade movement has for some time been losing energy.

American revenue reformers delude themselves if they imagine that protection can now be overthrown in the United States by a movement on the lines of the Cobden Club. The day for that has passed.

It is true that the British tariff reformers of forty years ago were enabled on these lines to arouse the popular enthusiasm necessary to overthrow protection. But not only did the fact that the British tariff made food dear enable them to appeal to sympathy and imagination with a directness and force impossible where the commodities affected by a tariff are not of such prime importance; but the feeling of that time in regard to such reforms was far more hopeful. The great social problems which to-day loom so dark on the horizon of the civilized world were then hardly perceived. In the destruction of political tyranny and the removal of trade

restrictions ardent and generous spirits saw the emancipation of labor and the eradication of chronic poverty,
and there was a confident belief that the industrial
inventions and discoveries of the new era which the
world had entered would elevate society from its very
foundations. The natural assumption that increase in
the general wealth must mean a general improvement in
the condition of the people was then confidently made.

But disappointment after disappointment has chilled
these hopes, and, just as faith in mere republicanism has
weakened, so the power of the appeal that free traders
make to the masses has weakened with the decline of
the belief that mere increase in the power of production
will increase the rewards of labor. Instead of the abolition of protection in Great Britain being followed, as
was expected, by the overthrow of protection everywhere,
it is not only stronger throughout the civilized world
than it was then, but is again raising its head in Great
Britain.

It is useless to tell working-men that increase in the
general wealth means improvement in their condition.
They know by experience that this is not true. The
working-classes of the United States have seen the
general wealth enormously increased, and they have also
seen that, as wealth has increased, the fortunes of the
rich have grown larger, without its becoming a whit
easier to get a living by labor.

It is true that statistics may be arrayed in such way as
to prove to the satisfaction of those who wish to believe
it, that the condition of the working-classes is steadily
improving. But that this is not the fact working-men
well know. It is true that the average consumption has
increased, and that the cheapening of commodities has
brought into common use things that were once considered luxuries. It is also true that in many trades

wages have been somewhat raised and hours reduced by combinations among workmen. But although the prizes that are to be gained in the lottery of life—or, if any one prefers so to call them, the prizes that are to be gained by superior skill, energy and foresight—are constantly becoming greater and more glittering, the blanks grow more numerous. The man of superior powers and opportunities may hope to count his millions where a generation ago he could have hoped to count his tens of thousands; but to the ordinary man the chances of failure are greater, the fear of want more pressing. It is harder for the average man to become his own employer, to provide for a family and to guard against contingencies. The anxieties attendant on the fear of losing employment are becoming greater and greater, and the fate of him who falls from his place more direful. To prove this it is not necessary to cite the statistics that show how pauperism, crime, insanity and suicide are increasing faster than our increase in population. Who that reads our daily papers needs any proof that the increase in the aggregate of wealth does not mean increased ease of gaining a living by labor?

Here is an item which I take from the papers as I write. I do not take it because equally striking items are rare, but because I find a comment on it which I should also like to quote:

STARVED TO DEATH IN OHIO.

DAYTON, O., *August* 26.—One of the most horrible deaths that ever occurred in a civilized community was that of Frank Waltzman, which happened in this city yesterday morning. He has seven children and a wife, and was once a prominent citizen of Xenia, O. He tried his hand at any kind of business where he could find opportunity, and finally was compelled to shovel gravel to get a crust for his children. He worked at this all last week, and on Saturday night was brought home in a wagon, unable to walk. This morning he was dead. An investigation of the affair established the fact that the man had starved to death. The family had been without food for nearly two weeks. His wife tells a horrible story of his death, saying that while he lay dying his children surrounded his couch and sobbed piteously for bread.

And here is the typical comment which the *New York Tribune*, shocked for a moment out of its attempt to convince working-men that the tariff has improved their condition, makes upon this item:

STARVED TO DEATH.

The *Tribune*, Tuesday, laid before its readers a very sad story of death by literal starvation, at Dayton, O. The details of this case must have struck many thoughtful persons as more resembling the catastrophes we are accustomed to regard as appertaining to European life than those indigenous here. The story is old enough in general outline. First, a merchant, prospering; then decline of business, bankruptcy, and by degrees destitution, until pride and shame together brought on the culminating disaster. A few years ago it would have been said that such a fact was impossible in America, and certainly there was a time when no one with power and will to work need have starved in any part of this country. During that period, too, the strong elasticity and recuperative power of Americans were the world's wonder. No man thought much of failure in business. The demand for enterprise of all kinds was such that no man of ordinary pluck and energy could be kept down. Perhaps this ability to recover was not so much a national peculiarity as an effect of the existing state of society. Certainly, as things settle more and more into regular grooves in the older States, the parallel between American and European civilization becomes closer, and the social problems which perplex those societies are beginning to overshadow this one also. Competition in our centers of population narrows more and more the field of unmoneyed enterprise. It is no longer so easy for those who fall to rise again. And social conventions fetter men more and tend to hold them within narrower bounds.

The poor fellow who starved to death at Dayton the other day suffered an Old-World fate. He was down and could not get up.

He was deprived of his old resources and could not invent new ones. His large family increased his difficulties. He could not compete successfully with younger and less handicapped contemporaries, and so he sank, as thousands have done in the great capitals of Europe, but as hitherto very few, it is to be hoped, have sunk in an American community. Yet this is the tendency of a rapid increase of population and wealth. The struggle becomes fiercer all the time; and while the exactions of society enslave and hamper the ambitious increasingly, the average fertility of resource and swift adaptability decline, just as the average skill of workmen declines with the perfection of mechanical appliances. Commerce and the artificial requirements of social tyranny have already educated among us a class of people whose lives are a perpetual struggle and as perpetual an hypocrisy. They could live comfortably if they could give up display, but they cannot do it, and so they make themselves wretched and demoralize themselves at the same time. The sound, healthy American characteristics are being eliminated in this way, and we are rearing up instead a generation of feeble folks who may in turn become the parents of such hewers of wood and drawers of water as the Old-World city masses have long been. And here, as there, our remedy and regeneration must come from the more vigorous and better-trained products of the country life.

I will not ask how regeneration is to come from the more vigorous products of the country life, when every census shows a greater and greater proportion of our population concentrating in cities, and when country roads to the remotest borders are filled with tramps. I merely reprint this article as a sample of the recognition one meets everywhere, even on the part of those who formally deny it, of the obvious fact, that it is becoming harder and harder for the man who has nothing but his own exertions to depend on to get a living in the United States. This fact destroys the assumption that our protective tariff raises and maintains wages, but it also makes it impossible to assume that the abolition of protection would in any way alter the tendency which as wealth increases makes the struggle for existence harder and harder. This tendency shows itself throughout the civilized world, and arises from the more unequal distribution which everywhere accompanies the increase of wealth. How could the abolition of protection affect it? The worst that can, in this respect, be said of protection is that it somewhat accelerates this tendency. The best that could be promised for the abolition of protection is that it might somewhat restrain it. In England the same tendency has continued to manifest itself since the abolition of protection, despite the fact that in other ways great agencies for the relief and elevation of the masses have been at work. Increased emigration, the greater diffusion of education, the growth of trades-unions, sanitary improvements, the better organization of charity, and governmental regulation of labor and its conditions have during all these years directly tended to improve the condition of the working-class. Yet the depths of poverty are as dark as ever, and the contrast between want and wealth more glaring. The Corn-Law Reformers thought to make hunger impossible, but though the corn-laws have long since been abolished, starvation still figures in the mortuary statistics of a country overflowing with wealth.

While "statisticians" marshal figures to show to Dives's satisfaction how much richer Lazarus is becoming, here is what the Congregational clergymen of the greatest and richest of the world's great cities declare in their "Bitter Cry of Outcast London":

While we have been building our churches and solacing ourselves with our religion and dreaming that the millennium was coming, the poor have been growing poorer, the wretched more miserable and the immoral more corrupt. The gulf has been daily widening which separates the lowest classes of the community from our churches and chapels and from all decency and civilization. It is easy to bring an array of facts which seem to point to the opposite conclusion. But what does it all amount to? We are simply living in a fools' paradise if we imagine that all these agencies combined are doing a thousandth part of what needs to be done. We must face the facts, and these compel the conclusion that this terrible flood of sin and misery is gaining on us. It is rising every day.

This is everywhere the testimony of disinterested and sympathetic observers. Those who are raised above the fierce struggle may not realize what is going on beneath them. But whoever chooses to look may see.

And when we take into account longer periods of time than are usually considered in discussions as to whether the condition of the working-man has or has not improved with improvement in productive agencies and increase in wealth, here is a great broad fact:

Five centuries ago the wealth-producing power of England, man for man, was small indeed compared with what it is now. Not merely were all the great inventions and discoveries which since the introduction of steam have revolutionized mechanical industry then undreamed of, but even agriculture was far ruder and less productive. Artificial grasses had not been discovered. The potato, the carrot, the turnip, the beet, and many other plants and vegetables which the farmer now finds most prolific, had not been introduced. The advantages which ensue from rotation of crops were unknown. Agricultural implements consisted of the spade, the sickle, the flail, the rude plow and the harrow. Cattle had not been bred to more than one-half the size they average now, and sheep did not yield half the fleece. Roads, where there were roads, were extremely bad, wheel vehicles scarce and rude, and places a hundred miles from each other were, in difficulties of transportation, practically as far apart as London and Hong Kong, or San Francisco and New York, are now.

Yet patient students of those times—such men as Professor Thorold Rogers, who has devoted himself to the

history of prices, and has deciphered the records of colleges, manors and public offices—tell us that the condition
of the English laborer was not only relatively, but absolutely better in those rude times than it is in England
to-day, after five centuries of advance in the productive
arts.   They tell us that the working-man did not work so
hard as he does now, and lived better; that he was
exempt from the harassing dread of being forced by loss
of employment to want and beggary, or of leaving a
family that must apply to charity to avoid starvation.
Pauperism as it prevails in the rich England of the nine-
teenth century was in the far poorer England of the
fourteenth century, absolutely unknown.   Medicine was
empirical and superstitious, sanitary regulations and
precautions were all but unknown.   There was frequently plague and occasionally famine, for, owing to the
difficulties of transportation, the scarcity of one district
could not be relieved by the plenty of another.   But
men did not, as they do now, starve in the midst of
abundance; and what is perhaps the most significant
fact of all is that not only were women and children not
worked as they are to-day, but the eight-hour system,
which even the working-classes of the United States,
with all the profusion of labor-saving machinery and
appliances, have not yet attained, was then the common
system !

If this be the result of five centuries of such increase in
productive power as has never before been known in the
world, what ground is there for hoping that the mere
abolition of protective tariffs would permanently benefit
working-men ?

And not merely do facts of this kind prevent us from
assuming that the abolition of protection could more than
temporarily benefit working-men, but they suggest the

question, whether it could more than temporarily increase
the production of wealth?

Inequality in the distribution of wealth tends to lessen
the production of wealth—on the one side, by lessening
intelligence and incentive among workers; and, on the
other side, by augmenting the number of idlers and those
who minister to them, and by increasing vice, crime and
waste. Now, if increase in the production of wealth tends
to increase inequality in distribution, not only shall we be
mistaken in expecting its full effect from anything which
tends to increase production, but there may be a point at
which increased inequality of distribution will neutralize
increased power of production, just as the carrying of too
much sail may deaden a ship's way.

Trade is a labor-saving method of production, and the
effect of tariff restrictions upon trade is unquestionably to
diminish productive power. Yet, important as may be the
effects of protection in diminishing the production of
wealth, they are far less important than the waste of productive forces which is commonly attributed to the very
excess of productive power. The existence of protective
tariffs will not suffice to explain that paralysis of industrial forces which in all departments of industry seems to
arise from an excess of productive power, over the demand
for consumption, and which is everywhere leading to combinations to restrain production. And considering this,
can we feel quite sure that the effect of abolishing protection would be more than temporarily to increase the production of wealth?

CHAPTER XXIII.

THE REAL STRENGTH OF PROTECTION.

THE pleas for protection are contradictory and absurd ; the books in which it is attempted to give it the semblance of a coherent system are confused and illogical.*

But we all know that the reasons men give for their conduct or opinions are not always the true reasons, and that beneath the reasons we advance to others or set forth to ourselves there often lurks a feeling or perception which we may but vaguely apprehend or may even be unconscious of, but which is in reality the determining factor.

I have been at pains to examine the arguments by which

---

* The latest apology for protection, "Protection *vs.* Free Trade —the scientific validity and economic operation of defensive duties in the United States," by ex-Governor Henry M. Hoyt of Pennsylvania (New York, 1886), is hardly below the average in this respect, yet in the very preface the author discloses his equipment for economic investigation by talking of value as though it were a measure of quantity, and supposing the case of a farmer who has $3500 *worth* of produce *which he cannot sell or barter*. With this beginning it is hardly to be wondered at that the 420 pages of his work bring him to the conclusion, which he prints in italics, that "the nearer we come to organizing and conducting our competing industries as if we were the only nation on the planet, the more we shall make and the more we shall have to divide among the makers." An asteroid of about the superficial area of Pennsylvania would doubtless seem the most desirable of worlds to this protectionist statesman and philosopher.

242

protection is advocated or defended, and this has been necessary to our inquiry, just as it is necessary that an advancing army should first take the outworks before it can move on the citadel. Yet though these arguments are not merely used controversially, but justify their faith in protection to protectionists themselves, the real strength of protection must be sought elsewhere.

One needs but to talk with the rank and file of the supporters of protection in such a way as to discover their thoughts rather than their arguments, to see that beneath all the reasons assigned for protection there *is* something which gives it vitality, no matter how clearly those reasons may be disproved.

The truth is, that the fallacies of protection draw their real strength from a great fact, which is to them as the earth was to the fabled Antæus, so that they are beaten down only to spring up again. This fact is one which neither side in the controversy endeavors to explain— which free traders quietly ignore and protectionists quietly utilize; but which is of all social facts most obvious and important to the working-classes—the fact that as soon, at least, as a certain stage of social development is reached, there are more laborers seeking employment than can find it—a surplus which at recurring periods of industrial depression becomes very large. Thus the opportunity of work comes to be regarded as a privilege, and work itself to be deemed in common thought a good.*

---

* The getting of work, not the getting of the results of work, is assumed by protectionist writers to be the end at which a true national policy should aim, though for obvious reasons they do not dwell upon this notion. Thus, Professor Thompson says (p. 211, "Political Economy"):

"The [free-trade] theory assumes that the chief end of national as of individual economy is to save labor, whereas the great problem is how to employ it productively. If buying in the cheapest market

Here, and not in the labored arguments which its advocates make or in the power of the special interests which it enlists, lies the real strength of protection. Beneath all the mental habits I have spoken of as disposing men to accept the fallacies of protection lies one still more important—the habit ingrained in thought and speech of looking upon work as a boon.

Protection, as we have seen, operates to reduce the power of a community to obtain wealth—to lessen the result which a given amount of exertion can secure. It "makes more work," in the sense in which Pharaoh made more work for the Hebrew brickmakers when he refused them straw; in the sense in which the spilling of grease over her floor makes more work for the housewife, or the rain that wets his hay makes more work for the farmer.

Yet, when we prove this, what have we proved to men whose greatest anxiety is to get work; whose idea of good times is that of times when work is plentiful?

A rain that wets his hay is to the farmer clearly an injury; but is it an injury to the laborer who gets by reason of it a day's work and a day's pay that otherwise he would not have got?

The spilling of grease upon her kitchen floor may be a bad thing for the housewife; but to the scrubbing woman who is thereby enabled to earn a needed half-dollar it may be a godsend.

Or if the laborers on Pharaoh's public works had been like the laborers on modern public works, anxious only that the job might last, and if outside of them had been a mass of less fortunate laborers, pressing, struggling, beg-

---

reduce the *amount of employment,* it will be, for the nation that does it, the dearest of all buying." Or, again (p. 235): "The national economy of labor consists, not in getting on with as little as possible, but in finding remunerative employment for as much of it as possible."

ging for employment in the brick-yards—would the edict that, by reducing the productiveness of labor, made more work have really been unpopular?

Let us go back to Robinson Crusoe. In speaking of him I purposely left out Friday. Our protectionist might have talked until he was tired without convincing Crusoe that the more he got and the less he gave in his exchange with passing ships the worse off he would be. But if he had taken Friday aside, recalled to his mind how Crusoe had sold Xury into slavery as soon as he had no further use for him, even though the poor boy had helped him escape from the Moors and had saved his life, and then had whispered into Friday's ear that the less work there was to do the less need would Crusoe have of him and the greater the danger that he might give him back to the cannibals, now that he was certain to have more congenial companions—would the idea that there might be danger in a deluge of cheap goods have seemed so ridiculous to Friday as it did to Crusoe?

Those who imagine that they can overcome the popular leaning to protection by pointing out that protective tariffs make necessary more work to obtain the same result, ignore the fact that in all civilized countries that have reached a certain stage of development the majority of the people are unable to employ themselves, and, unless they find some one to give them work, are helpless, and, hence, are accustomed to regard work as a thing to be desired in itself, and anything which makes more work as a benefit, not an injury.

Here is the rock against which "free traders" whose ideas of reform go no further than "a tariff for revenue only" waste their strength when they demonstrate that the effect of protection is to increase work without increasing wealth. And here is the reason why, as we have seen in the United States, in Canada and in Australia, the disposition to resort to protective tariffs increases as that early stage in which there is no difficulty of finding employment is passed, and the social phenomena of older countries begin to appear.*

There never yet lived a man who wanted work for its own sake. Even the employments, constructive or destructive, as may be, in which we engage to exercise our faculties or to dissipate *ennui*, must to please us show result. It is not the mere work of felling trees that tempts Mr. Gladstone to take up his ax as a relief from the cares of state and the strain of politics. He could get as much work—in the sense of exertion—from pounding a sand-bag with

---

* The growth of the protective spirit as social development goes on, which has been very obvious in the United States, is generally attributed to the influence of the manufacturing interests which begin to arise. But observation has convinced me that this cause is inadequate, and that the true explanation lies in habits of thought engendered by the greater difficulties of finding employment. I am satisfied, for instance, that protection is far stronger in California than it was in the earlier days of that State. But the Californian industries that can be protected by a national tariff are yet insignificant as compared with industries that cannot be protected. But when tramps abound and charity is invoked for relief works, one need not go far to find an explanation of the growth of a sentiment which favors the policy of "keeping work in the country." Nothing can be clearer than that our protective tariff adds largely to the cost of nearly everything that the American farmer has to buy, while adding little, if anything, to the price of what he has to sell, and it has been a favorite theory with those who since the war have been endeavoring to arouse sentiment against protection that the attention of the agricultural classes only needed to be called to this to bring out an overwhelming opposition to protective duties. But with all the admirable work that has been done in this direction, it is hard to see any result. The truth is, as may be discovered by talking with farmers, that the average farmer feels that "there are already too many people in farming," and hence is not ill disposed toward a policy which, though it may increase the prices he has to pay, claims to "make work" in other branches of industry.

a wooden mallet. But he could no more derive pleasure from this than the man who enjoys a brisk walk could find like enjoyment in tramping a treadmill. The pleasure is in the sense of accomplishment that accompanies the work —in seeing the chips fly and the great tree bend and fall.

The natural inducement to the work by which human wants are supplied is the produce of that work. But our industrial organization is such that what large numbers of men expect to get by work is not the produce or any proportional share of the produce of their work, but a fixed sum which is paid to them by those who take for their own uses the produce of their work. This sum takes to them the place of the natural inducement to work, and to obtain it becomes the object of their work.

Now the very fact that without compulsion no one will work unless he can get something for it, causes, in common thought, the idea of wages to become involved in the idea of work, and leads men to think and speak of wanting work when what they really want are the wages that are to be got by work. But the fact that these wages are based upon the doing of work, not upon its productiveness, dissociates the idea of return to the laborer from the idea of the actual productiveness of his labor, throwing this latter idea into the background or eliminating it altogether.

In our modern civilization the masses of men possess only the power to labor. It is true that labor is the producer of all wealth, in the sense of being the active factor of production; but it is useless without the no less necessary passive factor. With nothing to exert itself upon, labor can produce nothing, and is absolutely helpless. And so, the men who have nothing but the power to labor must, to make that power of any use to them, either hire the material necessary to the exertion of labor, or, as is the prevailing method in our industrial organization, sell their labor to those who have the material. Thus it comes that the majority of men must find some one who will set them to work and pay them wages, he keeping as his own what their expenditure of labor produces.

We have seen how in the exchange of commodities through the medium of money the idea arises, almost insensibly, that the buyer confers an obligation upon the seller. But this idea attaches to the buying and selling of labor with greater clearness and far greater force than to the buying and selling of commodities. There are several reasons for this. Labor will not keep. The man who does not sell a commodity to-day may sell it to-morrow. At any rate he retains the commodity. But the labor of the man who has stood idle to-day because no one would hire him cannot be sold to-morrow. The opportunity has gone from the man himself, and the labor that he might have exerted, had he found a buyer for it, is utterly lost. The men who have nothing but their labor are, moreover, the poorest class—the class who live from hand to mouth and who are least able to bear loss. Further than this, the sellers of labor are numerous as compared with buyers. All men in health have the power of labor, but under the conditions which prevail in modern civilization only a comparatively few have the means of employing labor, and there are always, even in the best of times, some men who find it difficult to sell their labor and who are thus exposed to privation and anxiety, if not to physical suffering.

Hence arises the feeling that the man who employs another to work is a benefactor to him—a feeling which even the economists who have made war upon some of the popular delusions growing out of it have done their best to foster, by teaching that capital employs and maintains labor. This feeling runs through all classes, and colors all our thought and speech. One cannot read our newspapers without seeing that the notice of a new building or projected enterprise of any kind usually concludes by stating that it will give employment to so many men, as though the giving of employment, the providing of work, were the measure of its public advantage, and something for which all should be grateful. This feeling, strong among employed, is stronger still among employers. The rich manufacturer, or iron-worker, or ship-builder, talks and thinks of the men to whom he has "given employment" as though he had actually given something which entitled him to their gratitude, and he is inclined to think, and in most cases does think, that in combining to demand higher wages or less hours, or in any way endeavoring to put themselves in the position of freely contracting parties, they are snapping at the hand that has fed them, although the obvious fact is that such an employer's men have given him a greater value than he has given them, else he could not have grown rich by employing them.

This habit of looking on the giving of employment as a benefaction and on work as a boon, lends easy currency to teachings which assume that work is desirable in itself —something which each nation ought to try to get the most of—and makes a system which professes to prevent other countries from doing for us work we might do for ourselves seem like a system for the enrichment of our own country and the benefit of its working-classes. It not only indisposes men to grasp the truth that protection can operate only to reduce the productiveness of labor; but it indisposes them to care anything about that. It is the need for labor, not the productiveness of labor, that they are accustomed to look upon as the thing to be desired.

So confirmed is this habit, that nothing is more common than to hear it said of a useless construction or expenditure that "it has done no good, except to provide employment," while the most popular argument for the eight-hour system is that machinery has so reduced the amount of work to be done that there is not now enough to go around unless divided into smaller "takes."

When men are thus accustomed to think and speak of work as desirable in itself, is it any wonder that a system which proposes to "make work" should easily obtain popularity?

Protectionism viewed in itself *is* absurd. But it is no more absurd than many other popular beliefs. Professor W. G. Sumner of Yale College, a fair representative of the so-called free traders who have been vainly trying to weaken the hold of protectionism in the United States without disturbing its root, essayed, before the United States Tariff Commission in 1882, to bring protectionism to a *reductio ad absurdum* by declaring that the protectionist theory involved such propositions as these : that a big standing army would tend to raise wages by withdrawing men from competition in the labor-market; that paupers in almshouses and convicts in prisons ought for the same reason to be maintained without labor; that it is better for the laboring-class that rich people should live in idleness than that they should work; that trades-unions should prevent their members from lessening the supply of work by doing too much; and that the destruction of property in riots must be a good thing for the laboring-class, by increasing the work to be done.

But whoever will listen to the ordinary talk of men and read the daily newspapers, will find that, so far from such notions seeming absurd to the common mind, they are accustomed ideas. Is it not true that the "good times during the war" are widely attributed to the "employment furnished by government" in calling so many men into the army, and to the brisk demand for commodities caused by their unproductive consumption and by actual destruction? Is it not true that all over the United States the working-classes are protesting against the employment of convicts

in this, that or the other way, and would much rather have
them kept in idleness than have them "take work from
honest men"?   Is it not true that the rich man who "gives
employment" to others by his lavish waste is universally
regarded as a better friend to the workers than the rich
man who "takes work from those who need it" by doing
it himself?

In themselves these notions may be what the Professor
declares them, "miserable fallacies which sin against common sense," but they arise from the recognition of actual
facts.   Take the most preposterous of them.   The burning
down of a city is indeed a lessening of the aggregate
wealth.   But is the waste involved in the burning down
of a city any more real than the waste involved in the
standing idle of men who would gladly be at work in
building up a city?   Where every one who needed to work
could find opportunity, there it would indeed be clear that
the maintenance in idleness of convicts, paupers or rich
men must lessen the rewards of workers; but where hundreds of thousands must endure privation because of their
inability to find work, the doing of work by those who can
support themselves, or will be supported without it, seems
like taking the opportunity to work from those who most
need or most deserve it.   Such "miserable fallacies" must
continue to sway men's minds until some satisfactory explanation is afforded of the facts that make the "leave to
toil" a boon.   To attempt, as do "free traders" of Professor Sumner's class, to eradicate protectionist ideas while
ignoring these facts, is utterly hopeless.   What they take
for a seedling that may be pulled up with a vigorous effort,
is in reality the shoot of a tree whose spreading roots reach
to the bed-rock of society.   A political economy that will
recognize no deeper social wrong than the framing of
tariffs on a protective instead of on a revenue basis, and
that, with such trivial exceptions, is but a justification of

"things as they are," is repellent to the instincts of the masses. To tell working-men, as Professor Sumner does, that "trades-unionism and protectionism are falsehoods," is simply to dispose them to protectionism, for whatever may be said of protection they well know that trades-unions have raised wages in many vocations, and that they are the only things that have yet given the working-classes any power of resisting a strain of competition that, unchecked, must force them to the maximum of toil for the minimum of pay. Such free-tradeism as Professor Sumner represents—and it is this that is taught in England, and that in the United States has essayed to do battle with protectionism—must, wherever the working-classes have political power, give to protection positive strength.

But it is not merely by indirection that what is known as the "orthodox political economy" strengthens protection. While condemning protective tariffs it has justified revenue tariffs, and its most important teachings have not merely barred the way to such an explanation of social phenomena as would cut the ground from under protectionism, but have been directly calculated to strengthen the beliefs which render protection plausible. The teaching that labor depends for employment upon capital, and that wages are drawn from capital and are determined by the ratio between the number of laborers and the amount of capital devoted to their employment;—all the teachings, in short, which have degraded labor to the position of a secondary and dependent factor in production, have tended to sanction that view of things which disposes the laboring-class to look with favor upon anything which, by preventing the coming into a country of the produce of other countries, seems, at least, to increase the requirement for work at home.

CHAPTER XXIV.

THE PARADOX.

IF our investigation has as yet led to no satisfactory conclusion it has at least explained why the controversy so long carried on between protectionists and free traders has been so indeterminate. The paradox we have reached is one toward which all the social problems of our day converge, and had our examination been of any similar question it must have come to just such a point.

Take, for instance, the question of the effects of machinery. The opinion that finds most influential expression is that labor-saving invention, although it may sometimes cause temporary inconvenience or even hardship to a few, is ultimately beneficial to all. On the other hand, there is among working-men a wide-spread belief that labor-saving machinery is injurious to them, although, since the belief does not enlist those powerful special interests that are concerned in the advocacy of protection, it has not been wrought into an elaborate system and does not get anything like the same representation in the organs of public opinion.

Now, should we subject this question to such an examination as we have given to the tariff question we should reach similar results. We should find the notion that invention ought to be restrained as incongruous as the notion that trade ought to be restrained—as incapable of

being carried to its logical conclusions without resulting
in absurdity.   And while the use of machinery enormously
increases the production of wealth, examination would
show in it nothing to cause inequality in distribution.
On the contrary, we should see that the increased power
given by invention inures primarily to labor, and that this
gain is so diffused by exchange that the effect of an
improvement which increases the power of labor in one
branch of industry must be shared by labor in all other
branches.   Thus the direct tendency of labor-saving
improvement is to augment the earnings of labor.   Nor is
this tendency neutralized by the fact that labor-saving
inventions generally require the use of capital, since competition, when free to act, must at length bring the profits of
capital used in this way to the common level.   Even the
monopoly of a labor-saving invention, while it can seldom
be maintained for any length of time, cannot prevent a
large (and generally much the largest) part of the benefits
from being diffused.*

From this we might conclude with certainty, that the
tendency of labor-saving improvements is to benefit all,
and especially to benefit the working-class, and hence
might naturally attribute any distrust of their beneficial
effects partly to the temporary displacements which, in
a highly organized society, any change in the forms of
industry must cause, and partly to the increased wants
called forth by the increased ability to satisfy want.

Yet, while as a matter of theory it is clear that labor-
saving inventions ought to improve the condition of all;
as a matter of fact it is equally clear that they do not.

In countries like Great Britain there is still a large
class living on the verge of starvation, and constantly

---

* For a fuller examination of the effects of machinery see my
"Social Problems."

slipping over it—a class who have not derived the slightest benefit from the immense increase of productive
power, since their condition never could have been any
worse than it is—a class whose habitual condition in
times of peace and plenty is lower, harder, more precarious and more degraded than that of any savages.

In countries like the United States, where such a class
did not previously exist, its development has been contemporaneous with wondrous advances of labor-saving
invention.   The laws against tramps which have been
placed upon the statute-books of our States, the restrictions upon child labor which have been found necessary,
the walking advertisements of our cities, the growing
bitterness of the strife which working-men are forced to
wage, indicate unmistakably that while discovery and
invention have been steadily increasing the productive
power of labor in every department of industry, the condition of the mere laborer has been growing worse.

It can be proved that labor-saving invention tends to
benefit labor, but that this tendency is in some way
aborted is even more clearly evident in the facts of
to-day than it was when John Stuart Mill questioned if
mechanical invention had lightened the day's toil of any
human being.   That in some places and in some occupations there has been improvement in the condition of
labor is true.   But not only is such improvement
nowhere commensurate with the increase of productive
power; it is clearly not due to it.   It exists only where it
has been won by combinations of workmen or by legal
interference.   It is trades-unions, not the increased power
given by machinery, that have in many occupations in
Great Britain reduced hours and increased pay; it is
legislation, not any improvement in the general condition of labor, that has stopped the harnessing of women
in mines and the working of little children in mills and

brick-yards. Where such influences have not been felt, it is not only certain that labor-saving inventions have not improved the condition of labor, but it seems as if they had exerted a depressing effect—operating to make labor a drug instead of to make it more valuable.

Thus, in relation to the effects of machinery, as in relation to the effects of tariffs, there are two sides to the shield. Conclusions to which we are led by a consideration of principles are contradicted by conclusions we are compelled to draw from existing facts. But, while discussion may go on interminably between those who, looking only at one side of the shield, refuse to consider what their opponents see, yet to recognize the contradictory aspects of such a question is to realize the possibility of an explanation that will include both.

The problem we must solve to explain why free trade or labor-saving invention or any similar cause fails to produce the general benefits we naturally expect, is a problem of the distribution of wealth. When increased production of wealth does not proportionately benefit the working-classes, it must be that it is accompanied by increased inequality of distribution.

In themselves free trade and labor-saving inventions do not tend to inequality of distribution. Yet it is possible that they may promote such inequality, not by virtue of anything inherent in their tendencies, but through their effect in increasing production, for, as already pointed out, increase or decrease in the production of wealth may of itself, under certain circumstances, alter the proportions of distribution. Let me illustrate :

Smith, a plumber, and Jones, a gas-fitter, form a partnership in the usual way, and go into the business of plumbing and gas-fitting. In this case whatever increases or decreases the profits of the firm will affect the partners equally, and whether these profits be much or little, the proportion which each takes will be the same.

But let us suppose their agreement to be of a kind occasionally made, that the plumber shall have two-thirds of the profits on all plumbing done by the firm, and the gas-fitter two-thirds of the profits on all gas-fitting. In such case, every job they do will not only increase or decrease the profits of the firm, but, according as it is a job of plumbing or of gas-fitting, will directly affect the distribution of profits between the partners.

Or, again, let us suppose that the partners differ in their ability to take risks. Smith has a family and must have a steady income, while Jones is a bachelor who could get along for some time without drawing from the firm. Better to assure Smith of a living, it is agreed that he shall draw a fixed sum before any profits are distributed, and, in return for this guaranty, shall get only a quarter of the profits remaining. In such a case, increase or decrease of profits would of itself alter the proportions of distribution. Increase of profits would affect distribution in favor of Jones, and might go so far as to raise his share to nearly 75 per cent. and reduce the share of Smith to little over 25 per cent. Decrease of profits on the other hand would affect distribution in favor of Smith, and might go so far as to give him 100 per cent., while reducing Jones's share to nothing. In such a case as this, any circumstance which affected the amount of profits would affect the terms of distribution, but not by virtue of anything peculiar to the circumstance. Its real cause would be something external to, and unconnected with, such circumstance.

The social phenomena we have to explain resemble those presented in this last case. The increased inequality of distribution which accompanies material progress is evidently connected with the increased production of wealth, and does not arise from any direct effect of the causes which increase wealth.

Our illustration, however, yet lacks something. In the case we have supposed, increase of their joint profits would benefit both partners, though in different degrees. Even when Smith's share diminished in proportion, it would increase in amount. But in the social phenomena we are considering, it is not merely that with increasing wealth the share that some classes obtain is not increased proportionately; it is that it is not increased absolutely, and that in some cases it is even absolutely, as well as proportionately, diminished.

To get an illustration that will cover this point as well, let us therefore take another case. Let us go back to Robinson Crusoe's island, which may well serve us as an example of society in its simplest and therefore most intelligible form.

The discovery of the island which we have heretofore supposed, involving calls by other ships, would greatly increase the wealth which the labor of its population of two could obtain. But it would not follow that in the increased wealth both would gain. Friday was Crusoe's slave, and no matter how much the opening of trade with the rest of the world might increase wealth, he could demand only the wages of a slave—enough to maintain him in working ability. So long as Crusoe himself lived he would doubtless take good care of the companion of his solitude, but when in the course of time the island had fully come into the circle of civilized life, and had passed into the possession of some heir of Crusoe's, or of some purchaser, living probably in England, and was cultivated with a view to making it yield the largest income, the gulf between the proprietor who owned it and the slave who worked upon it would not merely have enormously widened as compared with the time when

Crusoe and Friday shared with substantial equality the joint produce of their labor, but the share of the slave might have become absolutely less, and his condition lower and harder.

It is not necessary to suppose positive cruelty or wanton harshness. The slaves who in the new order of things took Friday's place might have all their animal wants supplied—they migh: have as much to eat as Friday had, might wear better clothes, be lodged in better houses, be exempt from the fear of cannibals, and in illness have the attendance of a skilled physician. And seeing this, island "statisticians" might collate figures or devise diagrams to show how much better off these toilers were than their predecessor, who wore goatskins, slept in a cave and lived in constant dread of being eaten, and the conclusions of these gentlemen might be paraded in all the island newspapers, with a chorus of: "Behold, in figures that cannot lie and diagrams that can be measured, how industrial progress benefits everybody, even the slave!"

But in things of which the statistician takes no account they would be worse off than Friday. Compelled to a round of dreary toil, unlightened by variety, undignified by responsibility, unstimulated by seeing results and partaking of them, their life, as compared with that of Friday, would be less that of men and more that of machines.

And the effect of such changes would be the same upon laborers such as we call free—free, that is to say, to use their own power to labor, but not free to that which is necessary to its use. If Friday, instead of setting Crusoe's foot upon his head, in token that he was thenceforward his slave, had simply acknowledged Crusoe's ownership of the island, what would have been the difference? As he could live upon Crusoe's property only on Crusoe's terms, his freedom would simply have amounted to the freedom to emigrate, to drown himself in the sea, or to give himself up to the cannibals. Men enjoying only such freedom—that is to say, the freedom to starve or emigrate as the alternative of getting some one else's permission to labor—cannot be enriched by improvements that increase the production of wealth. For they have no more power to claim any share of it than has the slave. Those who want them to work must give them what the master must give the slave if he wants him to work—enough to support life and strength; but when they can find no one who wants them to work they must starve, if they cannot beg. Grant to Crusoe ownership of the island, and Friday, the free man, would be as much subject to his will as Friday, the slave; as incapable of claiming any share of an increased production of wealth, no matter how great it might be nor from what cause it might come.

And what would be true in the case of one man would be true of any number. Suppose ten thousand Fridays, all free men, all absolute owners of themselves, and but one Crusoe, the absolute owner of the island. So long as his ownership was acknowledged and could be enforced, would not the one be the master of the ten thousand as fully as though he were the legal owner of their flesh and blood? Since no one could use *his* island without his consent, it would follow that no one could labor, or even live, without his permission. The order, "Leave my property," would be a sentence of death. This owner of the island would be to the other ten thousand "free men" who lived upon it, their land lord or land god, of whom they would stand in more real awe than of any deity that their religion taught them reigned above. For as a Scottish landlord told his tenants: "God Almighty may have made the land, but I own it. And if you don't do as I say, off you go!"

No increase of wealth could enable such "free" laborers to claim more than a bare living. The opening up of foreign trade, the invention of labor-saving machines, the discovery of mineral deposits, the introduction of more prolific plants, the growth of skill, would simply increase the amount their land lord would charge for the privilege of living on his island, and could in no wise increase what those who had nothing but their labor could demand. If Heaven itself rained down wealth upon the island that wealth would be his. And so, too, any economy that might enable these mere laborers to live more cheaply would simply increase the tribute that they could pay and that he could exact.

Of course, no man could utilize a power like this to its full extent or for himself alone. A single landlord in the midst of ten thousand poor tenants, like a single master amid ten thousand slaves, would be as lonely as was Robinson Crusoe before Friday came. The human being is by nature a social animal, and no matter how selfish such a man might be, he would desire companions nearer his own condition. Natural impulse would prompt him to reward those who pleased him, prudence would urge him to interest the more influential among his ten thousand Fridays in the maintenance of his ownership, while experience would show him, if calculation did not, that a larger income could be obtained by leaving to superior energy, skill and thrift some part of what their efforts secured. But while the single owner of such an island would thus be induced to share his privileges by means of grants, leases, exemptions or stipends, with a class more or less numerous, who would thus partake with him in the advantages of any improvement that increased the power of producing wealth, there would yet remain a class, the mere laborers of only ordinary ability, to whom such improvement could bring no benefit. And it would only be necessary to be a little chary in granting permission to work upon the island, so as to keep a small percentage of the population constantly on the verge of starvation and begging to be permitted to use their power to labor, to create a competition in which, bidding against each other, men would of themselves offer all that their labor could procure save a bare living, for the privilege of getting that.

We can sometimes see principles all the clearer if we imagine them brought out under circumstances to which we are not habituated; but, as a matter of fact, the social adjustment which in modern civilization creates a class who can neither labor nor live save by permission of others, never could have arisen in this way.

The reader of "The Further Adventures of Robinson Crusoe," as related by De Foe, will remember that during Crusoe's long absence, the three English rogues, led by Will Atkins, set up a claim to the ownership of the island, declaring that it had been given to them by Robinson Crusoe, and demanding that the rest of the inhabitants should work for them by way of rent. Though used in their own countries to the acknowledgment of just such claims, set up in the name of men gone, not to other lands, but to another world, the Spaniards, as well as the peaceable Englishmen, laughed at this demand, and, when it was insisted on, laid Will Atkins and his companions by the heels until they had got over the notion that other people should do their work for them. But if the three English rogues had got possession of all the firearms before asserting their claim to own the island, the rest of its population might have been compelled to acknowledge it. Thus a class of landowners and a class of non-landowners would have been established, to which arrangement the whole population might in a few generations have become so habituated as to think it the natural order, and when they had begun, in course of time, to colonize other islands, they would have established the same institution there. Now, what might thus have happened on Crusoe's island, had the three English rogues got possession of all the fire-arms, is precisely what on a larger scale, did happen in the development of European civilization, and what is happening in its extension to other parts of the world. Thus it is that we find in civilized countries a large class who, while they have power to labor, are denied any right to the use of the elements necessary to make that power available, and who, to obtain the use of those elements, must either give up in rent a part of the prod-uce of their labor, or take in wages less than their labor yields. A class thus helpless can gain nothing from advance in productive power. Where such a class exists, increase in the general wealth can only mean increased inequality in distribution. And though this tendency may be a little checked as to some of them by trades-unions or similar combinations which artificially lessen competition, it will operate to the full upon those outside of such combinations.

And, let me repeat it, this increased inequality in dis-tribution does not mean merely that the mass of those who have nothing but the power to labor do not propor-tionately share in the increase of wealth. It means that their condition must become absolutely, as well as relatively, worse. It is in the nature of industrial advance—it is of the very essence of those prodigious forces which modern invention and discovery are unloos-ing, that they must injure where they do not benefit. These forces are not in themselves either good or evil. They bring good or evil according to the conditions under which they are exerted. In a state of society in which all men stood upon an equality with relation to the

use of the material universe their effects could be only
beneficent. But in a state of society in which some men
are held to be the absolute owners of the material universe, while other men cannot use it without paying
tribute, the blessing these forces might bring is changed
into a curse—their tendency is to destroy independence,
to dispense with skill and convert the artisan into a
"hand," to concentrate all business and make it harder
for an employee to become his own employer, and to
compel women and children to injurious and stunting
toil. The change industrial progress is now working in
the conditions of the mere laborer, and which is only
somewhat held in check by the operations of trades-
unions, is that change which would convert a slave who
shared the varied occupations and rude comforts of his
goatskin-clothed master into a slave held as a mere
instrument of factory production. Compare the skilled
craftsman of the old order with the operative of the new
order, the mere feeder of a machine. Compare the
American farm "help" of an earlier state, the social
equal of his employer, with the cow-boy, whose dreary
life is enlivened only by a "round-up" or "drunk," or
with the harvest hand of the "wheat factory," who sleeps
in barracks or barns, and after a few months of employment goes on a tramp. Or compare the poverty of
Connemara or Skye with the infinitely more degraded
poverty of Belfast or Glasgow. Do this, and then say
if to those who can hope to sell their labor only for a
subsistence, our very industrial progress has not a dark
side.

And that this *must* be the tendency of labor-saving
invention or reform in a society where the planet is held
to be private property, and the children that come into
life upon it are denied all right to its use except as they
buy or inherit the title of some dead man, we may see

plainly if we imagine labor-saving invention carried to its furthest imaginable extent. When we consider that the object of work is to satisfy want, the idea that labor-saving invention can ever cause want by making work more productive seems preposterous. Yet, could invention go so far as to make it possible to produce wealth without labor, what would be the effect upon a class who can call nothing their own, save the power to labor, and who, let wealth be never so abundant, can get no share of it except by selling this power? Would it not be to reduce to naught the value of what this class have to sell; to make them paupers in the midst of all possible wealth—to deprive them of the means of earning even a poor livelihood, and to compel them to beg or starve, if they could not steal? Such a point it may be impossible for invention ever to reach, but it is a point toward which modern invention drives. And is there not in this some explanation of the vast army of tramps and paupers, and of deaths by want and starvation in the very midst of plenty?

The abolition of protection would tend to increase the production of wealth—that is sure. But under conditions that exist, increase in the production of wealth may itself become a curse—first to the laboring-class, and ultimately to society at large.

Is it not true, then, it may be asked, that protection, for the reason at least that it does check that freedom and extension of trade which are essential to the full play of modern industrial tendencies, is favorable to the working-classes? Much of the strength of protection among working-men comes, I think, from vague feelings of this kind.

My reply would be negative. Not only has protection —which is merely the protection of producing capitalists against foreign competition in the home market—tendencies in itself toward monopoly and inequality, but it is impotent to check the concentrating tendencies of modern inventions and processes. To do this by " protection" we must not only forbid foreign commerce, but restrain internal commerce. We must not only prohibit any new applications of labor-saving invention, but must prevent the use of the most important of those already adopted. We must tear up the railway and go back to the canal-boat and freight-wagon; cut down the telegraph-wire and rely upon the post-horse; substitute the scythe for the reaper, the needle for the sewing-machine, the hand-loom for the factory; in short, discard all that a century of invention has given us, and return to the industrial processes of a hundred years ago. This is as impossible as for the chicken to go back to the egg. A man may become decrepit and childish, but once manhood is reached he cannot again become a child.

No; it is not in going backward, it is in going forward, that the hope of social improvement lies.

CHAPTER XXV.

THE ROBBER THAT TAKES ALL THAT IS LEFT.

IN itself the abolition of protection is like the driving off of a robber.

But it will not help a man to drive off one robber, if another, still stronger and more rapacious, be left to plunder him.

Labor may be likened to a man who as he carries home his earnings is waylaid by a series of robbers. One demands this much, and another that much, but last of all stands one who demands all that is left, save just enough to enable the victim to maintain life and come forth next day to work. So long as this last robber remains, what will it benefit such a man to drive off any or all of the other robbers?

Such is the situation of labor to-day throughout the civilized world. And the robber that takes all that is left, is private property in land. Improvement, no matter how great, and reform, no matter how beneficial in itself, cannot help that class who, deprived of all right to the use of the material elements, have only the power to labor—a power as useless in itself as a sail without wind, a pump without water, or a saddle without a horse.

I have likened labor to a man beset by a series of robbers, because there are in every country other things than private property in land which tend to diminish

267

national prosperity and divert the wealth earned by labor into the hands of non-producers.　This is the tendency of monopoly of the processes and machinery of production and exchange, the tendency of protective tariffs, of bad systems of currency and finance, of corrupt government, of public debts, of standing armies, and of wars and preparations for war.　But these things, some of which are conspicuous in one country and some in another, cannot account for that impoverishment of labor which is to be seen everywhere.　They are the lesser robbers, and to drive them off is only to leave more for the great robber to take.

If the all-sufficient cause of the impoverishment of labor were abolished, then reform in any of these directions would improve the condition of labor; but so long as that cause exists, no reform can effect any permanent improvement.　Public debts might be abolished, standing armies disbanded, war and the thought of war forgotten, protective tariffs everywhere discarded, government administered with the greatest purity and economy, and all monopolies, save the monopoly of land, destroyed, without any permanent improvement in the condition of the laboring-class.　For the economic effect of all these reforms would simply be to diminish the waste or increase the production of wealth, and so long as competition for employment on the part of men who are powerless to employ themselves tends steadily to force wages to the minimum that gives the laborer but a bare living, this is all the ordinary laborer can get.　So long as this tendency exists—and it must continue to exist so long as private property in land exists—improvement (even if possible) in the personal qualities of the laboring masses, such as improvement in skill, in intelligence, in temperance or in thrift, cannot improve their material condition.　Improvement of this kind can benefit the

individual only while it is confined to the individual, and
thus gives him an advantage over the body of ordinary
laborers whose wages form the regulative basis of all
other wages.   If such personal improvements become
general the effect can only be to enable competition to
force wages to a lower level.   Where few can read and
write, the ability to do so confers a special advantage
and raises the individual who possesses it above the level
of ordinary labor, enabling him to command the wages
of special skill.   But where all can read and write, the
mere possession of this ability cannot save ordinary
laborers from being forced to as low a position as though
they could not read and write.

And so, where thriftlessness or intemperance prevails,
the thrifty or temperate have a special advantage which
may raise them above the conditions of ordinary labor;
but should these virtues become general that advantage
would cease.   Let the great body of working-men so
reform or so degrade their habits that it would become
possible to live on one-half the lowest wages now paid,
and that competition for employment which drives men
to work for a bare living must proportionately reduce
the level of wages.

I do not say that reforms that increase the intelligence
or improve the habits of the masses are even in this view
useless.   The diffusion of intelligence tends to make men
discontented with a life of poverty in the midst of wealth,
and the diminution of intemperance better fits them to
revolt against such a lot.   Public schools and temperance
societies are thus prerevolutionary agencies.   But they
can never abolish poverty so long as land continues to
be treated as private property.   The worthy people who
imagine that compulsory education or the prohibition of
the drink traffic can abolish poverty are making the
same mistake that the Anti-Corn-Law reformers made

when they imagined that the abolition of protection would make hunger impossible. Such reforms are in their own nature good and beneficial, but in a world like this, tenanted by beings like ourselves, and treated by them as the exclusive property of a part of their number, there must, under any conceivable conditions, be a class on the verge of starvation.

This necessity inheres in the nature of things; it arises from the relation between man and the external universe. Land is the superficies of the globe—that bottom of the ocean of air to which our physical structure confines us. It is our only possible standing-place, our only possible workshop, the only reservoir from which we can draw material for the supply of our needs. Considering land in its narrow sense, as distinguished from water and air, it is still the element necessary to our use of the other elements. Without land man could not even avail himself of the light and heat of the sun or utilize the forces that pulse through matter. And whatever be his essence, man, in his physical constitution, is but a changing form of matter, a passing mode of motion, constantly drawn from nature's reservoirs and as constantly returning to them again. In physical structure and powers he is related to land as the fountain-jet is related to the stream, or the flame of a gas-burner to the gas that feeds it.

Hence, let other conditions be what they may, the man who, if he lives and works at all, must live and work on land belonging to another, is necessarily a slave or a pauper.

There are two forms of slavery—that which Friday accepted when he placed Crusoe's foot upon his head, and that which Will Atkins and his comrades attempted to establish when they set up a claim to the ownership of the island and called on its other inhabitants to do all the work. The one, which consists in making property of man, is resorted to only when population is too sparse to make practicable the other, which consists in making property of land.

For while population is sparse and unoccupied land is plenty, laborers are able to escape the necessity of buying the use of land, or can obtain it on nominal terms. Hence to obtain slaves—people who will work for you without your working for them in return—it is necessary to make property of their bodies or to resort to predial slavery or serfdom, which is an artificial anticipation of the power that comes to the landowner with denser population, and which consists in confining laborers to land on which it is desired to utilize their labor. But as population becomes denser and land more fully occupied, the competition of non-landowners for the use of land obviates the necessity of making property of their bodies or of confining them to an estate in order to obtain their labor without return. They themselves will beg the privilege of giving their labor in return for being permitted what must be yielded to the slave—a spot to live on and enough of the produce of their own labor to maintain life.

This, for the owner, is much the more convenient form of slavery. He does not have to worry about his slaves —is not at the trouble of whipping them to make them work, or chaining them to prevent their escape, or chasing them with bloodhounds when they run away. He is not concerned with seeing that they are properly fed in infancy, cared for in sickness or supported in old age. He can let them live in hovels, let them work harder and fare worse, than could any half-humane owner of the bodies of men, and this without a qualm of conscience or any reprobation from public opinion. In short, when society reaches the point of development where a brisk

competition for the use of land springs up, the ownership of land gives more profit with less risk and trouble
than does the ownership of men. If the two young Englishmen I have spoken of had come over here and bought
so many American citizens, they could not have got from
them so much of the produce of labor as they now get by
having bought land which American citizens are glad to
be allowed to till for half the crop. And so, even if our
laws permitted, it would be foolish for an English duke
or marquis to come over here and contract for ten thousand American babies, born or to be born, in the expectation that when able to work he could get out of them
a large return. For by purchasing or fencing in a
million acres of land that cannot run away and do not
need to be fed, clothed or educated, he can, in twenty or
thirty years, have ten thousand full-grown Americans,
ready to give him half of all that their labor can produce
on his land for the privilege of supporting themselves and
their families out of the other half. This gives him
more of the produce of labor than he could exact from
so many chattel slaves. And as time goes on and American citizens become more plentiful, the ownership of this
land will enable him to get more of them to work for
him, and on lower terms. His speculation in land is as
much a speculation in the growth of men as though he
had bought children and contracted for infants yet to be
born. For if infants ceased to be born and men to grow
up in America, his land would be valueless. The profits
on such investment do not arise from the growth of
land or increase of its capabilities, but from growth of
population.

Land in itself has no value. Value arises only from
human labor. It is not until the ownership of land
becomes equivalent to the ownership of laborers that
any value attaches to it. And where land has a specula-

tive value it is because of the expectation that the growth of society will in the future make its ownership equivalent to the ownership of laborers.

It is true that all valuable things have the quality of enabling their owner to obtain labor or the produce of labor in return for them or for their use. But with things that are themselves the produce of labor such transactions involve an exchange—the giving of an equivalent of labor-produce in return for labor or its produce. Land, however, is not the produce of labor; it existed before man was, and, therefore, when the ownership of land can command labor or the products of labor, the transaction, though in form it may be an exchange, is in reality an appropriation. The power which the ownership of valuable land gives, is that of getting human service without giving human service, a power essentially the same as that power of appropriation which resides in the ownership of slaves. It is not a power of exchange, but a power of blackmail, such as would be asserted were some men compelled to pay other men for the use of the ocean, the air or the sunlight.

The value of such things as grain, cattle, ships, houses, goods or metals is a value of exchange, based upon the cost of production, and therefore tends to diminish as the progress of society lessens the amount of labor necessary to produce such things. But the value of land is a value of appropriation, based upon the amount that can be appropriated, and therefore tends to increase as the progress of society increases production. Thus it is, as we see, that while all sorts of products steadily fall in value, the value of land steadily rises. Inventions and discoveries that increase the productive power of labor lessen the value of the things that require labor for their production, but increase the value of land, since they

increase the amount that labor can be compelled to give
for its use. And so, where land is fully appropriated as
private property no increase in the production of wealth,
no economy in its use, can give the mere laborer more
than the wages of the slave. If wealth rained down
from heaven or welled up from the depths of the earth
it could not enrich the laborer. It could merely increase
the value of land.

Nor do we have to appeal to the imagination to see
this. In Western Pennsylvania it has recently been
discovered that if borings are made into the earth com-
bustible gas will force itself up—a sheer donation, as it
were, by Nature, of a thing that heretofore could be produced only by labor. The direct and natural tendency of
this new power of obtaining by boring and piping what
has heretofore required the mining and retorting of coal
is to make labor more valuable and to increase the earnings of the laborer. But land in Pennsylvania being
treated as private property, it can have no such effect.
Its effect, in the first place, is to enrich the owners of the
land through which the borings must be made, who, as
legal owners of the whole material universe above and
below their land, can levy a toll on the use of Natures'
gift. In the next place, the capitalists who have gone
into the business of bringing the gas in pipes to Pittsburgh and other cities have formed a combination similar
to that of the Standard Oil Company, by which they control the sale of the natural gas, and thus over and above
the usual returns of capital make a large profit. Still,
however, a residue of advantage is left, for the new fuel
is so much more easily handled, and produces so much
more uniform a heat, that the glass- and iron-workers of
Pittsburgh find it more economical than the old fuel,
even at the same cost. But they cannot long retain this
advantage. If it prove permanent, other glass- and iron-

workers will soon be crowding to Pittsburgh to share in it, and the result will be that the value of city lots in Pittsburgh will so increase as finally to transfer this residual advantage to the owners of Pittsburgh land.* And if the monopoly of the piping company is abolished, or if by legislative regulation its profits are reduced to the ordinary earnings of capital, the ultimate result will, in the same way, be not an advantage to workers, but an advantage to landowners.

Thus it is that railways cheapen transportation only to increase the value of land, not the value of labor, and that when their rates are reduced it is landowners not laborers who get the benefit. So it is with all improvements of whatever nature. The Federal Government has acted the part of a munificent patron to Washington City. The consequence is that the value of lots has advanced. If the Federal Government were to supply every Washington householder with free light, free fuel and free food, the value of lots would still further increase, and the owners of Washington "real estate" would ultimately pocket the donation.

The primary factors of production are land and labor. Capital is their product, and the capitalist is but an intermediary between the landlord and the laborer. Hence working-men who imagine that capital is the oppressor of labor are "barking up the wrong tree." In the first place, much that seems on the surface like oppression by capital is in reality the result of the helplessness to which labor is reduced by being denied all right to the use of land. "The destruction of the poor is their poverty."

---

* The largest owners of Pittsburgh land are an English family named Schenley, who draw in ground-rents a great revenue, thus (to the gratification of Pennsylvania protectionists) increasing our exports over our imports, just as though they owned so many Pennsylvanians.

It is not in the power of capital to compel men who can obtain free access to nature to sell their labor for starvation wages. In the second place, whatever of the earnings of labor capitalistic monopolies may succeed in appropriating, they are merely lesser robbers, who take what, if they were abolished, landownership would take.

No matter whether the social organization be simple or complex, no matter whether the intermediaries between the owners of land and the owners of the mere power to labor be few or many, wherever the available land has been fully appropriated as the property of some of the people, there must exist a class, the laborers of ordinary ability and skill, who can never hope to get more than a bare living for the hardest toil, and who are constantly in danger of failure to get even that.

We see that class existing in the simple industrial organization of western Ireland or the Scottish Highlands, and we see it, still lower and more degraded, in the complex industrial organization of the great British cities. In spite of the enormous increase of productive power, we have seen it developing in the United States, just as the appropriation of our land has gone on. This is as it must be, for the most fundamental of all human relations is that between man and the planet he inhabits.

How the recognition of the consequences involved in the division of men into a class of world-owners and a class who have no legal right to the use of the world explains many things otherwise inexplicable I cannot here point out, since I am dealing only with the tariff question. We have seen why what is miscalled "free trade"—the mere abolition of protection—can only temporarily benefit the working-classes, and we have now reached a position which will enable us to proceed with our inquiry and ascertain what the effects of true free trade would be.

CHAPTER XXVI.

"COME with me," said Richard Cobden, as John Bright turned heart-stricken from a new-made grave. "There are in England women and children dying with hunger—with hunger made by the laws. Come with me, and we will not rest until we repeal those laws."

In this spirit the free-trade movement waxed and grew, arousing an enthusiasm that no mere fiscal reform could have aroused. And intrenched though it was by restricted suffrage and rotten boroughs and aristocratic privilege, protection was overthrown in Great Britain.

And—there is hunger in Great Britain still, and women and children yet die of it.

But this is not the failure of free trade. When protection had been abolished and a revenue tariff substituted for a protective tariff, free trade had won only an outpost. That women and children still die of hunger in Great Britain arises from the failure of the reformers to go on. Free trade has not yet been tried in Great Britain. Free trade in its fullness and entirety would indeed abolish hunger.

This we may now see.

Our inquiry has shown that the reason why the abolition of protection, greatly as it would increase the production of wealth, can accomplish no permanent benefit for the laboring class, is, that so long as the land on which all must live is made the property of some, increase of productive power can only increase the tribute which those who own the land can demand for its use. So long as land is held to be the individual property of but a portion of its inhabitants no possible increase of productive power, even if it went to the length of abolishing the necessity of labor, and no imaginable increase of wealth, even though it poured down from heaven or gushed up from the bowels of the earth, could improve the condition of those who possess only the power to labor. The greatest imaginable increase of wealth could only intensify in the greatest imaginable degree the phenomena which we are familiar with as "over-production"—could only reduce the laboring-class to universal pauperism.

Thus it is, that to make either the abolition of protection or any other reform beneficial to the working-class we must abolish the inequality of legal rights to land, and restore to all their natural and equal rights in the common heritage.

How can this be done?

Consider for a moment precisely what it is that needs to be done, for it is here that confusion sometimes arises. To secure to each of the people of a country his equal right to the land of that country does not mean to secure to each an equal piece of land. Save in an extremely primitive society, where population was sparse, the division of labor had made little progress, and family groups lived and worked in common, a division of land into anything like equal pieces would indeed be impracticable. In a state of society such as exists in civilized countries to-day, it would be extremely difficult, if not altogether impossible, to make an equal division of land.

Nor would one such division suffice. With the first division the difficulty would only begin. Where population is increasing and its centers are constantly changing; where different vocations make different uses of land and require different qualities and amounts of it; where improvements and discoveries and inventions are constantly bringing out new uses and changing relative values, a division that should be equal to-day would soon become very unequal, and to maintain equality a redivision every year would be necessary.

But to make a redivision every year, or to treat land as a common, where no one could claim the exclusive use of any particular piece, would be practicable only where men lived in movable tents and made no permanent improvements, and would effectually prevent any advance beyond such a state. No one would sow a crop, or build a house, or open a mine, or plant an orchard, or cut a drain, so long as any one else could come in and turn him out of the land in which or on which such improvements must be fixed. Thus it is absolutely necessary to the proper use and improvement of land that society should secure to the user and improver safe possession.

This point is constantly raised by those who resent any questioning of our present treatment of land. They seek to befog the issue by persistently treating every proposition to secure equal rights to land as though it were a proposition to secure an equal division of land, and attempt to defend private property in land by setting forth the necessity of securing safe possession to the improver.

But the two things are essentially different.

In the first place equal rights to land could *not* be secured by the equal division of land, and in the second place it is *not* necessary to make land the private property of individuals in order to secure to improvers that safe possession of their improvements that is needed to induce men to make improvements. On the contrary, private property in land, as we may see in any country where it exists, enables mere dogs in the manger to levy blackmail upon improvers. It enables the mere owner of land to compel the improver to pay him for the privilege of making improvements, and in many cases it enables him to confiscate the improvements.

Here are two simple principles, both of which are self-evident:

I.—That all men have equal rights to the use and enjoyment of the elements provided by Nature.

II.—That each man has an exclusive right to the use and enjoyment of what is produced by his own labor.

There is no conflict between these principles. On the contrary they are correlative. To secure fully the individual right of property in the produce of labor we *must* treat the elements of nature as common property. If any one could claim the sunlight as his property and could compel me to pay him for the agency of the sun in the growth of crops I had planted, it would necessarily lessen my right of property in the produce of my labor. And conversely, where every one is secured the full right of property in the produce of his labor, no one can have any right of property in what is not the produce of labor.

No matter how complex the industrial organization, nor how highly developed the civilization, there is no real difficulty in carrying out these principles. All we have to do is to treat the land as the joint property of the whole people, just as a railway is treated as the joint property of many shareholders, or as a ship is treated as the joint property of several owners.

In other words, we can leave land now being used in the secure possession of those using it, and leave land

now unused to be taken possession of by those who wish
to make use of it, on condition that those who thus hold
land shall pay to the community a fair rent for the
exclusive privilege they enjoy—that is to say, a rent
based on the value of the privilege the individual
receives from the community in being accorded the
exclusive use of this much of the common property, and
which should have no reference to any improvement he
had made in or on it, or to any profit due to the use of
his labor and capital. In this way all would be placed
upon an equality in regard to the use and enjoyment of
those natural elements which are clearly the common
heritage, and that value which attaches to land, not
because of what the individual user does, but because of
the growth of the community, would accrue to the community, and could be used for purposes of common
benefit. As Herbert Spencer has said of it:

> Such a doctrine is consistent with the highest state of civilization;
> may be carried out without involving a community of goods, and
> need cause no very serious revolution in existing arrangements.
> The change required would be simply a change of landlords. Sepa-
> rate ownership would merge into the joint-stock ownership of the
> public. Instead of being in the possession of individuals, the coun-
> try would be held by the great corporate body—society. . . . A
> state of things so ordered would be in perfect harmony with the
> moral law. Under it all men would be equally landlords, all men
> would be alike free to become tenants. Clearly, therefore, on such
> a system the earth might be inclosed, occupied and cultivated, in
> entire subordination to the law of equal freedom.

That this simple change would, as Mr. Spencer says,
involve no serious revolution in existing arrangements is
in many cases not perceived by those who think of it for
the first time. It is sometimes said that while this principle is manifestly just, and while it would be easy to
apply it to a new country just being settled, it would be

exceedingly difficult to apply it to an already settled country where land had already been divided as private property, since, in such a country, to take possession of the land as common property and let it out to individuals would involve a sudden revolution of the greatest magnitude.

This objection, however, is founded upon the mistaken idea that it is necessary to do everything at once. But it often happens that a precipice we could not hope to climb, and that we might well despair of making a ladder long enough and strong enough to scale, may be surmounted by a gentle road. And there is in this case a gentle road open to us, which will lead us so far that the rest will be but an easy step. To make land virtually the common property of the whole people, and to appropriate ground-rent for public use, there is a much simpler and easier way than that of formally assuming the ownership of land and proceeding to rent it out in lots—a way that involves no shock, that will conform to present customs, and that, instead of requiring a great increase of governmental machinery, will permit of a great simplification of governmental machinery.

In every well-developed community large sums are needed for common purposes, and the sums thus needed increase with social growth, not merely in amount, but proportionately, since social progress tends steadily to devolve on the community as a whole functions which in a ruder stage are discharged by individuals. Now, while people are not used to paying rent to government, they are used to paying taxes to government. Some of these taxes are levied upon personal or movable property; some upon occupations or businesses or persons (as in the case of income taxes, which are in reality taxes on persons according to income); some upon the transportation or exchange of commodities, in which last category

fall the taxes imposed by tariffs; and some, in the
United States at least, on real estate—that is to say, on
the value of land and of the improvements upon it,
taken together.

That part of the tax on real estate which is assessed
on the value of land irrespective of improvements is, in
its nature, not a tax, but a rent—a taking for the common use of the community of a part of the income that
properly belongs to the community by reason of the
equal right of all to the use of land.

Now it is evident that, in order to take for the use of
the community the whole income arising from land, just
as effectually as it could be taken by formally appropriating and letting out the land, it is only necessary to
abolish, one after another, all other taxes now levied,
and to increase the tax on land values till it reaches, as
near as may be, the full annual value of the land.

Whenever this point of theoretical perfection is
reached, the selling value of land will entirely disappear,
and the charge made to the individual by the community for the use of the common property will become in
form what it is in fact—a rent.   But until that point is
reached, this rent may be collected by the simple increase
of a tax already levied in all our States, assessed (as
direct taxes are now assessed) upon the selling value of
land irrespective of improvements—a value that can be
ascertained more easily and more accurately than any
other value.

For a full exposition of the effects of this change in
the method of raising public revenues, I must refer the
reader to the works in which I have treated this branch
of the subject at greater length than is here possible.
Briefly, they would be threefold :

In the first place, all taxes that now fall upon the exertion of labor or use of capital would be abolished.   No

one would be taxed for building a house or improving a farm or opening a mine, for bringing things in from foreign countries, or for adding in any way to the stock of things that satisfy human wants and constitute national wealth. Every one would be free to make and save wealth; to buy, sell, give or exchange, without let or hindrance, any article of human production the use of which did not involve any public injury. All those taxes which increase prices as things pass from hand to hand, falling finally upon the consumer, would disappear. Buildings or other fixed improvements would be as secure as now, and could be bought and sold, as now, subject to the tax or ground-rent due to the community for the ground on which they stood. Houses and the ground they stand on, or other improvements and the land they are made on, would also be rented as now. But the amount the tenant would have to pay would be less than now, since the taxes now levied on buildings or improvements fall ultimately (save in decaying communities) on the user, and the tenant would therefore get the benefit of their abolition. And in this reduced rent the tenant would pay all those taxes that he now has to pay in addition to his rent—any remainder of what he paid on account of the ground going not to increase the wealth of a landlord, but to add to a fund in which the tenant himself would be an equal sharer.

In the second place, a large and constantly increasing fund would be provided for common uses, without any tax on the earnings of labor or on the returns of capital —a fund which in well-settled countries would not only suffice for all of what are now considered necessary expenses of government, but would leave a large surplus to be devoted to purposes of general benefit.

In the third place, and most important of all, the monopoly of land would be abolished, and land would be thrown open and kept open to the use of labor, since it would be unprofitable for any one to hold land without putting it to its full use, and both the temptation and the power to speculate in natural opportunities would be gone. The speculative value of land would be destroyed as soon as it was known that, no matter whether land was used or not, the tax would increase as fast as the value increased; and no one would want to hold land that he did not use. With the disappearance of the capitalized or selling value of land, the premium which must now be paid as purchase money by those who wish to use land would disappear, differences in the value of land being measured by what would have to be paid for it to the community, nominally in taxes but really in rent. So long as any unused land remained, those who wished to use it could obtain it, not only without the payment of any purchase price, but without the payment of any tax or rent. Nothing would be required for the use of land till less advantageous land came into use, and possession thus gave an advantage over and above the return to the labor and capital expended upon it. And no matter how much the growth of population and the progress of society increased the value of land, this increase would go to the whole community, swelling that general fund in which the poorest would be an equal sharer with the richest.

Thus the great cause of the present unequal distribution of wealth would be destroyed, and that one-sided competition would cease which now deprives men who possess nothing but power to labor of the benefits of advancing civilization, and forces wages to a minimum no matter what the increase of wealth. Labor, free to the natural elements of production, would no longer be incapable of employing itself, and competition, acting as fully and freely between employers as between employed,

would carry wages up to what is truly their natural rate—
the full value of the produce of labor—and keep them there.

Let us turn again to the tariff question.

The mere abolition of protection—the mere substitution of a revenue tariff for a protective tariff—is such a
lame and timorous application of the free-trade principle
that it is a misnomer to speak of it as free trade. A
revenue tariff is only a somewhat milder restriction on
trade than a protective tariff.

Free trade, in its true meaning, requires not merely
the abolition of protection but the sweeping away of all
tariffs—the abolition of all restrictions (save those
imposed in the interests of public health or morals) on
the bringing of things into a country or the carrying of
things out of a country.

But free trade cannot logically stop with the abolition
of custom-houses. It applies as well to domestic as to
foreign trade, and in its true sense requires the abolition
of all internal taxes that fall on buying, selling, transporting or exchanging, on the making of any transaction
or the carrying on of any business, save of course where
the motive of the tax is public safety, health or morals.

Thus the adoption of true free trade involves the
abolition of all indirect taxation of whatever kind, and
the resort to direct taxation for all public revenues.

But this is not all. Trade, as we have seen, is a mode
of production, and the freeing of trade is beneficial because it is a freeing of production. For the same reason,
therefore, that we ought not to tax any one for adding to
the wealth of a country by bringing valuable things into
it, we ought not to tax any one for adding to the wealth
of a country by producing within that country valuable
things. Thus the principle of free trade requires that we
should not merely abolish all indirect taxes, but that

we should abolish as well all direct taxes on things that
are the produce of labor; that we should, in short, give
full play to the natural stimulus to production—the
possession and enjoyment of the things produced—by
imposing no tax whatever upon the production, accumulation or possession of wealth (*i.e.*, things produced by
labor), leaving every one free to make, exchange, give,
spend or bequeath.

There are thus left, as the only taxes by which in
accordance with the free-trade principle revenue can be
raised, these two classes:

1. Taxes on ostentation.

Since the motive of ostentation in the use of wealth is
simply to show the ability to expend wealth, and since
this can be shown as well in the ability to pay a tax,
taxes on ostentation pure and simple, while not checking
the production of wealth, do not even restrain the enjoyment of wealth. But such taxes, while they have a place
in the theory of taxation, are of no practical importance.
Some trivial amount is raised in England from taxes on
footmen wearing powdered wigs, taxes on armorial bearings, etc., but such taxes are not resorted to in this
country, and are incapable anywhere of yielding any
considerable revenue.

2. Taxes on the value of land.

Taxes on the value of land must not be confounded
with taxes on land, from which they differ essentially.
Taxes on land—that is to say, taxes levied on land by
quantity or area—apply equally to all land, and hence
fall ultimately on production, since they constitute a
check to the use of land, a tax that must be paid as the
condition of engaging in production. Taxes on land
values, however, do not fall upon all land, but only upon
valuable land, and on that in proportion to its value.
Hence they do not in any degree check the ability of

labor to avail itself of land, and are merely an appropriation, by the taxing power, of a portion of the premium which the owner of valuable land can charge labor for its use. In other words, a tax on land, according to quantity, could ultimately be transferred by owners of land to users of land and become a tax upon production. But a tax on land values must, as is recognized by all economists, fall on the owner of land and cannot be by him in any way transferred to the user. The landowner can no more compel those to whom he may sell or let his land to pay a tax levied on its value, than he could compel them to pay a mortgage.

A tax on land values is of all taxes that which best fulfils every requirement of a perfect tax. As land cannot be hidden or carried off, a tax on land values can be assessed with more certainty and can be collected with greater ease and less expense than any other tax, while it does not in the slightest degree check production or lessen its incentive. It is, in fact, a tax only in form, being in nature a rent—a taking for the use of the community of a value that arises not from individual exertion but from the growth of the community. For it is not anything that the individual owner or user does that gives value to land. The value that he creates is a value that attaches to improvements. This, being the result of individual exertion, properly belongs to the individual, and cannot be taxed without lessening the incentive to production. But the value that attaches to land itself is a value arising from the growth of the community and increasing with social growth. It, therefore, properly belongs to the community, and can be taken to the last penny without in the slightest degree lessening the incentive to production.

Taxes on land values are thus the only taxes from which, in accordance with the principle of free trade,

any considerable amount of revenue can be raised, and
it is evident that to carry out the free-trade principle to
the point of abolishing all taxes that hamper or lessen
production would of itself involve very nearly the same
measures which we have seen are required to assert the
common right to land and place all citizens upon an
equal footing.

To make these measures identically the same, it is only
necessary that the taxation of land values, to which true
free trade compels us to resort for public revenues,
should be carried far enough to take, as near as might
practically be, the whole of the income arising from the
value given to land by the growth of the community.

But we have only to go one step further to see that
free trade does, indeed, require this, and that the two
reforms are thus absolutely identical.

Free trade means free production. Now fully to free
production it is necessary not only to remove all taxes
on production, but also to remove all other restrictions
on production. True free trade, in short, requires that
the active factor of production, Labor, shall have free
access to the passive factor of production, Land. To
secure this all monopoly of land must be broken up, and
the equal right of all to the use of the natural elements
must be secured by the treatment of the land as the
common property in usufruct of the whole people.

Thus it is that free trade brings us to the same simple
measure as that which we have seen is necessary to
emancipate labor from its thraldom and to secure that
justice in the distribution of wealth which will make
every improvement or reform beneficial to all classes.

The partial reform miscalled free trade, which consists
in the mere abolition of protection—the mere substitution of a revenue tariff for a protective tariff—cannot
help the laboring-classes, because it does not touch the

fundamental cause of that unjust and unequal distribution which, as we see to-day, makes "labor a drug and
population a nuisance" in the midst of such a plethora
of wealth that we talk of over-production. True free
trade, on the contrary, leads not only to the largest production of wealth, but to the fairest distribution. It is
the easy and obvious way of bringing about that change
by which alone justice in distribution can be secured, and
the great inventions and discoveries which the human
mind is now grasping can be converted into agencies for
the elevation of society from its very foundations.

This was seen with the utmost clearness by that knot
of great Frenchmen who, in the last century, first raised
the standard of free trade. What they proposed was
not the mere substitution of a revenue tariff for a protective tariff, but the total abolition of all taxes, direct and
indirect, save a single tax upon the value of land—the
impôt unique. They realized that this unification of taxation meant not merely the removal from commerce and
industry of the burdens placed upon them, but that it
also meant the complete reconstruction of society—the
restoration to all men of their natural and equal rights
to the use of the earth. It was because they realized
this, that they spoke of it in terms that applied to any
mere fiscal change, however beneficial, would seem wildly
extravagant, likening it, in its importance to mankind,
to those primary inventions which made the first
advances in civilization possible—the use of money and
the adoption of written characters.

And whoever will consider how far-reaching are the
benefits that would result to mankind from a measure
which, removing all restrictions from the production of
wealth, would also secure equitable distribution, will see
that these great Frenchmen were not extravagant.

True free trade would emancipate labor.

CHAPTER XXVII.

THE LION IN THE WAY.

WE may now see why the advocacy of free trade has been so halting and half-hearted.

It is because the free-trade principle carried to its logical conclusion would destroy that monopoly of nature's bounty which enables those who do no work to live in luxury at the expense of "the poor people who have to work," that so-called free traders have not ventured to ask even the abolition of tariffs, but have endeavored to confine the free-trade principle to the mere abolition of protective duties. To go further would be to meet the lion of "vested interests."

In Great Britain the ideas of Quesnay and Turgot found a soil in which, at the time, they could grow only in stunted form. The power of the landed aristocracy was only beginning to find something of a counterpoise in the growth of the power of capital, and in politics, as in literature, Labor had no voice. Adam Smith belonged to that class of men of letters always disposed by strong motives to view things which the dominant class deem essential in the same light as they do, and who before the diffusion of education and the cheapening of books could have had no chance of being heard on any other terms. Under the shadow of an absolute despotism more liberty of thought and expression may sometimes be enjoyed than where power is more diffused, and forty years ago it would doubtless have been safer to express in Russia opinions adverse to serfdom than in South Carolina to have questioned slavery. And so, while Quesnay, the favorite physician of the master of France, could in the palace of Versailles carry his free-trade propositions to the legitimate conclusion of the *impôt unique*, Adam Smith, had he been so radical, could hardly have got the leisure to write "The Wealth of Nations" or the means to print it.

I am not criticizing Adam Smith, but pointing out conditions which have affected the development of an idea. The task which Adam Smith undertook—that of showing the absurdity and impolicy of protective tariffs —was in his time and place a sufficiently difficult one, and even if he saw how much further than this the principles he enunciated really led, the prudence of the man who wishes to do what may be done in his day and generation, confident that where he lays the foundation others will in due time rear the edifice, might have prompted him to avoid carrying them further.

However this may be, it is evidently because free trade really goes so far, that British free traders, so called, have been satisfied with the abolition of protection, and, abbreviating the motto of Quesnay, "Clear the ways and let things alone," into "Let things alone," have shorn off its more important half. For one step further —the advocacy of the abolition of revenue tariffs, as well as of protective tariffs—would have brought them upon dangerous ground. It is not only, as English writers intimate to excuse the retaining of a revenue tariff, that direct taxation could not be resorted to without arousing the British people to ask themselves why they should continue to support the descendants of royal favorites, and to pay interest on the vast sums spent during former

generations in worse than useless wars; but it is that
direct taxation could not be advocated without danger
to even more important "vested interests." One step
beyond the abolition of protective duties, and the British
free-trade movement must have come full against that
fetish which for some generations the British people
have been taught to reverence as the very Ark of the
Covenant—private property in land.

For in the British kingdoms (save in Ireland and the
Scottish Highlands) private property in land was not
instituted in the short and easy way in which Will
Atkins endeavored to institute it on Crusoe's island. It
has been the gradual result of a long series of usurpations and spoliations. In the view of British law there
is to-day but one owner of British soil, the Crown—that
is to say, the British people. The individual landholders
are still in constitutional theory what they once were in
actual fact—mere tenants. The process by which they
have become virtual owners has been that of throwing
upon indirect taxation the rents and taxes they were
once held to pay in return for their lands, while they
have added to their domains by fencing in the commons,
in much the same manner as some of the same class
have recently fenced in large tracts of our own public
domain.

The entire abolition of the British tariff would involve
as a necessary consequence the abolition of the greater
part of the internal indirect taxation, and would thus
compel heavy direct taxation, which would fall not upon
consumption but upon possession. The moment this
became necessary, the question of what share should be
borne by the holders of land must inevitably arise in
such a way as to open the whole question of the rightful
ownership of British soil. For not only do all economic
considerations point to a tax on land values as the

proper source of public revenues; but so do all British traditions. A land tax of four shillings in the pound of rental value is still nominally enforced in England, but being levied on a valuation made in the reign of William III., it amounts in reality to not much over a penny in the pound. With the abolition of indirect taxation this is the tax to which men would naturally turn. The resistance of landholders would bring up the question of title, and thus any movement which went so far as to propose the substitution of direct for indirect taxation must inevitably end in a demand for the restoration to the British people of their birthright.

This is the reason why in Great Britain the free-trade principle was aborted into that spurious thing "British free trade," which calls a sudden halt to its own principles, and after demonstrating the injustice and impolicy of all tariffs, proceeds to treat tariffs for revenue as something that must of necessity exist.

In assigning these reasons for the failure to carry the free-trade movement further than the abolition of protection, I do not, of course, mean to say that such reasons have consciously swayed free traders. I am definitely pointing out what by them has been in many cases doubtless only vaguely felt. We imbibe the sympathies, prejudices and antipathies of the circle in which we move, rather than acquire them by any process of reasoning. And the prominent advocates of free trade, the men who have been in a position to lead and educate public opinion, have belonged to the class in which the feelings I speak of hold sway—for that is the class of education and leisure.

In a society where unjust division of wealth gives the fruits of labor to those who do not labor, the classes who control the organs of public education and opinion—the classes to whom the many are accustomed to look for

light and leading, must be loath to challenge the primary
wrong, whatever it may be. This is inevitable, from the
fact that the class of wealth and leisure, and consequently of culture and influence, must be, not the class
which loses by the unjust distribution of wealth, but the
class which (at least relatively) gains by it.

Wealth means power and "respectability," while
poverty means weakness and disrepute. So in such a
society the class that leads and is looked up to, while
it may be willing to tolerate vague generalities and
impracticable proposals, must frown on any attempt to
trace social evils to their real cause, since that is the
cause that gives their class superiority. On the other
hand, the class that suffers by these evils is, on that
account, the ignorant and uninfluential class, the class
that, from its own consciousness of inferiority, is prone
to accept the teachings and imbibe the prejudices of the
one above it; while the men of superior ability that arise
within it and elbow their way to the front are constantly
received into the ranks of the superior class and interested in its service, for this is the class that has rewards
to give. Thus it is that social injustice so long endures
and is so difficult to make head against.

Thus it was that in our Southern States while slavery
prevailed, the influence, not only of the slaveholders
themselves, but of churches and colleges, the professions
and the press, condemned so effectually any questioning
of slavery, that men who never owned and never
expected to own a slave were ready to persecute and
ostracize any one who breathed a word against property
in flesh and blood—ready, even, when the time came, to
go themselves and be shot in defense of the "peculiar
institution."

Thus it was that even slaves believed abolitionists the
worst of humankind, and were ready to join in the sport

of tarring and feathering one. And so, an institution in which only a comparatively small class were interested, and which was in reality so unprofitable, even to them, that now that slavery has been abolished, it would be hard to find an ex-slaveholder who would restore it if he could, not only dominated public opinion where it existed, but exerted such influence at the North, where it did not exist, that "abolitionist" was for a long time suggestive of "atheist," "communist" and "incendiary."

The effect of the introduction of steam and labor-saving machinery upon the industries of Great Britain was such a development of manufactures as to do away with all semblance of benefit to the manufacturing classes from import duties, to raise up a capitalistic power capable of challenging the dominance of the "landed interest," and by concentrating workmen in towns to make of them a more important political factor. The abolition of protection in Great Britain was carried, against the opposition of the agricultural landholders, by a combination of two elements, capital and labor, neither of which would, of itself, have been capable of winning the victory. But, of the two, that which was represented by the Manchester manufacturers possessed much more effective and independent strength than that whose spirit breathed in the Anti-Corn-Law rhymes. Capital furnished the leadership, the organizing ability and the financial means for agitation, and when it was satisfied, the further progress of the free-trade movement had to wait for the growth of a power which, as an independent factor, is only now beginning to make its entrance into British politics. Any advance toward the abolition of revenue duties would not only have added the strength of the holders of municipal and mining land to that of the holders of agricultural land, but would also have arrayed in opposition the very class most efficient in the

free-trade movement. For, save where their apparent
interests come into clear and strong opposition, as they
did in Great Britain upon the question of protective
duties, capitalists as a class share the feelings that ani-
mate landholders as a class. Even in England, where the
division between the three economic orders—landholders,
capitalists and laborers—is clearer than anywhere else,
the distinction between landholders and capitalists is
more theoretical than real. That is to say, the landholder is generally a capitalist as well, and the capitalist
is generally in actuality or expectation to some extent a
landholder, or by the agency of leases and mortgages is
interested in the profits of landholding. Public debts
and the investments based thereon constitute, moreover,
a further powerful agency in disseminating through
the whole "House of Have" a bitter antipathy to anything that might bring the origin of property into discussion.

In the United States the same principles have operated,
though owing to differences in industrial development
the combinations have been different. Here the interest
that could not be "protected" has been the agricultural,
and the active and powerful manufacturing interest has
been on the side of protective duties. And though the
"landed interest" here has not been so well intrenched
politically as in Great Britain, yet not only has landownership been more widely diffused, but our rapid
growth has interested a larger proportion of the present
population in anticipating, by speculation based on
increasing land values, the power of levying tribute on
those yet to come. Thus private property in land has
been in reality even stronger here than in Great Britain,
while it has been to those interested in it that the opponents of protection have principally appealed. Under
such circumstances there has been here even less disposi-

tion than in Great Britain to carry the free-trade principle to its legitimate conclusions, and free trade has
been presented to the American people in the emasculated shape of a "revenue reform" too timid to ask for
even "British free trade."

CHAPTER XXVIII.

FREE TRADE AND SOCIALISM.

THROUGHOUT the civilized world, and preëminently in Great Britain and the United States, a power is now arising which is capable of carrying the principles of free trade to their logical conclusion. But there are difficulties in the way of concentrating this power on such a purpose.

It requires reflection to see that manifold effects result from a single cause, and that the remedy for a multitude of evils may lie in one simple reform. As in the infancy of medicine, men were disposed to think each distinct symptom called for a distinct remedy, so when thought begins to turn to social subjects there is a disposition to seek a special cure for every ill, or else (another form of the same short-sightedness) to imagine the only adequate remedy to be something which presupposes the absence of those ills; as, for instance, that all men should be good, as the cure for vice and crime; or that all men should be provided for by the state, as the cure for poverty.

There is now sufficient social discontent and a sufficient desire for social reform to accomplish great things if concentrated on one line. But attention is distracted and effort divided by schemes of reform which though they may be good in themselves are, with reference to

299

the great end to be attained, either inadequate or super. adequate.

Here is a traveler who, beset by robbers, has been left bound, blindfolded and gagged. Shall we stand in a knot about him and discuss whether to put a piece of court-plaster on his cheek or a new patch on his coat, or shall we dispute with each other as to what road he ought to take and whether a bicycle, a tricycle, a horse and wagon, or a railway, would best help him on? Should we not rather postpone such discussion until we have cut the man's bonds? Then he can see for himself, speak for himself, and help himself. Though with a scratched cheek and a torn coat, he may get on his feet, and if he cannot find a conveyance to suit him, he will at least be free to walk.

Very much like such a discussion is a good deal of that now going on over "the social problem"—a discussion in which all sorts of inadequate and impossible schemes are advocated to the neglect of the simple plan of removing restrictions and giving Labor the use of its own powers.

This is the first thing to do. And, if not of itself sufficient to cure all social ills and bring about the highest social state, it will at least remove the primary cause of wide-spread poverty, give to all the opportunity to use their labor and secure the earnings that are its due, stimulate all improvement, and make all other reforms easier.

It must be remembered that reforms and improvements in themselves good may be utterly inefficient to work any general improvement until some more fundamental reform is carried out. It must be remembered that there is in every work a certain order which must be observed to accomplish anything. To a habitable house a roof is as important as walls; and we express in a word the end to which a house is built when we speak of putting a roof over our heads. But we cannot build a house from roof down; we must build from foundation up.

To recur to our simile of the laborer habitually preyed upon by a series of robbers. It is surely wiser in him to fight them one by one, than all together. And the robber that takes all he has left is the one against whom his efforts should first be directed. For no matter how he may drive off the other robbers, that will not avail him except as it may make it easier to get rid of the robber that takes all that is left. But by withstanding this robber he will secure immediate relief, and being able to get home more of his earnings than before, will be able so to nourish and strengthen himself that he can better contend with robbers—can, perhaps, buy a gun or hire a lawyer, according to the method of fighting in fashion in his country.

It is in just such a way as this that Labor must seek to rid itself of the robbers that now levy upon its earnings. Brute strength will avail little unless guided by intelligence.

The first attempts of working-men to improve their condition are by combining to demand higher wages of their direct employers. Something can be done in this way for those within such organizations; but it is after all very little. For a trades-union can only artificially lessen competition within the trade; it cannot affect the general conditions which force men into bitter competition with each other for the opportunity to gain a living. And such organizations as the Knights of Labor, which are to trades-unions what the trades-union is to its individual members, while they give greater power, must encounter the same difficulties in their efforts to raise wages directly. All such efforts have the inherent disadvantage of struggling against general tendencies. They are like the attempts of a man in a crowd to gain room by forcing back those who press upon him—like attempts

to stop a great engine by the sheer force of human muscle, without cutting off steam.

This, those who are at first inclined to put faith in the
power of trades-unionism are beginning to see, and the
logic of events must more and more lead them to see.
But the perception that to accomplish large results general tendencies must be controlled, inclines those who do
not analyze these tendencies into their causes to transfer
faith from some form of the voluntary organization of
labor to some form of governmental organization and
direction.

All varieties of what is vaguely called socialism recognize with more or less clearness the solidarity of the
interests of the masses of all countries. Whatever may
be objected to socialism in its extremest forms, it has at
least the merit of lessening national prejudices and aim-
ing at the disbandment of armies and the suppression of
war. It is thus opposed to the cardinal tenet of protectionism that the interests of the people of different
"nations" are diverse and antagonistic. But, on the
other hand, those who call themselves socialists, so far
from being disposed to look with disfavor upon governmental interference and regulation, are disposed to sym-
pathize with protection as in this respect in harmony
with socialism, and to regard free trade, at least as it has
been popularly presented, as involving a reliance on that
principle of free competition which to their thinking
means the crushing of the weak.

Let us endeavor, as well as can in brief be done, to
trace the relations between the conclusions to which we
have come and what, with various shades of meaning, is
termed "socialism." *

---

* The term "socialism" is used so loosely that it is hard to attach
to it a definite meaning. I myself am classed as a socialist by those

In socialism as distinguished from individualism there is an unquestionable truth—and that a truth to which (especially by those most identified with free-trade principles) too little attention has been paid.   Man is primarily an individual—a separate entity, differing from his fellows in desires and powers, and requiring for the exercise of those powers and the gratification of those desires individual play and freedom.   But he is also a social being, having desires that harmonize with those of his fellows, and powers that can be brought out only in concerted action.   There is thus a domain of individual action and a domain of social action—some things which can best be done when each acts for himself, and some things which can best be done when society acts for all its members.   And the natural tendency of advancing civilization is to make social conditions relatively more important, and more and more to enlarge the domain of social action.   This has not been sufficiently regarded, and at the present time, evil unquestionably results from leaving to individual action functions that by reason of the growth of society and the development of the arts have passed into the domain of social action; just as, on the other hand, evil unquestionably results from social interference with what properly belongs to the individual.

---

who denounce socialism, while those who profess themselves socialists declare me not to be one.   For my own part I neither claim nor repudiate the name, and realizing as I do the correlative truth of both principles can no more call myself an individualist or a socialist than one who considers the forces by which the planets are held to their orbits could call himself a centrifugalist or a centripetalist. The German socialism of the school of Marx (of which the leading representative in England is Mr. H. M. Hyndman, and the best exposition in America has been given by Mr. Laurence Gronlund) seems to me a high-purposed but incoherent mixture of truth and fallacy, the defects of which may be summed up in its want of radicalism—that is to say, of going to the root.

Society ought not to leave the telegraph and the railway to the management and control of individuals; nor yet ought society to step in and collect individual debts or attempt to direct individual industry.

But while there is a truth in socialism which individualists forget, there is a school of socialists who in like manner ignore the truth there is in individualism, and whose propositions for the improvement of social conditions belong to the class I have called "super-adequate." Socialism in its narrow sense—the socialism that would have the state absorb capital and abolish competition—is the scheme of men who, looking upon society in its most complex organization, have failed to see that principles obvious in a simpler stage still hold true in the more intimate relations that result from the division of labor and the use of complex tools and methods, and have thus fallen into fallacies elaborated by the economists of a totally different school, who have taught that capital is the employer and sustainer of labor, and have striven to confuse the distinction between property in land and property in labor-products. Their scheme is that of men who, while revolting from the heartlessness and hopelessness of the "orthodox political economy," are yet entangled in its fallacies and blinded by its confusions. Confounding "capital" with "means of production," and accepting the dictum that "natural wages" are the least on which competition can force the laborer to live, they essay to cut a knot they do not see how to unravel, by making the state the sole capitalist and employer, and abolishing competition.

The carrying on by government of all production and exchange, as a remedy for the difficulty of finding employment on the one side, and for overgrown fortunes on the other, belongs to the same category as the prescription that all men should be good. That if all men

were assigned proper employment and all wealth fairly
distributed, then none would need employment and there
would be no injustice in distribution, is as indisputable a
proposition as that if all were good none would be bad.
But it will not help a man perplexed as to his path to tell
him that the way to get to his journey's end is to get
there.

That all men should be good is the greatest desidera-
tum, but it can be secured only by the abolition of conditions which tempt some and drive others into evil-doing.
That each should render according to his abilities and
receive according to his needs, is indeed the very highest
social state of which we can conceive, but how shall we
hope to attain such perfection until we can first find
some way of securing to every man the opportunity to
labor and the fair earnings of his labor? Shall we try to
be generous before we have learned how to be just?

All schemes for securing equality in the conditions of
men by placing the distribution of wealth in the hands of
government have the fatal defect of beginning at the
wrong end. They presuppose pure government; but it
is not government that makes society; it is society that
makes government; and *until* there is something like substantial equality in the distribution of wealth, we cannot
expect pure government.

But to put all men on a footing of substantial equality,
so that there could be no dearth of employment, no "over-
production," no tendency of wages to the minimum of
subsistence, no monstrous fortunes on the one side and
no army of proletarians on the other, it is not necessary
that the state should assume the ownership of all the
means of production and become the general employer
and universal exchanger; it is necessary only that the
equal rights of all to that primary means of production
which is the source all other means of production are

derived from, should be asserted. And this, so far from involving an extension of governmental functions and machinery, involves, as we have seen, their great reduction. It would thus tend to purify government in two ways—first, by the betterment of the social conditions on which purity in government depends, and second, by the simplification of administration. This step taken, and we could safely begin to add to the functions of the state in its proper or coöperative sphere.

There is in reality no conflict between labor and capital;* the true conflict is between labor and monopoly. That a rich employer "squeezes" needy workmen may be true. But does this squeezing power result from his riches or from their need? No matter how rich an employer might be, how would it be possible for him to squeeze workmen who could make a good living for themselves without going into his employment? The competition of workmen with workmen for employment, which is the real cause that enables, and even in most cases forces, the employer to squeeze his workmen, arises from the fact that men, debarred of the natural opportunities to employ themselves, are compelled to bid against one another for the wages of an employer. Abolish the monopoly that forbids men to employ themselves, and capital could not possibly oppress labor. In no case could the capitalist obtain labor for less than the laborer could

---

* The great source of confusion in regard to such matters arises from the failure to attach any definite meaning to terms. It must always be remembered that nothing that can be classed either as labor or as land can be accounted capital in any definite use of the term, and that much that we commonly speak of as capital—such as solvent debts, government bonds, etc.—is in reality not even wealth —which all true capital must be. For a fuller elucidation of this, as of similar points, I must refer the reader to my "Progress and Poverty."

get by employing himself. Once remove the cause of that injustice which deprives the laborer of the capital his toil creates, and the sharp distinction between capitalist and laborer would, in fact, cease to exist.

They who, seeing how men are forced by competition to the extreme of human wretchedness, jump to the conclusion that competition should be abolished, are like those who, seeing a house burn down, would prohibit the use of fire.

The air we breathe exerts upon every square inch of our bodies a pressure of fifteen pounds. Were this pressure exerted only on one side, it would pin us to the ground and crush us to a jelly. But being exerted on all sides, we move under it with perfect freedom. It not only does not inconvenience us, but it serves such indispensable purposes that, relieved of its pressure, we should die.

So it is with competition. Where there exists a class denied all right to the element necessary to life and labor, competition is one-sided, and as population increases must press the lowest class into virtual slavery, and even starvation. But where the natural rights of all are secured, then competition, acting on every hand —between employers as between employed; between buyers as between sellers—can injure no one. On the contrary it becomes the most simple, most extensive, most elastic, and most refined system of coöperation, that, in the present stage of social development, and in the domain where it will freely act, we can rely on for the coördination of industry and the economizing of social forces.

In short, competition plays just such a part in the social organism as those vital impulses which are beneath consciousness do in the bodily organism. With it, as with them, it is only necessary that it should be free.

The line at which the state should come in is that where free competition becomes impossible—a line analogous to that which in the individual organism separates the conscious from the unconscious functions.   There is such a line, though extreme socialists and extreme individualists both ignore it.   The extreme individualist is like the man who would have his hunger provide him food; the extreme socialist is like the man who would have his conscious will direct his stomach how to digest it.

Individualism and socialism are in truth not antagonistic but correlative.   Where the domain of the one principle ends that of the other begins.   And although the motto *Laissez faire* has been taken as the watchword of an individualism that tends to anarchism, and so-called free traders have made "the law of supply and demand" a stench in the nostrils of men alive to social injustice, there is in free trade nothing that conflicts with a rational socialism.   On the contrary, we have but to carry out the free-trade principle to its logical conclusions to see that it brings us to such socialism.

The free-trade principle is, as we have seen, the principle of free production—it requires not merely the abolition of protective tariffs, but the removal of all restrictions upon production.

Within recent years a class of restrictions on production, imposed by concentrations and combinations which have for their purpose the limiting of production and the increase of prices, have begun to make themselves felt and to assume greater and greater importance.

This power of combinations to restrict production arises in some cases from temporary monopolies granted by our patent laws, which (being the premium that society holds out to invention) have a compensatory principle, however faulty they may be in method.

Such cases aside, this power of restricting production

is derived, in part, from tariff restrictions. Thus the American steel-makers who have recently limited their production, and put up the price of rails 40 per cent. at one stroke, are enabled to do this only by the heavy duty on imported rails. They are able, by combination, to put up the price of steel rails to the point at which they could be imported plus the duty, but no further. Hence, with the abolition of the duty this power would be gone. To prevent the play of competition, a combination of the steel-workers of the whole world would then be necessary, and this is practically impossible.

In other part, this restrictive power arises from ability to monopolize natural advantages. This would be destroyed if the taxation of land values made it unprofitable to hold land without using it. In still other part, it arises from the control of businesses which in their nature do not admit of competition, such as those of railway, telegraph, gas and other similar companies.

I read in the daily papers that half a dozen representatives of the "anthracite coal interest" met last evening (March 24, 1886), in an office in New York. Their conference, interrupted only by a collation, lasted till three o'clock in the morning. When they separated they had come to "an understanding among gentlemen" to restrict the production of anthracite coal and advance its price.

Now how comes it that half a dozen men, sitting around some bottles of champagne and a box of cigars in a New York office, can by an "understanding among gentlemen" compel Pennsylvania miners to stand idle, and advance the price of coal along the whole eastern seaboard? The power thus exercised is derived in various parts from three sources.

1. From the protective duty on coal. Free trade would abolish that.

2. From the power to monopolize land, which enables them to prevent others from using coal deposits which they will not use themselves. True free trade, as we have seen, would abolish that.

3. From the control of railways, and the consequent power of fixing rates and making discriminations in transportation.

The power of fixing rates of transportation, and in this way of discriminating against persons and places, is a power essentially of the same nature as that exercised by governments in levying import duties. And the principle of free trade as clearly requires the removal of such restrictions as it requires the removal of import duties. But here we reach a point where positive action on the part of government is needed. Except as between terminal or "competitive" points where two or more roads meet (and as to these the tendency is, by combination or "pooling," to do away with competition), the carrying of goods and passengers by rail, like the business of telegraph, telephone, gas, water or similar companies, is in its nature a monopoly. To prevent restrictions and discriminations, governmental control is therefore required. Such control is not only not inconsistent with the free-trade principle; it follows from it, just as the interference of government to prevent and punish assaults upon persons and property follows from the principle of individual liberty. Thus, if we carry free trade to its logical conclusions we are inevitably led to what monopolists, who wish to be "let alone" to plunder the public, denounce as "socialism," and which is, indeed, socialism, in the sense that it recognizes the true domain of social functions.

Whether businesses in their nature monopolies should be regulated by law or should be carried on by the community, is a question of method. It seems to me, however, that experience goes to show that better results can be secured, with less risk of governmental corruption, by state management than by state regulation. But the great simplification of government which would result from the abolition of the present complex and demoralizing modes of taxation would vastly increase the ease and safety with which either of these methods could be applied. The assumption by the state of all those social functions in which competition will not operate would involve nothing like the strain upon governmental powers, and would be nothing like as provocative of corruption and dishonesty, as our present method of collecting taxes. The more equal distribution of wealth that would ensue from the reform which thus simplified government, would, moreover, increase public intelligence and purify public morals, and enable us to bring a higher standard of honesty and ability to the management of public affairs. We have no right to assume that men would be as grasping and dishonest in a social state where the poorest could get an abundant living as they are in the present social state, where the fear of poverty begets insane greed.

There is another way, moreover, in which true free trade tends strongly to socialism, in the highest and best sense of the term. The taking for the use of the community of that value of privilege which attaches to the possession of land, would, wherever social development has advanced beyond a certain stage, yield revenues even larger than those now raised by taxation, while there would be an enormous reduction in public expenses consequent, directly and indirectly, upon the abolition of present modes of taxation. Thus would be provided a fund, increasing steadily with social growth, that could be applied to social purposes now neglected. And among the purposes which will suggest themselves to the reader by which the surplus income of the community could be used to increase the sum of human knowledge, the diffusion of elevating tastes, and the gratification of healthy desires, there is none more worthy than that of making honorable provision for those deprived of their natural protectors, or through no fault of their own incapacitated for the struggle of life.

We should think it sin and shame if a great steamer, dashing across the ocean, were not brought to a stop by a signal of distress from the meanest smack; at the sight of an infant lashed to a spar, the mighty ship would round to, and men would spring to launch a boat in angry seas. Thus strongly does the bond of our common humanity appeal to us when we get beyond the hum of civilized life. And yet—a miner is entombed alive, a painter falls from a scaffold, a brakeman is crushed in coupling cars, a merchant fails, falls ill and dies, and organized society leaves widow and children to bitter want or degrading alms. This ought not to be. Citizenship in a civilized community ought of itself to be insurance against such a fate. And having in mind that the income which the community ought to obtain from the land to which the growth of the community gives value is in reality not a tax but the proceeds of a just rent, an English Democrat (William Saunders, M.P.) puts in this phrase the aim of true free trade: " *No taxes at all, and a pension to everybody.*"

This is denounced as " the rankest socialism " by those whose notion of the fitness of things is, that the descendants of royal favorites and blue-blooded thieves should be kept in luxurious idleness all their lives long, by pensions wrung from struggling industry, while the laborer and his wife, worn out by hard work, for which they have received scarce living wages, are degraded by a parish dole, or separated from each other in a "work-house."

If this is socialism, then, indeed, is it true that free trade leads to socialism.

CHAPTER XXIX.

PRACTICAL POLITICS.

ON a railway train I once fell in with a Pittsburgh brass band that was returning from a celebration. The leader and I shared the same seat, and between the tunes with which they beguiled the night, we got into a talk which, from politics, touched the tariff. I neither expressed my own opinions nor disputed his, but asked him some questions as to *how* protection benefited labor. His answers seemed hardly to satisfy himself, and suddenly he said :

"Look here, stranger, may I ask *you* a question? I mean no offense, but I'd like to ask you a straightforward question. Are you a free trader?"

"I am."

"A real free trader—one that wants to abolish the tariff?"

"Yes, a real free trader. I would have trade between the United States and the rest of the world as free as it is between Pennsylvania and Ohio."

"Give me your hand, stranger," said the band-leader, jumping up. "I like a man who's out and out."

"Boys," he exclaimed, turning to some of his bandsmen, "here's a sort of man you never saw; here's a real free trader, and he ain't ashamed to own it." And when the "boys" had shaken hands with me, very much as they might have shaken hands with the "Living Skeleton" or the "Chinese Giant," "Do you know, stranger," the band-master continued, "I've been hearing of free traders all my life, but you're the first I ever met. I've seen men that other people called free traders, but when it came their turn they always denied it. The most they would admit was that they wanted to trim the tariff down a little, or fix it up better. But they always insisted we must have a tariff, and I'd got to believe that there were no real free traders; that they were only a sort of bugaboo."

My Pittsburgh friend was in this respect, I think, no unfair sample of the great body of the American people of this generation. The only free traders most of them have seen and heard have been anxious to deny the appellation—or at least to insist that we always must have a tariff, and to deprecate sudden reductions.

Is it any wonder that the fallacies of protection run rampant when such is the only opposition they meet? Dwarfed into mere revenue reform the harmony and beauty of free trade are hidden; its moral force is lost; its power to remedy social evils cannot be shown, and the injustice and meanness of protection cannot be arraigned. The "international law of God" becomes a mere fiscal question which appeals only to the intellect and not to the heart, to the pocket and not to the conscience, and on which it is impossible to arouse the enthusiasm that is alone capable of contending with powerful interests. When it is conceded that custom-houses must be maintained and import duties levied, the average man will conclude that these duties might as well be protective, or at least will trouble himself little about them. When told that they must beware of moving too quickly, people are not likely to move at all.

Such advocacy is not of the sort that can compel discussion, awaken thought, and press forward a great cause against powerful opposition. Half a truth is not half so strong as a whole truth, and to minimize such a principle as that of free trade in the hope of disarming opposition, is to lessen its power of securing support in far greater degree than to lessen the antagonism it must encounter. A principle that in its purity will be grasped by the popular mind loses its power when befogged by concessions and enervated by compromises.

But the mistake which such advocates of free trade make has a deeper root than any misapprehension as to policy. They are, for the most part, men who derive their ideas from the emasculated and incoherent political economy taught in our colleges, or from political traditions of "States' rights" and "strict construction" now broken and weak. They do not present free trade in its beauty and strength because they do not so see it. They have not the courage of conviction, because they have not the conviction. They have opinions, but these opinions lack that burning, that compelling force that springs from a vital conviction. They see the absurdity and waste of protection, and the illogical character of the pleas made for it, and these things offend their sense of fitness and truth; but they do not see that free trade really means the emancipation of labor, the abolition of poverty, the restoring to the disinherited of their birthright. Such free traders are well represented by journals which mildly oppose protection when no election is on, but which at election-times are as quiet as mice. They are in favor of what they call free trade, as a certain class of good people are in favor of the conversion of the Jews. When entirely convenient they will speak, write, attend a meeting, eat a dinner or give a little money for the cause, but they will hardly break with their party or "throw away" a vote.

Even the most energetic and public-spirited of these men are at a fatal disadvantage when it comes to a popular propaganda. They can well enough point out the abuses of protection and expose its more transparent sophistries, but they cannot explain the social phenomena in which protection finds its real strength. All they can promise the laborer is that production shall be increased and many commodities cheapened. But how can this appeal to men who are accustomed to look upon "over-production" as the cause of wide-spread distress, and who are constantly told that the cheapness of commodities is the reason why thousands have to suffer for the want of them? And when confronted by the failure of revenue reform to eradicate pauperism and abolish starvation— when asked why in spite of the adoption in Great Britain of the measures he proposes, wages there are so low and poverty so dire, the free trader of this type can make no answer that will satisfy the questioner, even if he can give one satisfactory to himself. The only answer his philosophy can give—the only answer he can obtain from the political economy taught by the "free-trade" text-books—is that the bitter struggle for existence which crushes men into pauperism and starvation is of the nature of things. And whether he attributes this nature of things to the conscious volition of an intelligent Creator or to the working of blind forces, the man who either definitely or vaguely accepts this answer is incapable of feeling himself or of calling forth in others the spirit of Cobden's appeal to Bright.

Thus it is that free trade, narrowed to a mere fiscal reform, can appeal only to the lower and weaker motives —to motives that are inadequate to move men in masses. Take the current free-trade literature. Its aim is to show the impolicy of protection, rather than its injustice; its appeal is to the pocket, not to the sympathies.

Yet to begin and maintain great popular movements it is the moral sense rather than the intellect that must be appealed to, sympathy rather than self-interest. For however it may be with any individual, the sense of justice is with the masses of men keener and truer than intellectual perception, and unless a question can assume the form of right and wrong it cannot provoke general discussion and excite the many to action. And while material gain or loss impresses us less vividly the greater the number of those we share it with, the power of sympathy increases as it spreads from man to man— becomes cumulative and contagious.

But he who follows the principle of free trade to its logical conclusion can strike at the very root of protection; can answer every question and meet every objection, and appeal to the surest of instincts and the strongest of motives. He will see in free trade not a mere fiscal reform, but a movement which has for its aim and end nothing less than the abolition of poverty, and of the vice and crime and degradation that flow from it, by the restoration to the disinherited of their natural rights and the establishment of society upon the basis of justice. He will catch the inspiration of a cause great enough to live for and to die for, and be moved by an enthusiasm that he can evoke in others.

It is true that to advocate free trade in its fullness would excite the opposition of interests far stronger than those concerned in maintaining protective tariffs. But on the other hand it would bring to the standard of free trade, forces without which it cannot succeed. And what those who would arouse thought have to fear is not so much opposition as indifference. Without opposition that attention cannot be excited, that energy evoked, that are necessary to overcome the inertia that is the strongest bulwark of existing abuses. A party can no more be rallied on a question that no one disputes than steam can be raised to working pressure in an open vessel.

The working-class of the United States, who have constituted the voting strength of protection, are now ready for a movement that will appeal to them on behalf of real free trade. For some years past educative agencies have been at work among them that have sapped their faith in protection. If they have not learned that protection *cannot* help them, they have at least become widely conscious that protection *does* not help them. They have been awakening to the fact that there is some deep wrong in the constitution of society, although they may not see clearly what that wrong is; they have been gradually coming to feel that to emancipate labor radical measures are needed, although they may not know what those measures are.

And scattered through the great body thus beginning to stir and grope are a rapidly increasing number of men who *do* know what this primary wrong is—men who see that in the recognition of the equal right of all to the element necessary to life and labor is the hope, and the only hope, of curing social injustice.

It is to men of this kind that I would particularly speak. They are the leaven which has in it power to leaven the whole lump.

To abolish private property in land is an undertaking so great that it may at first seem impracticable.

But this seeming impracticability consists merely in the fact that the public mind is not yet sufficiently awakened to the justice and necessity of this great change. To bring it about is simply a work of arousing thought. How men vote is something we need not much concern ourselves with. The important thing is how they think.

Now the chief agency in promoting thought is discussion. And to secure the most general and most effective discussion of a principle it must be embodied in concrete form and presented in practical politics, so that men, being called to vote on it, shall be forced to think and talk about it.

The advocates of a great principle should know no thought of compromise. They should proclaim it in its fullness, and point to its complete attainment as their goal. But the zeal of the propagandist needs to be supplemented by the skill of the politician. While the one need not fear to arouse opposition, the other should seek to minimize resistance. The political art, like the military art, consists in massing the greatest force against the point of least resistance; and, to bring a principle most quickly and effectively into practical politics, the measure which presents it should be so moderate as (while involving the principle) to secure the largest support and excite the least resistance. For whether the first step be long or short is of little consequence. When a start is once made in a right direction, progress is a mere matter of keeping on.

It is in this way that great questions always enter the phase of political action. Important political battles begin with affairs of outposts, in themselves of little moment, and are generally decided upon issue joined not on the main question, but on some minor or collateral question. Thus the slavery question in the United States came into practical politics upon the issue of the extension of slavery to new territory, and was decisively settled upon the issue of secession. Regarded as an end, the abolitionist might well have looked with contempt on the proposals of the Republicans, but these proposals were the means of bringing to realization what the abolitionists would in vain have sought to accomplish directly.

So with the tariff question. Whether we have a protective tariff or a revenue tariff is in itself of small

importance, for, though the abolition of protection
would increase production, the tendency to unequal distribution would be unaffected and would soon neutralize
the gain. Yet, what is thus unimportant as an end, is
all-important as a means. Protection is a little robber,
it is true; but it is the sentinel and outpost of the great
robber—the little robber who cannot be routed without
carrying the struggle into the very stronghold of the
great robber. The great robber is so well intrenched,
and people have so long been used to his exactions, that
it is hard to arouse them to assail him directly. But to
help those engaged in a conflict with this little robber
will be to open the easiest way to attack his master, and
to arouse a spirit that must push on.

To secure to all the free use of the power to labor and
the full enjoyment of its products, equal rights to land
must be secured.

To secure equal rights to land there is in this stage of
civilization but one way. Such measures as peasant
proprietary, or "land limitation," or the reservation to
actual settlers of what is left of the public domain, do
not tend toward it; they lead away from it. They can
affect only a comparatively unimportant class, and that
temporarily, while their outcome is not to weaken landownership but rather to strengthen it, by interesting a
larger number in its maintenance. The only way to
abolish private property in land is by the way of taxation. That way is clear and straightforward. It consists simply in abolishing, one after another, all imposts
that are in their nature really taxes, and resorting for
public revenues to economic rent, or ground value. To
the full freeing of land, and the complete emancipation
of labor, it is, of course, necessary that the whole of this
value should be taken for the common benefit; but that
will inevitably follow the decision to collect from this

source the revenues now needed, or even any considerable part of them, just as the entrance of a victorious
army into a city follows the rout of the army that
defended it.

In the United States the most direct way of moving
on property in land is through local taxation, since that
is already to some extent levied upon land values. And
that is doubtless the way in which the final and decisive
advance will be made. But national politics dominate
State politics, and a question can be brought into discussion much more quickly and thoroughly as a national
than as a local question.

Now to bring an issue into politics it is not necessary
to form a party. Parties are not to be manufactured;
they grow out of existing parties by the bringing forward of issues upon which men will divide. We have,
ready to our hand, in the tariff question, a means of
bringing the whole subject of taxation, and, through it,
the whole social question, into the fullest discussion.

As we have seen in the inquiry through which we have
passed, the tariff question necessarily opens the whole
social question. Any discussion of it to-day must go
further and deeper than the Anti-Corn-Law agitation in
Great Britain, or than the tariff controversies of Whigs
and Democrats, for the progress of thought and the
march of invention have made the distribution of wealth
the burning question of our times. The making of the
tariff question a national political issue must now mean
the discussion in every newspaper, on every stump, and
at every cross-roads where two men meet, of questions of
work and wages, of capital and labor, of the incidence of
taxation, of the nature and rights of property, and of the
question to which all these questions lead—the question
of the relation of men to the planet on which they live.
In this way more can be accomplished for popular eco-

nomic education in a year than could otherwise be
accomplished in decades.

Therefore it is that I would urge earnest men who aim
at the emancipation of labor and the establishment of
social justice, to throw themselves into the free-trade
movement with might and main, and to force the tariff
question to the front. It is not merely that the free-
trade side of the tariff controversy best consorts with the
interests of labor; it is not merely that until working-men
get over thinking of labor as a poor thing that needs to be
"protected," and of work as a dole from gracious capitalists or paternal governments, they cannot rise to a
sense of their rights; but it is that the movement for
free trade is in reality the van of the struggle for the
emancipation of labor. *This is the way the bull must go to
untwist his rope.* It makes no difference how timorously
the issue against protection is now presented; it is still
the thin end of the wedge. It makes no difference how
little we can hope at once to do; social progress is by
steps, and the step to which we should address ourselves
is always the next step.*

---

* There is no reason why at least the bulk of the revenues needed
for the national government under our system should not be collected
from a percentage on land values, leaving the rest for the local
governments, just as State, county and municipal taxes are collected
on one assessment and by one set of officials. On the contrary there
is, over and above the economy that would thus be secured, a strong
reason for the collection of national revenues from land values in
the fact that the ground values of great cities and mineral deposits
are due to the general growth of population.

But the total abolition of the tariff need not await any such adjustment. The issuance of paper money, a function belonging properly
to the General Government, would, properly used, yield a considerable income; while independent sources of any needed amount of
revenue could be found in various taxes, which though not economically perfect, as is the tax on land values, are yet much less
objectionable than taxes on imports. The excise tax on spirituous

Nor does it matter that those now active in the free-trade movement have no sympathy with our aims; nor that they denounce and misrepresent us. It is our policy to support them, and strengthen them, and urge them on. No matter how soon they may propose to stop, the direction they wish to take is the direction in which we must go if we would reach our goal. In joining our forces to theirs, we shall not be putting ourselves to their use, we shall be making use of them.

But these men themselves, when fairly started and borne on by the impulse of controversy, will go further than they now dream. It is the law of all such movements that they must become more and more radical. And while we are especially fortunate in the United States in a class of protectionist leaders who will not yield an inch until forced to, our political conditions differ

---

liquors ought to be abolished, as it fosters corruption, injuriously affects many branches of manufacture and puts a premium on adulteration; but either by a government monopoly, or by license taxes on retail sales, a large revenue might be derived from the liquor traffic with much greater advantage to public health and morals than by the present system. There are also some stamp taxes which are comparatively uninjurious and can be collected easily and cheaply.

But of all methods of raising an independent Federal revenue, that which would yield the largest return with the greatest ease and least injury is a tax upon legacies and successions. In a large population the proportion of deaths is as regular as that of births, and with proper exemptions in favor of widows, minor children and dependent relatives, such a tax would bear harshly on no one, and from the publicity which must attach to the transfer of property by death or in view of death it is easily collected and little liable to evasion. The appropriation of land values would of itself strike at the heart of overgrown fortunes, but until that is accomplished, a tax of this kind would have the incidental advantage of interfering with their transmission.

Of all excuses for the continuance of any tariff at all, the most groundless is that it is necessary to secure Federal revenues. Even the income tax, bad as it is, is in all respects better than a tariff.

from those of Great Britain in 1846, when, the laboring-
class being debarred from political power, a timely sur-
render on the part of the defenders of protection checked
for a while the natural course of the movement, and thus
prevented the demand for the abolition of protection from
becoming at once a demand for the abolition of landlord-
ism.   The class that in Great Britain is only coming into
political power has, with us, political power already.

Yet even in Great Britain the inevitable tendencies of
the free-trade movement may clearly be seen.   Not only
has the abolition of protection cleared the ground for the
far greater questions now beginning to enter British
politics; not only has the impulse of the free-trade agitation led to reforms which are placing political power in
the hands of the many; but the work done by men who,
having begun by opposing protection, were not content
to stop with its abolition, has been one of the most
telling factors in hastening the revolution now in its
incipient stages—a revolution that cannot stop short of
the restoration to the British people of their natural
rights to their native land.

Richard Cobden saw that the agitation of the tariff
question must ultimately pass into the agitation of the
land question, and from what I have heard of him I am
inclined to think that were he in life and vigor to-day, he
would be leading in the movement for the restoration to
the British people of their natural rights in their native
land.   But, however this may be, the British free-trade
movement left a "remnant" who, like Thomas Briggs,*

---

* Author of "Property and Taxation," etc., and a warm supporter
of the movement for the restoration of their land to the British
people.   Mr. Briggs was one of the Manchester manufacturers active
in the Anti-Corn-Law movement, and, regarding that victory as a
mere beginning, has always insisted that Great Britain was yet under
the blight of protectionism, and that the struggle for true free trade
was yet to come.

have constantly advocated the carrying of free trade to its final conclusions. And one of the most effective of the revolutionary agencies now at work in Great Britain is the Liverpool Financial Reform Association, whose *Financial Reform Almanac* and other publications are doing so much to make the British people acquainted with the process of usurpation and spoliation by which the land of Great Britain has been made the private property of a class, and British labor saddled with the support of a horde of aristocratic paupers. Yet the Liverpool Financial Reform Association is composed of men who, for the most part, would shrink from any deliberate attack upon property in land. They are simply free traders of the Manchester school, logical enough to see that free trade means the abolition of revenue tariffs as well as of protective tariffs. But in striking at indirect taxation they are of necessity dealing tremendous blows at private property in land, and sapping the very foundations of aristocracy, since, in showing the history of indirect taxation, they are showing how the tenants of the nation's land made themselves virtual owners; and in proposing the restoration of the direct tax upon land values they are making an issue which will involve the complete restoration of British land to the British people.

Thus it is that when men take up the principle of freedom they are led on and on, and that the hearty advocacy of freedom to trade becomes at length the advocacy of freedom to labor. And so must it be in the United States. Once the tariff question becomes a national issue, and in the struggle against protection, free traders will be forced to attack indirect taxation. Protection is so well intrenched that before a revenue tariff can be secured the active spirits of the free-trade party will have far passed the point when that would satisfy them; while before the abolition of indirect taxation is reached, the incidence of taxation and the nature and effect of private property in land will have been so well discussed that the rest will be but a matter of time.

Property in land is as indefensible as property in man. It is so absurdly impolitic, so outrageously unjust, so flagrantly subversive of the true right of property, that it can only be instituted by force and maintained by confounding in the popular mind the distinction between property in land and property in things that are the result of labor. Once that distinction is made clear—and a thorough discussion of the tariff question must now make it clear—and private property in land is doomed.

CHAPTER XXX.

CONCLUSION.

A WEALTHY citizen whom I once supported, and called on others to support, for the Presidential chair, under the impression that he was a Democrat of the school of Jefferson, has recently published a letter advising us to steel-plate our coasts, lest foreign navies come over and bombard us. This counsel of timidity has for its hardly disguised object the inducing of such an enormous expenditure of public money as will prevent any demand for the reduction of taxation, and thus secure to the tariff rings a longer lease of plunder. It well illustrates the essential meanness of the protectionist spirit—a spirit that no more comprehends the true dignity of the American Republic and the grandeur of her possibilities than it cares for the material interests of the great masses of her citizens—"the poor people who have to work."

That which is good harmonizes with all things good; and that which is evil tends to other evil things. Properly does Buckle, in his "History of Civilization," apply the term "protective" not merely to the system of robbery by tariffs, but to the spirit that teaches that the many are born to serve and the few to rule; that props thrones with bayonets, substitutes small vanities and petty jealousies for high-minded patriotism, and converts

327

the flower of European youth into uniformed slaves, trained to kill each other at the word of command. It is not accidental that Mr. Tilden, anxious to get rid of the surplus revenue in order to prevent a demand for the repeal of protective duties, should propose wasting it on steel-clad forts, rather than applying it to any purpose of general utility. Fortifications and navies and standing armies not merely suit the protectionist purpose in requiring a constant expenditure, and developing a class who look on warlike expenditures as conducive to their own profit and importance, but they are of a piece with a theory that teaches us that our interests are antagonistic to those of other nations.

Unembarrassed by hostile neighbors; unentangled in European quarrels; already, in her sixty millions of people, the most powerful nation on earth, and rapidly rising to a position that will dwarf the greatest empires, the American Republic can afford to laugh to scorn any suggestion that she should ape the armaments of Old-World monarchies, as she should laugh to scorn the parallel suggestion that her industries could be ruined by throwing open her ports to the commerce of the world.

The giant of the nations does not depend for her safety upon steel-clad fortresses and armor-plated ships which the march of invention must within a few years make, even in war-time, mere useless rubbish; but in her population, in her wealth, in the intelligence and inventiveness and spirit of her people, she has all that would be really useful in time of need. No nation on earth would venture wantonly to attack her, and none could do so with impunity. If we ever again have a foreign war it will be of our own making. And too strong to fear aggression, we ought to be too just to commit it.

In throwing open our ports to the commerce of the world we shall far better secure their safety than by fortifying them with all the "protected" plates that our steel ring could make. For not merely would free trade give us again that mastery of the ocean which protection has deprived us of, and stimulate the productive power in which real fighting strength lies; but while steel-clad forts could afford no defense against the dynamite-dropping balloons and death-dealing air-ships which will be the next product of destructive invention, free trade would prevent their ever being sent against us. The spirit of protectionism, which is the real thing that it is sought to defend by steel-plating, is that of national enmity and strife. The spirit of free trade is that of fraternity and peace.

A nobler career is open to the American Republic than the servile imitation of European follies and vices. Instead of following in what is mean and low, she may lead toward what is grand and high. This league of sovereign States, settling their differences by a common tribunal and opposing no impediments to trade and travel, has in it possibilities of giving to the world a more than Roman peace.

What are the real, substantial advantages of this Union of ours? Are they not summed up in the absolute freedom of trade which it secures, and the community of interests that grows out of this freedom? If our States were fighting each other with hostile tariffs, and a citizen could not cross a State boundary-line without having his baggage searched, or a book printed in New York could not be sent across the river to Jersey City without being held in the post-office until duty was paid, how long would our Union last, or what would it be worth? The true benefits of our Union, the true basis of the interstate peace it secures, is that it has prevented the establishment of State tariffs and given us free trade over the better part of a continent.

We may "extend the area of freedom" whenever we choose to—whenever we apply to our intercourse with other nations the same principle that we apply to intercourse between our States. We may annex Canada to all intents and purposes whenever we throw down the tariff wall we have built around ourselves. We need not ask for any reciprocity; if we abolish our custom-houses and call off our baggage searchers and Bible confiscators, Canada would not and could not maintain hers. This would make the two countries practically one. Whether the Canadians chose to maintain a separate Parliament and pay a British lordling for keeping up a mock court at Rideau Hall, need not in the slightest concern us. The intimate relations that would come of unrestricted commerce would soon obliterate the boundary-line; and mutual interest and mutual convenience would speedily induce the extension over both countries of the same general laws and institutions.

And so would it be with our kindred over the sea. With the abolition of our custom-houses and the opening of our ports to the free entry of all good things, the trade between the British Islands and the United States would become so immense, the intercourse so intimate, that we should become one people, and would inevitably so conform currency and postal system and general laws that Englishman and American would feel themselves as much citizens of a common country as do New Yorker and Californian. Three thousand miles of water are no more of an impediment to this than are three thousand miles of land. And with relations so close, ties of blood and language would assert their power, and mutual interest, general convenience and fraternal feeling might soon lead to a pact, which, in the words of our own, would unite all the English-speaking peoples in a league "to establish justice, insure domestic tranquillity, provide for the common defense, promote the general welfare, and secure the blessings of liberty."

Thus would free trade unite what a century ago protectionism severed, and in a federation of the nations of English speech—the world-tongue of the future—take the first step to a federation of mankind.

And upon our relations with all other nations our repudiation of protection would have a similar tendency. The sending of delegations to ask the trade of our sister republics of Spanish America avails nothing so long as we maintain a tariff which repels their trade. We have but to open our ports to draw their trade to us and avail ourselves of all their natural advantages. And more potent than anything else would be the moral influence of our action. The spectacle of a continental republic such as ours really putting her faith in the principle of freedom, would revolutionize the civilized world.

For, as I have shown, that violation of natural rights which imposes tariff duties is inseparably linked with that violation of natural rights which compels the masses to pay tribute for the privilege of living. The one cannot be abolished without the other. And a republic wherein the free-trade principle was thus carried to its conclusion, wherein the equal and unalienable rights of men were thus acknowledged, would indeed be as a city set on a hill.

The dangers to the Republic come not from without but from within. What menaces her safety is no armada launched from European shores, but the gathering cloud of tramps in her own highways. That Krupp is casting monstrous cannon, and that in Cherbourg and Woolwich projectiles of unheard-of destructiveness are being stored, need not alarm her, but there is black omen in the fact that Pennsylvania miners are working for 65 cents a day. No triumphant invader can tread our soil till the blight of "great estates" has brought "failure of the crop of men;" if there be danger that our cities blaze, it is from torches lit in faction fight, not from foreign shells.

Against such dangers forts will not guard us, iron-clads protect us, or standing armies prove of any avail. They are not to be avoided by any aping of European protectionism; they come from our failure to be true to that spirit of liberty which was invoked at the formation of the Republic. They are only to be avoided by con-forming our institutions to the principle of freedom.

For it is true, as was declared by the first National Assembly of France, that "*ignorance, neglect, or contempt of human rights are the sole causes of public misfortunes and corruptions of government.*"

Here is the conclusion of the whole matter: That we should do unto others as we would have them do to us— that we should respect the rights of others as scrupu-lously as we would have our own rights respected, is not a mere counsel of perfection to individuals, but it is the law to which we must conform social institutions and national policy if we would secure the blessings of abun-dance and peace.

INDEX.

333